Team of Destiny

Team of Destiny

Walter Johnson, Clark Griffith, Bucky Harris, and the 1924 Washington Senators

GARY SARNOFF

ROWMAN & LITTLEFIELD
Lanham • Boulder • New York • London

Published by Rowman & Littlefield
An imprint of The Rowman & Littlefield Publishing Group, Inc.
4501 Forbes Boulevard, Suite 200, Lanham, Maryland 20706
www.rowman.com

86-90 Paul Street, London EC2A 4NE, United Kingdom

British Library Cataloguing in Publication Information Available

Library of Congress Cataloging-in-Publication Data Available

ISBN 978-1-5381-8234-5 (cloth) | ISBN 978-1-5381-8235-2 (ebook)

In memory of Timothy G. Smith, a huge baseball fan
and a great friend to many.

Contents

Acknowledgments

Like any other author, I needed support in writing this book, and I was fortunate to have a great team in helping make it a reality. I first want to thank my publisher, Rowman & Littlefield, and acquisitions editors Christen Karniski and Samantha Delwarte and production editor Jessica McCleary for believing in my story. I also want to thank my editor, Andrea Howe, for her hard work and expertise.

My gratitude goes out to the helpful staff members at the Giamatti Research Center at the Baseball Hall of Fame in Cooperstown, the Reading Room at the Library of Congress, the Washingtonian Room at the Martin Luther King Library in Washington, D.C., the Tampa-Hillsboro Public Library, and Tampa's Henry B. Plant Museum.

Plus, I want to pass along a thank-you to Washington sports Hall of Famer Phil Hochberg for his help and Ted Leavengood and Robert Wiggins for sharing their research.

I'm also grateful to Matt Mendelsohn for his support and contribution to the book. Finally, I want to offer my appreciation to Charles C. Alexander, Ronald T. Waldo, Thomas Wolf, and Bruce Adams.

The 1924 Washington Senators Roster

Player	Pos	B-T	HT	WT	Age	Seasons*
Ossie Bluege	INF	R-R	5'11	162	23	3
Carl East	RF	L-R	6'2	178	29	2
Showboat Fisher	RF	L-R	5'10	170	25	2
Goose Goslin	LF	L-R	5'11	185	23	4
Pinky Hargrave	C	R-R	6'0	170	28	2
Bucky Harris	2B-MGR	R-R	5'9	156	27	6
Walter Johnson	P	R-R	6'1	200	36	18
Joe Judge	1B	L-L	5'8	155	30	10
Wade Lefler	PH	L-R	5'11	162	28	1
Nemo Leibold	OF	L-R	5'6	157	32	12
Fred Marberry	P	R-R	6'1	190	25	2
Joe Martina	P	R-R	6'0	183	34	1
Wid Matthews	CF	L-L	5'8	155	27	2
Earl McNeely	CF	R-R	5'9	155	26	1
Ralph Miller	INF	R-R	6'0	190	28	3
George Mogridge	P	L-L	6'2	165	35	12
Curley Ogden	P	R-R	6'1	180	23	3
Roger Peckinpaugh	SS	R-R	5'10	165	33	14
Doc Protho	3B	R-R	5'10	175	30	3
Sam Rice	OF	L-R	5'9	150	34	10
Lance Richbourg	OF	L-R	5'10	160	26	2
Muddy Ruel	C	R-R	5'9	150	28	9
Allen Russell	P	R-R	5'11	165	30	10
Mule Shirley	1B	L-L	5'11	180	23	1
Carr Smith	OF	R-R	6'0	175	23	2
By Speece	P	R-R	5'11	170	27	1
Bennie Tate	C	L-R	5'9	165	22	1
Tommy Taylor	INF	R-R	5'10	170	31	1
Tom Zachary	P	L-L	6'1	187	28	7
Paul Zahniser	P	R-R	5'10	170	27	2

*Season in majors including 1924

Team of Destiny. The 1924 Washington Senators won the American League pennant and World Series. It was the only time the Senators were baseball's world champions. *Library of Congress, Prints & Photographs Division*

Introduction

There was an assumption during the first decade of the twentieth century: The lack of success of the American League's Washington franchise must have been due to the team's nickname. The name "Senators" meant losing, bad luck, and the Wagner brothers. Under the ownership of the Wagner brothers, the National League version of the Washington Senators during the 1890s never posted a winning record and finished their seasons lightyears away from first place. Washington baseball fans expressed their dissatisfaction by staying away from the ballpark, thus leading to the city of Washington losing its baseball team when the National League reduced its league membership from twelve to eight teams after the 1899 season. Then in 1901 came the arrival of a new league and the return of major-league baseball to the nation's capital with the Washington Senators of the American League. Like the franchise of the 1890s, the Senators finished low in the standings during their first few years of existence. Before the 1905 season started, the team decided to scrap their nickname and have a contest for a new one. Among the thousand names suggested, the "Nationals" was selected; however, this did not sit well with some sportswriters and fans, who insisted on keeping the name "Senators." So, although the team's name officially became the Washington Nationals, the names Senators and Nationals would be used interchangeably.

But the new name, and the arrival of the great Walter Johnson in 1907, failed to change Washington's fortunes. In 1912, Clark Griffith was hired to manage the team, which did improve under his leadership, but not enough to win the first major-league pennant in city history. Then in 1924 it all came together for Washington.

In 1951 Clark Griffith pointed out a photo of the 1924 team on his office wall at Griffith Stadium to President Truman. This one had a special place among the many baseball memories for Griffith. Baseball fans throughout the country and around the world cheered for the 1924 Washington Senators, causing a New York sportswriter to dub them "The People's Team."[1] In 1933 longtime *Washington Post* sportswriter Frank Young referred to them as the "Team of Destiny," because, "during the pennant race it looked as though it was in the books for the Senators to win."[2]

What is so special about this team, and why tell their story? It's a heartwarming story of overcoming the greatest odds. Heading into the 1924 season, nobody thought the Washington Senators had a chance to even contend, let alone win the American League pennant and the World Series. The New York Yankees, the defending World Champions, had won three consecutive American League pennants and were expected to repeat in 1924.

Conversely, most picked the Senators to post another losing record and finish in the lower half of the American League standings. Having a reputation for losing caused the Senators to become such a laughingstock that a 1909 vaudeville line described Washington, D.C., as "First in War, First in Peace and last in the American League."[3] When Clark Griffith arrived in Washington to manage the team in 1912, they had a quick jaunt into winning seasons and even pennant contention before dropping back into the second division (the lower half of the league standings).

During the eight seasons prior to 1924, the Senators finished with a losing record in six of those seasons, so it was no surprise that most expected another loser in 1924. However, Griffith, who advanced from manager to co-owner and team president, made a big push toward winning by hiring Bucky Harris, the team's twenty-seven-year-old second baseman, as manager. Harris had only four full seasons of Major League Playing experience, so this move was laughed at by the sportswriters, who called it "Griffith's Folly."[4] But it would be Griffith who had the last laugh. Through Harris's confidence, leadership, and inspiration, the Senators went on to edge out the Yankees for the American League pennant and went into extra innings in the seventh and deciding game with the New York Giants in a nail-biting World Series.

But Harris wasn't the only one to push the Senators to victory. In fact, the Team of Destiny's heart was best exemplified by Walter Johnson, perhaps the greatest pitcher in baseball history, who had the misfortune of pitching for the Washington Senators—and during the prime of his career.

Since arriving in Washington to pitch for the Senators in 1907, Johnson had earned the admiration of baseball fans for his blazing fastball, modesty, sportsmanship, and kind disposition. When Griffith arrived to manage the Senators in 1912, Johnson was entering his prime, and he nearly singlehandedly pushed the Senators into contention. However, in 1920 the great pitcher sustained the only arm injury of his career, and his status as a superstar pitcher plummeted into mediocrity. Following four average seasons, the thirty-six-year-old announced that 1924 would be his final season. Sadly, it was believed he would go down in history as the great pitcher who never had the opportunity to pitch on a pennant-winning team and experience his career-long dream of pitching a win in a World Series game. But Johnson fully recovered from his injury that year, and he pitched as he did in the good old days, winning twenty-three games. Then, after being the tough-luck loser in two starts, Johnson entered the deciding Game 7 of the 1924 World Series with the score tied 3–3 in the top of the ninth. Another opportunity to fulfill his dream of winning a World Series game had arrived.

CHAPTER 1

New Year's Eve 1923

Bright stars freckled the sky on a damp, crystal-cold evening. The citizens of Washington, D.C., were vibrant and ready to erupt with more traditional noisy fun and revelry than they had shown since before Prohibition. Hotel ballrooms, dining rooms, and cafes, charging $4–$10 to attend their parties, were expected to be packed to capacity, totaling more than twenty-five thousand guests. The most fashionable of the gatherings were projected to be at the New Willard, Hamilton, Washington, and Shoreham hotels and Le Paradis Café. The largest gathering, according to the *Washington Post*, would be at the Wardman Park Hotel because they had the biggest space available. In addition to hotel and restaurant parties, houses of worship scheduled watch parties and services to sing triumphant songs. Residents throughout the city prepared to host crowded parties, expecting them to extend from their living rooms, through the front doorways and onto the front porches. "Leap, the baby year," as the local newspapers called the coming year, was going to be born, and "old man 1923" was about to pass into history.[1] Most Washingtonians were ready to celebrate, and others were content to simply cause mischief. Pranksters kept firefighters busy by reporting twenty-four false alarms during the evening. As funny as practical jokers thought this was, the consequences facing the offenders were costly: a $100 fine and six months in jail. Anyone who reported a violator leading to an arrest and conviction would receive a $35 reward.

America, deep into the prosperous Roaring Twenties, was looking forward to a bright future in 1924. The Great War was now more than five years in the past, the postwar recession and blues were solved, and people's standard of living was vastly improving. Many households, especially in rural areas, were receiving electricity for the first time, leading to the escalation in sales of vacuum cleaners, electric lamps, radios, refrigerators, and freezers. The automobile ratio per household was skyrocketing. According to the *Washington Post* the auto industry

1

had its finest year in 1923, with nearly four million cars and trucks manufactured on the assembly lines, bringing total cars in use in the United States to fourteen million, 90 percent of the world's supply. The first quarter forecast for 1924 estimated auto production to surpass the entire output of 1923.[2]

The booming radio and automobile sales led to the rise of sports popularity. People could listen to or even attend games in higher numbers than ever before. "Sports in the year 1923 was marked by growth in almost every aspect," claimed a *Washington Star* sportswriter.[3] And because of a spike in sports enthusiasm, Major League Baseball looked to increase its ballparks' seating capacities. The New York Yankees built a magnificent new stadium, and the Washington Senators Baseball Club planned to make improvements to its ballpark, including a necessary infield upgrade, an investment certain to satisfy the infielders and Washington's starting second baseman Stanley "Bucky" Harris.

Harris was among the Washington New Year's Eve partygoers who booked a reservation at a hotel ballroom. He escorted the lovely Elizabeth Sutherland, daughter of former West Virginia congressman Howard Sutherland. They were one of the thousand couples attending one of the scheduled parties at the Wardman Park Hotel. Harris sported a black eye he had received in a rough basketball game the night before in Utica. His previous contracts with the Washington Senators prohibited playing basketball and stipulated a $1,000 fine for breaking the rule, but this clause was absent in his current contract. He took advantage of the oversight by signing with a professional team in Great Neck, New York. He wanted the extra money, and in his opinion, playing basketball would keep him in good physical condition during the winter. "Basketball is a great game to prevent a man from putting on extra weight," he believed.[4] Harris knew he would be in hot water if his boss, Senators team president Clark Griffith, found out, though he didn't think word about his infraction would ever reach Griffith's ears.

The Wardman Park Hotel, located in the charming Woodley Park neighborhood in Washington's northwest section, housed most of the visiting American League teams when in town to play the Senators. It was also where Harris used to quarter during the baseball season. He knew the hotel staff and knew they would ask about his black eye. The chances of a hotel staff member engaging with Griffith was unlikely, so he felt no risk in explaining if asked.

Inside the ballroom, large chandeliers hung from the ceiling, curtains decked the windows, plants surrounded the spacious dance floor, and each table had a floral centerpiece. Hotel manager Elmer Dyer made sure each place setting included noisemakers, confetti, and souvenirs for the guests to express their joy at midnight. On hand to entertain throughout the evening was Irving Boernstein and his orchestra, scheduled to perform until 6:00 a.m., assuming the guests lasted that long.

A few minutes before the clock struck twelve, stray shouts and chatter echoed around the city. Inside the large Wardman Park ballroom, the lights were dimmed, and at midnight the partygoers laughed, clicked glasses, and cried "Happy New Year!"[5]

The entire city seemed set on outdoing other cities in its volume of greeting. A clamor of screams, church bells, automobile horns, whistles, firecrackers, pistol shots, and other noise making devices welcomed 1924. But not everybody was celebrating. There were two holdups and five burglaries. At a storefront along Connecticut Avenue, located only two miles from the Wardman Park, a man hurled a rock through a store's front window and cleaned out the shop. As he prepared to make his getaway, he was apprehended by a police officer. Another man used a diamond cutter to carve a hole in the front window of a jewelry store and grabbed a thousand dollars' worth of diamonds and watches that were on display. He was also caught in the act and placed under arrest.

The revelers continued to party into the wee hours in the Wardman Park ballroom. Ed Eynon, the secretary of the Washington ball club, was not someone Harris expected to bump into that night, but he encountered Eynon at the hotel. Surprised by the presence of the team's club secretary and unprepared to tell a white lie, when Eynon asked about the eye injury, Harris was honest with his answer.

The next day, Harris knew that Eynon had tattled when he received a phone call. "Hello Mr. Griffith," he feebly said into the phone. "Bucky, you've been playing basketball," Griffith said. "Yes sir, but it wasn't in my contract," replied Harris.[6] Griffith ordered him to come to his office. When the two men met, Griffith spoke to his young ballplayer in his usual calm manner. He didn't yell; he didn't rave. "While you may not have broken your contract," Griffith clarified, "you did a thing that I disapprove of." Harris knew his decision to play basketball was wrong. He took full responsibility for his poor judgment and apologized. "Forget it," Griffith told him.[7]

Griffith moved to a different subject. He informed Harris that he was going to send him to the Senators' spring training site in Tampa within the next two weeks, more than a month before the rest of the team was due to report. "You look underweight," Griffith told Harris. He also mentioned that he wanted him to rest before spring training and the season. And he finished by letting him know that he was going to send him with Mike Martin, the team's trainer. "Must be as an insurance so I will not footloose," Harris thought to himself.[8]

In 1912, Clark Griffith had arrived to manage the Washington Senators, a team without direction that was viewed as a laughingstock among the fans and sportswriters. The franchise's image was typified by a well-known vaudeville punchline describing Washington as "First in War, First in Peace, and last in the American League."[9] Wanting to pull the franchise out of the bottom of the league, the team's board of directors needed a savvy baseball man with a reputation for winning. After deciding Griffith was their man, he was offered an incentive to buy 10 percent of the ball club if he agreed to accept the team's managerial position. Intrigued by the offer, Griffith accepted, mortgaged his farm in Montana to raise the funds to invest in the franchise, and went to work on building a winner.

While the team didn't win any pennants under Griffith, he did make the team respectable and even contenders for a few seasons. Despite slipping to a seventh-place finish in 1919, Griffith was not discouraged. He was sure the only way to lead the Senators to the promised land of World Champions was to have complete control, so he decided the way to go was to buy out the board of directors, which he did in December of 1919.

Griffith believed the formula for success was to start fresh, with a youthful team of energetic players, such as Bucky Harris. To give full attention to the team's day-to-day operations and fulfilling his vision, he needed someone else to manage the Senators, but that proved to be more difficult than what he had envisioned. After stepping down as manager following the 1920 season, Griffith went through a manager a year in each of the previous three seasons.

Who would be Washington's next manager when the 1924 season began? With spring training only one and a half months away, Griffith had yet to decide who was going to pilot his ball club.

On the second day of the year, Griffith met with the club's other majority owner, William Richardson, and the minority owners. They reviewed the team's finances, noting the 1923 home season attendance was more than one-hundred thousand less than the previous year, its lowest since they formed the new ownership group in 1919. Griffith pitched a ballpark remodeling project to make it one of the most attractive parks in the American League. He planned to invest $110,000 on enlarging the park's capacity, heightening the right field wall, constructing a new set of left field bleachers, and improving the infield through resodding and leveling. The sum of $76,000 was earmarked to purchase rookie ballplayers. This would be a huge investment, but despite the lack of attendance in 1923, the Senators did make a substantial profit, and the team would save $20,000 on the contract of Donie Bush, the manager Griffith had just terminated.[10]

The team's stockholders went along with the plan and reelected the current club directors: Clark Griffith as president, William Richardson as vice president, and Ed Eynon as secretary. They knew the expenses meant no dividend checks, which didn't make them happy, but they had hopes for the future being better. One person who was content with the direction of the club and remained confident in Griffith was the team's other majority owner.

William "Billy" Richardson, a forty-five-year-old native Philadelphian, didn't appear to be athletic. However, Richardson played baseball as a youth at Philadelphia's Navy Athletic Club and favored daily dips in the surf in Atlantic City, where he owned a summer home. He began working in the grain business as an office boy at the age of thirteen. Through tireless energy and determination, he rose rapidly in the grain industry to become a prominent grain dealer and exporter in his hometown. While not rated as a millionaire, and uninterested in becoming one, Richardson was said to have a comfortable fortune. "I have all the money I need," he once told a reporter.[11] An ardent baseball fan, he traveled to Washington for a few days each season to watch the Senators, and he'd watch his team when they came through Philadelphia to play the Athletics. He would accompany Griffith each year to the baseball winter meetings, mostly to observe and socialize. Constantly occupied with his own business affairs, he was content with blending into the background and letting Griffith make the ball club's decisions, including whom to hire as the team's next manager. But when asked at last December's baseball winter meetings in Chicago, Richardson voiced his opinion: "I've been urging Griffith to manage the club next year," he told a group of reporters, who laughed at his answer. "I was quite serious when I suggested to Griffith that he should become the manager of our club," Richardson continued. "I really hope he will go through with it. I think he can take the very good material we have and finish high in the race, or at least make the club pennant contenders."[12]

With his decision to send Harris to Tampa in mid-January and the investors meeting out of the way, Griffith turned his attention to the players' season contracts, completing his team's spring training schedule, and the hottest topic: hiring a manager. With time running out, the focus of the local press shifted to someone on the current roster, and the popular choice was Washington's thirty-three-year-old veteran shortstop, Roger Peckinpaugh. "Griffith could make no better choice," opined a local sportswriter.[13]

Was Griffith considering Peckinpaugh? During a busy day when giving the matter some thought, he received a letter from Walter Johnson, arguably the greatest pitcher the game had ever seen, he was now thirty-six and past his prime. His career had been in decline due to a sore arm ever since he hurled the only no-hitter of his brilliant career on July 1, 1920. Although he was still taking his turn in the starting pitching rotation and still throwing faster than any pitcher in the league, his fastball no longer hopped and made life miserable for opposing batters. His straight fastballs allowed opponents to dig in and get base hits. The good news was that his 1923 season had been his best since his injury—and Griffith believed he would have an even better season in 1924.

When Griffith read Johnson's letter, his heart sank. Johnson's letter informed him about his plan to retire after the 1924 season: "As things are now

I have a home in Kansas, another in Washington and spend some time in Nevada," Johnson explained. "I have a family, with two children of school age, and no permanent place of residence. It is an injustice to them to have to be chasing all around the country. I want to settle down in one place to make it my all-around home and I hope to do it on the west coast."[14]

The thought of losing Johnson to retirement troubled Griffith. Not ready to lose his great hurler, he believed some talking to his pitcher would bring a change of heart, and this meant he would have to keep this news away from the press, thinking the more the press took up the issue, the more likely Johnson would be to hang up his glove and cleats.

As Griffith continued to work through his daily schedule and ponder the managerial issue, Bucky Harris was getting ready to leave for Tampa. Asked why he was leaving a month before he had to report for spring training, Harris replied in an issued statement: "In an effort to get a complete rest before swinging into action."[15] On January 16, Harris and trainer Mike Martin boarded the Dixie Flyer at D.C.'s Union Station, and reached their destination the next day.

West of Hillsboro River and across Tampa's Lafayette Bridge stood the Tampa Bay Hotel, a five-story red-bricked building with thirteen minarets topped by onion-shaped silver domes. The inside of the hotel displayed a revival style with ornate Victorian and Moorish architectural features, including keyhole-shaped doorways and gingerbread woodwork. Opened for business in 1891, the Tampa Bay Hotel was considered one of the best lodges in the world. It was one of the first hotels to have electricity, telephones, private baths, and full-sized tubs. "The most beautiful hotel I've ever seen," a hotel guest wrote in a letter. "It's a resemblance of the stories of the Arabian Knights, where some genie waved a wand and a palace appeared."[16]

In 1898, Teddy Roosevelt and the Rough Riders came to town to prepare for combat in Cuba during the Spanish-American War. Roosevelt and the other generals stayed at the Tampa Bay Hotel in what a famous newspaper writer called "The Rocking-Chair Campaign."[17] During the evenings, Roosevelt and the other high-ranking officers would sit in the rocking chairs on the hotel's vine-draped porch and rock during their discussions. The troops camped on the grounds among the ants and mosquitos and in conditions described as a hot Valley Forge. With the sweltering weather and the water supply low, many became ill, but they kept their spirits up. Some of the troop members managed to muster enough energy to play the first baseball game on the premises.

After the turn of the century, the hotel began to lose its appeal and popularity. In 1905, when the hotel's investment company was unable to pay its land taxes, the city of Tampa purchased the hotel and its land for $125,000.36.[18] The city kept the hotel but turned the land into a ballpark, naming it Plant Field, in honor of Henry B. Plant, the man who built the Tampa Bay Hotel, and began to seek a major-league team to train in Tampa during the spring. In 1913 the Cubs came for the first of four consecutive springs. In 1919 the city of Tampa received an agreement from the World Champion Boston Red Sox, who had the world's best draw in Babe Ruth. In an intersquad game on April 1, 1919, Ruth hit a tremendous drive off teammate "Sad Sam" Jones that was believed to be the longest hit ever made. According to a *Tampa Bay Tribune* sportswriter, "On his first trip to the pan he dropped a sky-scrapper on the race track in deep right. The pill bounded almost back to heaven and soared over the high board fence. (Red Sox outfielder Harry) Hooper refused to chase the ball and rested while a dozen urchins scurried as the Colossus cantered around the bases just for the fun of the affair."[19]

But just as everyone thought Ruth would never hit one like that again, he belted one to right-center field three days later against the New York Giants in front of forty-two hundred fans at Plant Field. The drive traveled 587 feet and outdistanced his previous drive by 20–25 feet. Giants outfielder Ross Youngs looked skyward and began to run, then stopped. "I believe that it's the longest hit I ever saw," said Giants manager John McGraw.[20]

The Red Sox didn't return to Tampa in 1920, opening the door for the Senators to come to town. Griffith wanted a warmer climate than Augusta, Georgia, his team's previous spring training site, and Tampa was the ideal place.

The morning after arriving in town, Martin and Harris headed to the ballpark, said to be within a stone's throw of the hotel. The two men found the field to be a wreck. The playing field was never in tip-top shape, but its off-season events, including local baseball and football games, high school track meets, and automobile races on the half-mile ring around the field, as well as a state fair, had wreaked havoc on Plant Field.

The only bright spot was the structure along the field. A fire had destroyed the old wooden grandstand before spring training in 1923, and Griffith took advantage by requesting a newly built replacement made of concrete and steel. "If you build a suitable ballpark, I'll bring my ball club here for five years," he told the Tampa city officials. "If you bring your ball club here for five years, we'll build you a park," an official replied.[21] Tampa held up their end of the deal by investing $25,000 to construct a 160-foot-long concrete-and-steel 4,000-seat grandstand that required only three beams to support the steel framework beneath the roof. A pavilion was erected on each side of the grandstand, large enough to hold another 1,500 spectators. Beneath the grandstand were thirty concession booths and a spacious clubhouse, large enough to accommodate thirty-five ballplayers and with hot and cold running water from eight showerheads. "We have seen ballparks in St. Petersburg and Daytona and they do not begin to compete with the Griffmen's spring training home," penned a

Washington Times sportswriter. "Tampa today has a better home than Chattanooga and Memphis of the Southern League."[22]

Martin and Harris went to work, beginning with watering, rolling, and rebuilding the field. At the end of their long day, Martin placed a "Keep Off" sign in the middle of the field for all to see. During their evenings, the two men would head to the hotel's porch, sit in the same rocking chairs made famous by Roosevelt and his fellow officers during the Rocking-Chair Campaign, and talk about conditioning. "He told me things about athletes that were new to me," Harris would later admit.[23]

Mike Martin was a stocky, gray-haired man who worked hard on responsibilities that went beyond the health of the players. During spring training he'd wake up early, grab a quick bite to eat, then head to the ballpark to prepare the field before the first player hit the breakfast table. He would work through lunch and finish the day by cleaning up the field following the players' daily workout. Over twenty-five years as a trainer, he handled an assortment of different athletes, including bikers back in the days of the six-day bike racing vogue and jockeys in the market weight for big handicaps back in the old days of Sheepshead Bay Race Track in New York. In 1905 he came on board with Griffith, then the manager of the New York Highlanders (who would later change the name to Yankees). Griffith took Martin along when he went to Cincinnati, then to Washington. While with the Senators, Martin was placed in charge of conditioning the pitchers during spring training for eight years before the job was turned over to the coaches. This year Griffith was considering placing the pitchers under Martin's care again.

Harris and Martin also discussed the upcoming season and the Washington managerial position, wondering who would get the job. Harris, Martin, and everyone else were fully aware about Griffith being in hot pursuit of White Sox second baseman Eddie Collins, an eighteen-year veteran regarded as the greatest second baseman up to that time. Noted for being a great all-around player, intelligent, and a leader who made the players around him even better, Collins was showing no signs of slowing down at age thirty-seven. In 1923 he posted a .360 batting average, led the league with forty-eight stolen bases, was outstanding in the field, and finished second to Babe Ruth for league MVP honors. Griffith's plan, if he could get Collins, was to appoint him as a player-manager, and of course, this meant Collins would take over Harris's position as Washington's starting second baseman. "Would you be satisfied to switch to third base if we should land Eddie Collins?" Griffith asked Harris. "Certainly, I'll play anywhere or do anything you want me to do," Harris replied.[24] But while he had agreed to make the switch, he told Martin that he would be uncomfortable and unhappy at third base. He was also unsure how he would get along with Collins because he knew nothing about his personality. Harris's own preference for Washington's next manager was former White Sox manager Kid Gleason. "He's a good manager and a good fit for the Nats," he told Martin. Griffith, considered another managerial possibility, would also satisfy Harris.[25]

Who would be the next manager of the Washington Senators? With a mere three weeks until spring training the position remained unfilled. Rumors heated up again about the possibility of Eddie Collins. The gossip began last October when Chicago and New York newspapers broke a story about Collins heading to Washington. They spread the word that, in exchange for Collins, Harris would be sent to Boston in what would be a three-way deal with the Red Sox, Senators, and White Sox. "It's a shock to me, for I did not expect to be placed on the open market," Collins told a reporter in a phone interview from his winter home in Lansdowne, Pennsylvania. "I do not know of any deal pending for me to go to Washington, and naturally don't know what to say," Collins continued. "I would be glad to manage a big-league club, but that is for someone else to say. I like Chicago and would be delighted to play under [Frank] Chance [the new White Sox manager], but that is for someone else to say."[26]

"Collins is not on the open market," refuted White Sox secretary Harry Grabiner. "We have had proposals from almost every club in the American League for his services, but we want him ourselves." Grabiner admitted that the Senators were one of those teams to make an offer. "The Washington club made no offer that would tempt us to let go of a second baseman of Collins's caliber," Grabiner said.[27]

Unable to swing a deal for Collins, the attention turned to former White Sox manager Kid Gleason, who had retired after the 1923 season. When asked about managing in Washington, Gleason smiled at the group of reporters at the December Baseball Winter Meetings. "I do not want to manage, but I do desire to stay in the game," Gleason replied.[28]

"Who is going to be the next manager of your ball club?" a writer asked Griffith. "Is it going to be Walter Johnson?" another writer asked. Griffith laughed when hearing this. "I have a few men in mind," replied Griffith. "That is all I will say."[29]

Would Eddie Collins be the Washington manager? The *New York World* was about to break a story about a trade sending Collins to the Senators for Harris and outfielder Sam Rice or a pitcher. Another story began to circulate about a trade involving the White Sox and Yankees. The story was that Collins and a White Sox catcher would go to the Yankees in exchange for outfielder Bob Meusel, second baseman Aaron Ward, and pitchers Waite Hoyt or "Sad Sam" Jones.

The baseball trade talk reached the Tampa newspapers and made its way to the Tampa Bay Hotel, where Harris saw his name among the potential trade stories. If Washington did land Eddie Collins, why would they need him? He saw his name mentioned in an article about a trade to the New York Yankees, no doubt to make room for Collins.

Keeping up with the rumors and the team's managerial status was *Washington Herald* sportswriter John Dugan. Wondering how this trade and managerial talk was affecting Washington baseball fans, Dugan went around the city to find out. His conclusion was, "Baseball enthusiasm in the District is now at a low ebb. With little more than two weeks before the Nationals start training camp, the fans are showing no interest in the prospects of the 1924.

"A week's tour of government departments, businesses houses, factories, workshops, office buildings and general sporting circles displays an awful lack of baseball enthusiasm."

The fans noted several reasons for their lack of interest, but the most popular were the failure to appoint a manager and no roster changes for a team that finished with a losing record in 1923. "With the same roster as 1923, and with the managerial question still in the air, the prospects of the most ardent fans are not bright," Dugan wrote. "Since Philadelphia, St. Louis and Chicago have improved, little hope is held for the Griffs. It looks like at this writing as though the Nationals will have their hands full in beating out the Boston Red Sox (who had finished last in the American League in 1923)."[30]

Fans finally had something to be excited about when, on January 30, local newspapers mentioned Jack Barry. The starting shortstop for Connie Mack's famous $100,000 infield and dominant Philadelphia Athletics teams from the first half of the previous decade, Barry seemed a popular choice. "The signing of Barry would find the fans flocking back to the club," wrote Dugan.[31] Barry had managing experience from when he had piloted the Red Sox to ninety wins and a second-place finish in 1917, the only season he managed in the Majors. He left the Red Sox to enlist in the service in 1918. In 1921 he became head coach at the College of Holy Cross, a job he thoroughly enjoyed, but said he would leave the position if someone came along with the right offer. It was also said that he was "anxious to get back into the harness as a Major-League pilot."[32] A reliable source claimed Barry had come to town to meet with Griffith and left town satisfied with the terms offered; however, no agreement was ever made.

During the first weekend of February, Griffith traveled to Boston for an American League meeting. Collins was rumored to be registered for the meeting, and Barry, who would not be attending, was just an hour away. When the meeting concluded, there was no news about Collins or Barry, but there was news about Griffith offering his team's managing job to Ed Barrow, the former Red Sox manager and currently the Yankees business manager. Barrow declined, saying, "I am a stock holder and the club secretary in addition to being the business manager of the New York Yankees."[33]

The story of Barrow's rejection was in the *Tampa Tribune*. Harris knew this meant Collins was out of the picture. With spring training just eight days away, he assumed that Griffith had no other choice but to manage his ball club.

On Saturday, February 9, Harris was resting in his hotel room when he received a telegram from George Preston Marshall, a successful Washington businessman who was close with the Senators and traveled to Tampa each year to observe spring training. "Congratulations," was the only word in his telegram.[34] Without much to go by, Harris assumed the congratulation was for being traded to the Yankees, baseball's 1923 World Champions and winners of the previous three American League pennants.

Leaving Washington, where Harris was happy and the team's starting second baseman for the past four seasons, would be hard. He liked D.C., Griffith, and the Washington baseball fans, but this was the business of baseball. Of course, going to New York would be nice. After all, they had Babe Ruth and were World Champions.

As Harris began to think about packing and heading to the Yankees spring training camp in New Orleans, another telegram arrived. He assumed this message was his reporting orders from the Yankees and everything else he needed to know. He opened the envelope, pulled out a letter, and began to read. He blinked. Was this for real? One of his hands began to tremble to the point where he had to sit down to regain his composure. He later described it: "I knew then how a man feels when he gets word an unknown relative left him a fortune."[35]

"I have had you in mind for a long time as a manager in the making," Griffith explained in the telegram. "I had hesitated in getting in touch with you, or announcing my plans, until I satisfied myself that the worry or the responsibility of the job wouldn't affect your playing. How do you feel about the matter?"

Included with the letter were the details of a new contract. As Harris studied the contract terms, the phone rang. "Well, how about it?" Griffith asked on the other end of the telephone line. "Do you want the job?"

"Do I want the job?" Harris asked. "Certainly!"[36]

Unable to hear Harris's reply due to a bad connection, Griffith asked again. "I want that job!" Harris shouted into the telephone receiver. Griffith was still unable to hear. Harris hung up and raced downstairs to the telegraph office, located in the hotel lobby. "Send this telegram right away and repeat it every hour for the next four hours," he instructed the clerk while handing over a twenty-dollar bill. He then wrote his message on the telegram: *I'll take that job and win Washington's first American League pennant.*[37]

CHAPTER 2

Spring Training (February–April)

Hotel guests stood on rugs that were spread along a hardwood floor and surrounded several marble pillars and plants in the lobby of the Tampa Bay Hotel. Other guests were seated on a circular relic couch fastened to a pedestal supporting a sculpture of Esmeralda from Hugo's *Hunchback of Notre Dame*. Their attention was focused on the Washington baseball club's new manager, who was engaged in a discussion with Hank Wright, a *Tampa Tribune* sportswriter. "In being appointed manager of the Washington ball club, I was afforded the greatest thrill in my life," Harris said, whose face beamed with excitement, scarcely a day after receiving the news. "Matching wits against such successful managers as Ty Cobb and Tris Speaker should keep one busy, so I shall start at once in an effort to get the very best results . . . possible. My great hope is to have the support of the fans and press."[1]

"Harris is a fighter but has always maintained cordial relations with his teammates through an inherently helpful attitude of kindly consideration of them," Griffith said back in Washington, and he assured the local sportswriters that Harris would do a good job. "He has never had trouble of any kind with club members. I believe in Harris that I have the very best man obtainable for the manager for the Washington ball club, and I am convinced this will be demonstrated to the satisfaction of everybody in time."[2]

The sportswriters were skeptical. Player-managers weren't uncommon during this era, with four of the other fifteen major-league teams currently managed by active players, but those player-managers were seasoned veterans who were at least thirty years old. Harris had just four full years of major-league playing experience, and at only twenty-seven, he was the youngest player-manager, a fact leading a writer to wonder if recently hired forty-nine-year-old coach Jack Chesbro would serve as Washington's "assistant manager." "No mention of 'assistant manager' was mentioned in my talk with Chesbro in Boston," Griffith clarified. "There is no such position on the Washington club. Chesbro will coach the pitchers, and if he proves to be the kind of coach I think he is, he will be kept mighty busy in that capacity."[3]

"Harris is not going to be a one-year manager," Griffith continued. "I want that understood at the start. He is going to have plenty of time to show his fitness for the job. I shall leave it up to him as to whether he wants a two-year or three-year contract."[4]

Griffith's confidence in his own decision was unimpressive to the sportswriters, who dubbed his managerial choice "Griffith's folly."[5] A *Chicago Tribune* writer believed that, due to the lack of experience and because the Senators made no roster moves during the winter to better the team, Bucky Harris was set to fail. "Our sympathies to Stanley Harris, the youthful manager of the national capital team. He hasn't a thing better than what was handed to him this spring."[6]

While most snickered, Harris did have backers, including opposing players. Detroit outfielder Harry Heilmann, the American League's leading hitter in 1923, sent a congratulatory telegram to Harris. Donie Bush, the Washington manager canned after the 1923 season, sent a letter to the Washington sportswriters in support of Harris: "There is no one in baseball I can wish more success than Stanley. He is a good, hustling, smart ballplayer, and I know he will be a good manager. All I wish is the fans of Washington to give him the same loyal support I enjoyed in 1923."[7] Washington sportswriter Denman Thompson was bold about telling his readers how he felt: "Harris is a keen student of baseball, and while aggressive to a degree, he has a pleasant personality that enables him to get along amicably with his teammates and fight hard for everything in sight without incurring the ill will of the umpire." Thompson emphasized one of Harris's best attributes was his mental poise. "Although unmarried, bright lights and late hours never had much effect on him, and when the team is on the road, he seldom gets out in the evenings, preferring to indulge in fanning bees in hotel lobbies or with fellow players."[8]

With a week until the rookies arrived to officially open the 1924 spring training season, Harris began to make plans. While eagerly counting down the days until the rookies reported, he continued to work with Martin on field preparations at Plant Field. During the evenings, swaying in the rocking chairs on the Tampa Bay Hotel porch, Martin educated Harris on physical fitness, and Harris picked Martin's mind on the physical condition and training plans for each Washington ballplayer.

The rookies and coaches were due to arrive on Sunday evening, February 17. Since the veterans didn't have to arrive so early, Walter Johnson and eight teammates would head to Hot Springs, Arkansas, to condition and relax prior to their required reporting date in Tampa.

When reporting day arrived a dozen rookies checked in to the Tampa Bay Hotel. Both coaches, Nick Altrock and Jack Chesbro, were also on hand, as was comical veteran Al Schacht, a pitcher for the Senators during the 1919–1921 seasons who was hoping to revive his major-league career after spending the past two years in the minors. Clark Griffith was also in Tampa, accompanied by his wife, nephew, and niece.

Despite the best efforts by Harris, Martin, and the Tampa grounds crew, the Plant Field surface was still in poor condition. True, their efforts during the past month showed, but the playing field was still in need of some work. At 9:30 on Monday morning, the rookies took the field for the first spring workout, though the field contained pockmarks and dead grass and the infield dirt was rock-hard from baking in the sun all year. That night, Harris and Griffith had dinner, then met behind closed doors for two hours. When they emerged, they spoke to the press. "I told Stanley I expect to have him with the Washington club for the remainder of his career," said Griffith. "I told him to write his own ticket. He chose a two-year term, and that was perfectly agreeable to me."[9]

On the second day of spring training, Harris had his team work on base running, which did not thrill the players, who had to perform the drill on the rock-hard infield surface. Harris, who decided to join the veterans in Hot Springs, left in the middle of the practice session, leaving his two coaches and Martin in charge.

Before boarding a train, Harris was questioned by a host of sportswriters. "I think we will have a better chance this year than most people give us credit for," he said. "With Johnson, Mogridge, Russell, and Zachary as pitchers and Ruel to receive them, we have an experienced bunch of battery men, while Rice, Goslin, Peckinpaugh, Judge, and myself certainly form a splendid nucleus for both the infield and garden." He also said his Washington team would hustle every day. "No game is lost, no matter what the score may be, nor what the inning," Harris said.[10]

Shortly after boarding the train, Harris began to think about the club's veterans. How would they accept him as the manager? Suddenly the excitement and enthusiasm he felt for the entire week turned to fear. How would Roger Peckinpaugh, a veteran with managing experience who many believed would get the managing job, think about being passed over? Harris and Peckinpaugh had always gotten along well and partnered so well in the field, they set a record for converting double plays the previous season. How would Walter Johnson feel about taking orders from someone nine years younger?

Nestled in the Ouachita Mountains of central Arkansas is the town of Hot Springs, a place known for its sparkling hot flowing springs, mineral baths, and recreation. For more than half a century, tourists had been coming to the resort town in search of better health. It also served as a hotspot for ballplayers and major-league baseball teams. In 1886, Cap Anson brought his Chicago White Stockings to town for spring training, a choice that other teams copied in later years. By the 1920s, Hot Springs no longer served as a spring training site, but ballplayers were still coming to the popular destination for relaxation and to tune up for the season.

Believing it a sure way to ready Roger Peckinpaugh for the 1923 season and help him improve upon his disappointing 1922 showing, Griffith instructed his shortstop to visit Hot Springs before reporting to Tampa. Peckinpaugh's 1923 season stats didn't improve by a lot, but he did report to spring training in better shape than he had in 1922.

In 1923, Washington's two top hurlers were out of shape upon arriving in Tampa. Walter Johnson talked about having weak legs and Tom Zachary claimed to have a sore arm. Johnson's legs were never quite right during the 1923 season. "He told me that he made up his mind last fall that he would quit baseball if he found his legs had gone back on him," said Harris.[11] To be sure, his top two pitchers were ready for the 1924 season, Griffith ordered the pitching duo to head to Hot Springs.

Harris arrived to join his teammates in a one-week training period before heading back to Tampa. When he appeared at the Eastman Hotel, he was greeted by first baseman Joe Judge, outfielder Sam Rice, and pitchers Johnson, Zachary, and Paul Zahniser. The Nats' new manager immediately learned that the veterans would support Griffith's managerial choice. "Every one of them congratulated me," Harris would later say. "They declared that they would be glad to 'work their heads off for me.' I knew they meant it, too."[12] The group talked about wasting no time in hitting the hiking trail and playing catch, but their trunks containing the necessary paraphernalia had yet to arrive. "Let's go hit the baths," someone suggested, and the group journeyed to one of the bath-houses to take advantage of one of the twenty-one mineral baths offered.[13]

Three more players arrived the following day: third baseman Doc Protho, catcher Muddy Ruel, and pitcher George Mobridge. A few days later, Roger Peckinpaugh stepped off a train to complete the party. Some wondered if there would be friction between Harris and Peckinpaugh, who had been passed over for the managing position. Peckinpaugh set the record straight: "I'm mighty glad that Stanley got the job," he told reporters. "I think he'll make a strong manager. He has all the strong qualifications of a good leader, for he knows baseball thoroughly. Every man on the club likes him and will play hard to help him bring our team near the top." When asked where Washington would finish in the standings, he declined to predict, adding "We should do a little better though, for Mogridge, Johnson, Zachary, and Judge were out of the game a great part of last season." A writer told him he looked like he was in great shape, far better than last spring and the year before. "I spent the winter in Cleveland [his hometown], getting plenty of exercise by hunting and trapping through the Ohio woods."[14]

The Senators' Hot Springs schedule called for the ten players to be at breakfast by 7:00 a.m., rest for thirty minutes, and then hit the trails for a long hike, increasing the distance every day. About a mile into the hike, they'd break out their gloves and play catch. At the end of the long day, the players would reward themselves with a hot bath and massage. "That Johnson is a house of work," Harris told the sportswriters back at the Eastman Hotel. "He led us all over the mountains, setting the pace every inch of the way. And when we were dog tired and ready to return to our hotel for our baths, Walter left us and went to the golf links, played eighteen holes, returned to the hotel and then went out again this afternoon. Is there any wonder if he is in great shape?"[15] The sportswriters reported Johnson's face was the color of old bronze due to his perfect health and an active outdoor life. Johnson said he felt better than at any time during the past four years. "I spent the entire winter in the Nevada Mountains," Johnson said. "Day in and day out I trampled over those big hills. I spent a lot of the time hunting, and I had a lot of good luck. But even when I didn't hunt, I trudged through the woods and over mountains. That is the reason for my excellent physical condition. I haven't any surplus of weight to speak of, my wind is good and I am as strong as an ox. When the curtain goes up on the 1924 season, I'll be in condition to step out there and win a lot of ball games."

Harris, overhearing the conversation, chimed in. "I'll be mighty disappointed if you don't land twenty or more games," the manager said.

"I won't disappoint you," Johnson promised.[16]

Each evening, Harris spoke to the sportswriters about his ball club. He talked about Walter Johnson, moving Sam Rice from right field to center field, and about three players vying for the starting job in right field. "Of course, I will not find the answer to the riddle of who is to get the job until we are all in training camp in Tampa," Harris added. The writers wanted a prediction on where his team would finish in the standings. "I'm not going to make any rash statements regarding where we'll finish in the scramble for the American League bunting, nor am I going to say what I am going to do with this ball club," Harris told them. "Ball games are not won in hotel lobbies. Of course, I have high hopes and so have all the players. I promise the fans that we'll try, and try mighty hard."[17]

The ten Washington ballplayers were not the only major leaguers in town. The Cleveland Indians, expected to be one of the top contenders to dethrone the Yankees in the 1924 American League pennant race, sent two dozen players with Indians coach Jack McCallister to Hot Springs. "No ballplayers will require speed by climbing the sheer sides of mountains," said McCallister. "Such work may develop endurance. Our players are seeking fleetness."[18]

Harry Heilmann, who hit .403 to beat out Babe Ruth by ten points for the 1923 American League batting title, was also in town. Dressed in golf clothes and ready to hit the links, he glanced at a newspaper statement from Tigers player-manager Ty Cobb about his hired hands being prohibited from playing golf. "Amen," Heilmann told a Washington reporter. "I take his statement to mean that we can't play at Augusta. I rounded the course today, anyway; Pretty nice course, isn't it?" Heilmann was reported to be at 210 pounds, ten pounds over his playing weight. "I spent the winter working very hard," Heilmann continued. "I'm in the insurance business in Detroit. I didn't devote a thought to baseball all winter, so I can't say I did a lot of outdoor work in preparation for the season.

"What do I think of Washington's chances? Well, that's a question I will not answer."[19]

Babe Ruth was also in Hot Springs, working his way into shape by playing golf, horseback riding, and hitting the shooting gallery on Main Street every night. He was said to be overweight and admitted he was up to 233 pounds. To help him lose the extra pounds, each day he'd put on a robe, said to be the size of a circus tent, head to a bath pavilion, and get into a tub filled with water that was so hot, he'd protest. After a while, he'd step out of the tub and slip on what looked like a shower curtain over his entire body, leaving only his face exposed. Steam was then turned on, causing Ruth's face to turn as red as a lobster. Yankees pitcher Joe Bush would then stroll in and say, "I don't think he is done quite yet. I'd give that steam valve another turn." After this treatment, Ruth was wrapped in acres of linen and laid on a warm slab to perspire as much as possible. After thirty minutes, the wraps would be removed, and Ruth would take a cold shower. He would then step on a scale and find that he had lost eight pounds. "Well, I know where to find it again," he'd say, and then head to the dinner table.[20] He had an active nightlife in Hot Springs, resulting in a case of influenza that put him in bed for the second straight spring. "My God, I'm sick," he said when he decided to get out of bed and take a stroll. After a few steps along the sidewalk, he put his arms around two bystanders and said, "Please help me to my room." A doctor was summoned. "Ruth is in better shape to recover from this attack than he was last year," the doctor said. "There is a danger, of course, that pneumonia may develop. We cannot tell about that until tomorrow at the earliest."[21]

Back in Tampa, the rookies continued to work under the direction of coaches Nick Altrock and Jack Chesbro and team trainer Mike Martin. Each day the rookies would play catch, field bunts, toss around a medicine ball, and jog twice around the field. Griffith, in Tampa with his family, watched the practices and spoke with the press each day. One day the sportswriters caught him by surprise by asking about Walter Johnson's plans to retire after the season. Stunned by the question, Griffith played innocent. "It's news to me," he said. "I've never been informed that Johnson has such plans."[22]

Back in Hot Springs, Johnson let the cat out of the bag, telling a few reporters about informing Griffith of his intentions through a letter in January. "My plans, however, are not now as definite as my intentions," Johnson said. "What I propose to do is buy into one of the Pacific Coast League clubs. There are two teams that no one has a chance to acquire and a couple of others are not good propositions, but there are three or four others that could be considered." According to experts, there were no Pacific Coast League teams for sale, nor would there be after the season. And in an era when ballplayers didn't have exorbitant salaries, buying a team in the Pacific Coast League, the highest caliber of minor-league talent, meant that Johnson would need financial backing. "I have friends who assured me of all the financial support necessary to swing such a deal as I have in mind," Johnson said, "and there will be someone to run the business end of the club while I manage the team and play some, too."[23]

"If Walter wants to retire he is free to do so, of course, and the Washington club would do nothing to stand in his way," said Griffith, "but we will not cross that bridge until we come to it. So as far as I know, Johnson has no definite plans about quitting the Nationals. He is under contract to play for me this year, and until the term of that agreement ends he will be a member of the Washington club."[24]

On March 9, the Hot Springs contingent arrived in Tampa. "You will be surprised at the fine physical condition of the boys as a result of their stay in Arkansas," Harris told a sportswriter. "The exercise we took combined with the radioactive water had a marvelous effect on all of us. The players act as if they feel ten years younger."[25] All ten players were said to be in excellent shape and ready to endure more than hiking and playing catch.

While talking to the press, Harris spotted Al Schacht in the lobby, the pitcher who was hoping to revive his major-league career. "Hey, Al," Harris called out. Schacht excused himself from his conversation and walked over to Harris. "Al," Harris said in a low earnest voice—almost a whisper, "I met some of the most beautiful women you had ever seen in Hot Springs."

"You did?" Schacht whispered.

"Yep," replied Harris, "and I told them all about you. They are going to arrive here in a few days and rent a cottage and you and I are going to visit them." Schacht was a bachelor who loved to talk about romance and his love for women. "I am a lover of beauty," he once said. "Feminine beauty, especially, has been one of my great weaknesses. Blessed with a soft romantic nature, the mere mention of a girl's name would stir me to deep thoughts of love in my younger days."[26]

All Washington veterans and rookies, comprising a squad of thirty-two, checked in to the Tampa Bay Hotel, including slugging outfielder Goose Goslin, who looked good according to the sportswriters. Goslin said he felt great before hurrying to the batting cage at Plant Field to do what he loved most—batting. "It's said he would rather bat than eat," a sportswriter quipped, and Goslin batted for thirty consecutive minutes with so much gusto that when he swung and missed, he landed on the seat of his pants. Fearing he'd wear out, Mike Martin ordered Goslin to stop and save it for the next day.[27]

The following morning the Senators held their first full-team practice, where thrilled voices of local baseball fans in the grandstand mingled with the pleasant sound of the bat meeting the horsehide, which echoed across the hotel's premises. "I am more than delighted and pleased at the work done since I left Tampa," said Harris. "I know Mike Martin, Jack Chesbro, and Nick Altrock have done wonders with the boys. They look to be in prime shape right now."[28]

Following a few more practices, the Senators opened their exhibition season with a 9–4 win over Brooklyn at Plant Field. The next day was another win, 10–6, over the Boston Braves. Leading the hitting attack was left fielder Goose Goslin, who in the 1923 season hit .300, drove home ninety-nine runs, and tied teammate Sam Rice with eighteen triples to lead the American League. In the field, Goslin had improved from the days when he was a liability, when it was a mystery whether he would catch a routine fly ball hit in his direction. He possessed a powerful throwing arm, perhaps the best among all American League outfielders, and he could throw with amazing accuracy from long distances. His biggest enigma was his lack of hustle and discipline, something that dated back to his childhood, when he would disobey his dad's orders while growing up on the family's New Jersey farm. In 1922, his disregard for curfew during spring training, resulted in suspension. In 1923, manager Donie Bush fined Goslin during spring training after the team's hard-hitting outfielder exchanged blows with a teammate. Now, under new manager Bucky Harris, Goslin was off to a good start, although he had been complaining about a sore throat and illness.

Harris informed Schacht that their rendezvous was set. On a Saturday morning, before the Senators played the Braves at Plant Field, Schacht went to town to get a haircut and a shave and to have his best suit pressed. Later that day he was in the hotel dining room when Harris confirmed, "It's all set Al." Following dinner, Schacht purchased a quart of liquor for twelve dollars. Then Harris and Schacht climbed into a cab and traveled to a cottage. On the way, Harris suggested they make a stop at a fruit stand to purchase a dozen oranges. After they traveled five more miles, Schacht was getting restless. "Where is this joint, anyway?" he asked.

"Now take it easy, Al," Harris replied. "You won't mind how far it is when you see these gals. Just think of it, Al. Two gorgeous women and all for you and me."

"Say, Bucky, are these girls married?" Schacht asked.

"What's the difference?" said Harris. "They're married but they're both getting divorces."

"We're not taking any chances, are we?" asked Schacht.

"You don't think for a minute that I, manager of a ball club, would take any chances of getting mixed up in a scandal, do you?" replied Harris.

"OK, Bucky, OK," Schacht said with a laugh. "I was only curious, that's all." When they finally reached the destination, the cab stopped in front of a lot, and Schacht added to his expensive evening by paying the driver five dollars.

The lot was completely dark, and Schacht was unable to see a house. The two men walked onto the lot, Harris carrying the bottle of liquor while Schacht handled the dozen oranges. They came across a few trees and a row of bushes, where Walter Johnson and others from the Hot Springs group hid, covering their mouths to squelch their laughter.

Harris and Schacht finally encountered a cottage with a single light from within gleaming through a window. Schacht peeked in the window and saw a man pacing. "Hey Bucky, look," Schacht said as he grabbed Harris's arm. Harris shook off Schact's hand and continued walking toward the front door.

Harris rang the bell, and a man opened the front door. Schacht was ready to run until Harris grabbed his arm. "Is Marge in?" Harris asked.

"So, you're the dirty bums who are trying to break up my home!" the man shouted. The man then reached into his pocket, pulled out a revolver, aimed it at Harris and fired two shots. "My God, I'm shot! He got me!" said Harris, who fell off the porch and lay very still.

"Now I'll get you, you rat!" the man said to Schacht.

Schacht leaped from the porch and ran as fast as he could, gunshots from his teammates firing blanks chasing him. They all fired, except for Johnson, who was overwhelmed by laughter at the sight.

As he hurried back to the hotel, Schacht heard a car, saw its headlights, and to be safe, he darted for bushes like a scared rabbit. When he finally reached the hotel, he was surprised to see a gathering of teammates in the lobby, all with broad smiles across their faces. One of them spoke up: "You look pale, Al." Laughter than filled the corridor, and Schacht, knowing he was the victim of a practical joke, laughed along.[29]

The Senators continued to win during their spring exhibition season. On March 21, Goslin went 3 for 4 in Washington's 8–2 win over the Milwaukee Brewers of the American Association, and the following day the Senators defeated the St. Louis Cardinals, 8–6. The team was said to be responding well to

Harris, though the burden of managing seemed to be affecting Harris's performance on the field. It hadn't been uncommon for him to make an error every now and then, but never a throwing error—until he started managing. And his spring batting average was a disappointing .255.

On March 25, the Nats dressed in Tampa and bused twenty-eight miles to Plant City to play the Indianapolis Indians, managed by Donie Bush. Going up against his predecessor, this game was more than an exhibition to Harris. In the fourth inning, Goslin loafed after hitting a routine infield grounder, and when he noticed he had a chance to beat the throw, he turned on the speed, but was thrown by less than a half step. Harris, seething over the lack of hustle on the play, sternly rebuked the outfielder and removed him from the game. When his team bowed in defeat, it was reported to be "a bitter pill for Harris to swallow."[30]

One day later, Harris broke out of his slump by going 4 for 4 and Johnson pitched four strong innings in a 7–6 win over the New York Giants at Plant Field. Harris said he was pleased with his team's showing, but he did have one issue: "More pep on the coaching line is what my club needs," he said, "and I firmly believe a lot of punch will be added to the club if I can induce Ben Egan to become a member of my coaching staff."[31]

Ben Egan, a former major-league catcher who once managed the Jersey City Skeeters of the International League, had crossed paths with the rookie manager when Harris was with Buffalo. "Egan is a splendid fellow," said Harris. "I have known him for years and know that in addition to being a shrewd judge of pitching prospects and clever teacher of young hurlers, he is a very valuable man to have around when the players begin to lag a trifle on the paths. If anyone can put fire into a base runner, Egan is the man."

"Does his job include 'assistant manager?'" a sportswriter asked.

"There will be no assistant manager on this ball club while I am in charge," answered Harris. "Assistant to the manager, yes; but assistant manager, no. I will be in complete control of the Nationals."[32]

The sportswriters wanted to know if Egan's hiring meant either of the two current coaches must go. "No," said Harris, "Altrock is a valuable asset and Chesbro is patient in helping the mound-men."[33] But Chesbro was said to have a "weak voice" when coaching on the baselines, and his future as a Washington coach looked doubtful. The word was Chesbro's future in Washington would be in scouting.[34]

As the season in Tampa reached its final week, Harris said the team was rounding nicely into shape for the start of the season, but mentioned that he wanted to polish off the rough edges before the season opened on April 15. He wanted to work with his outfielders on throwing to the correct base, his infielders on fielding mechanics, and his pitchers on holding runners. Something else he wanted to focus on was base running, said to be a sore spot for Washington in 1923.

The Senators checked out of the Tampa Bay hotel with a final bill of $20,000. The team would now head north, making stops along the way to play exhibition games before arriving in Washington for the start of the season. The first stop was Savannah, Georgia, for a game against the Rochester Tribe. When the ninth inning ended with the game tied, Goslin said he felt tired and weak and wanted to be removed from the game, a request his manager denied. After the game, Harris made an announcement: Goslin would not be making the rest of the team's road trip. He said he had ordered the outfielder to return to Washington to get into shape while working under the supervision of newly hired coach Ben Egan. "I would be shamed to start in a league game with a man too unfit for duty," said Harris. "Goose is overweight and certainly has not strengthened his legs sufficiently to withstand the strain of play in the field. Without making it generally known, I had warned Goose a couple of times during the stay at Tampa, but apparently, the warnings had no effect. Now I am through with warnings."[35]

When Goslin arrived in Washington, he went to see a doctor, who found the cause of his fatigue was a case of tonsillitis. If he went through surgery to remove his sore tonsils, he would miss the start of the season, so Goslin elected to undergo treatment with an understanding that surgery would be necessary after the season. He missed no time and went to the stadium to work under the supervision of a coach Egan and a physician. He took batting practice during his workout and hit one over the recently heightened right field wall. He said the treatment was working and he felt better and was ready for the season.

On April 12, the Senators arrived at the refurbished Griffith Stadium for a two-game home exhibition series against the Boston Braves to conclude their preseason. The team noticed a fresh paint job, the new left field pavilion, the higher right field wall, and the new infield turf. A month before, the old "lumpy, bumpy, jumpy infield," said to be the worst in the league, was greatly improved when avid baseball fan Edward B. McLean presented the Senators with an entire nine-hundred-square-foot golf green from his Friendship mansion. "This means no more hoppers around second base and short, no more ducking heads or zig-zag grounders from hill to hill," said team secretary Ed Eynon.[36] For his hard work and investment to improve the ballpark, Griffith was praised by a Washington sportswriter: "He has built a most modern and interesting park. This ballpark, with the improvements made since last fall, is now the ultimate word in baseball parks."[37]

Although they were exhibition games, the press counted the two games against the Braves as Harris's Griffith Stadium managerial debut. In the team's final dress rehearsal, the Senators won both games, much to the delight of the eight thousand fans who braved the cold weather.

With the start of the new season just two days away, sportswriters were pestering Harris for a prediction. Frank Morse, a West Coast sportswriter and former football All-American at Princeton in the 1890s, asked Harris how the team looked for the upcoming season. "Got any chance?" he wanted to know.

"Well, we'll be hustling all the time," answered Harris. "Anyone who plays us will know they're in for a battle."

"I've heard this before," Morse replied with a smile, "but along midsummer Washington clubs are generally only playing the schedule out."[38]

When asked to say a final word about the upcoming season by a local writer, Harris said he would be glad to make a statement but no predictions. "I believe that I have a club that will bear watching in the pennant race," he said. "I believe we have a better club than four of the teams in this race. We might even be better than New York, Detroit and Cleveland, if the breaks come our way."[39]

CHAPTER 3

Opening Day (April)

There seems to be a club owner's policy there. When the team fails, they change managers rather than get better players. I hope they give Harris a fair opportunity. They can't possibly expect him to win the pennant with the team he has.[1]

—Babe Ruth

Washington Herald sportswriter John Dugan reported a lack of baseball enthusiasm in the District back in February, but with a manager now in place and the arrival of Opening Day, the Washington baseball fans were reenergized. All box seats and grandstand tickets for the home opener were purchased prior to game day. Fans who didn't get in on advanced ticket sales endured the chilly spring weather to line up at the ticket window before 9:00 a.m., the hour the Senators' box office opened for business, and shortly after the ticket window shutters were unlocked, the few hundred remaining left field bleachers and $1 standing-room tickets were gone to complete the sellout.

A *Washington Herald* reporter believed, "Washington's opening baseball game has become more spectacular than an inauguration."[2] The home opener became a gala in 1910, when President Taft became the first president to throw out the pregame ceremonial pitch from the ballpark's presidential box. The Opening Day tradition had continued with the two presidents who followed Taft—Woodrow Wilson and Warren Harding—and now the honor fell to Calvin Coolidge, who was expected to arrive fifteen minutes before game time. Other pregame festivities scheduled to celebrate the occasion included a performance by the Navy Band, a presentation of two floral pieces for Bucky Harris, and the usual Opening Day routine of both teams parading to the center field flagpole to raise the American flag.

Around 11:00 a.m., fans began to park at designated street parking on College, Rhode Island, Third, and Tenth streets. At noon, the ballpark gates opened and fans began to file in by the hundreds. They were greeted by vendors who shrilled their cries and shouts of "Ya can't tell the players without a sco' cawd!"[3] Red-capped ushers led dignified officials to their seats. Men, women, and children from all walks of life took their seats to observe the performance of the Navy Band stationed on the field.

By this time, the ballplayers began to arrive at the ballpark. Upon his arrival, Walter Johnson was greeted by a well-dressed young man who asked if he'd dare cross the gamblers. "Why, what do you mean?" asked a confused Johnson. "Well, all the wise bettors in town are wagering that the first ball you pitch this afternoon will be a strike," the young man explained. "Why not cross them up by throwing a wide one?" Johnson politely declined the advice and walked away.[4] The last thing the great pitcher wanted was to settle betting wagers and mix gambling with baseball.

Major League Baseball was thriving four years after the game's integrity was nearly ruined by the news of eight members of the Chicago White Sox confessing to fixing the 1919 World Series in exchange for a big payday. Fearing a shellacking at the ticket window, the Major-League club owners hired Kenesaw Mountain Landis, a highly-respected federal judge who loved the game, as baseball's first commissioner, a decision that appealed to the fans and press. The integrity of Landis, and Babe Ruth's uncanny ability to consistently hit the ball over the fence, restored the fans' confidence, and they responded by attending ballgames in record numbers. To continue to protect the game, Major League Baseball was doing all it could to stamp out gambling pools as fast as possible. "It's hard to uncover all of it,"[5] admitted American League President Ban Johnson, but organized baseball acted whenever a possible threat came to light. For instance, Phil Douglas had won fifteen regular season games and two World Series games for the 1921 New York Giants and was 11–4 in 1922 when he got into hot water with Giants manager John McGraw for his drinking episodes. McGraw gave Douglas a blistering lecture that made the pitcher angry enough to rebel. Douglas wrote a letter to former teammate Les Mann in which he informed Mann that he was willing to intentionally lose to deny McGraw the 1922 pennant. Mann gave the letter to his manager, who sent it to Landis. "Phil Douglas, you are permanently out of baseball," said Landis when the pitcher confessed in a personal meeting with the commissioner.[6]

By 1924, most believed that the game's integrity was fully restored and hoped that the 1919 World Series fix would soon be forgotten, but a continuous source of frustration for Commissioner Landis was that somehow the 1919 scandal wouldn't go away. Buck Weaver, the White Sox third baseman who was banned for not reporting his knowledge of the fix, repeatedly applied for reinstatement, and Joe Jackson, another of the eight, and one of the game's greatest, made news when he hired an attorney and filed a lawsuit against the White Sox for back pay he felt he was owed. In the spring of 1923, Jackson paid a visit to the Senators before a spring exhibition game in Savannah. He sat alone, refused to discuss his lawsuit, and spoke only to Donie Bush to congratulate him on becoming the Senators' manager and to wish him luck in the coming season. In January of 1924, a jury reached a verdict in Jackson's favor; however, the trial judge overruled the decision on the grounds that Jackson's testimony clashed with the one he gave to a grand jury in 1920. Jackson ended up settling with the White Sox for an undisclosed amount.[7]

Players from both teams emerged from their respective team dugouts and took the field for their pregame warmup. The Senators were decked in new plain white uniforms without pinstripes, wording, or chest emblem. The new uniforms did have a blue "W" on each sleeve and included midnight blue and white horizontal striped socks and midnight blue caps with a white "W" above the bill. Shortly after three o'clock, Secretary of the Navy Curtis Wilbur arrived and the Navy Band broke into "Anchors Aweigh." When the band took a break, E. Lawrence Phillips, the Griffith Stadium field announcer, raised his megaphone and began to announce the starting lineups. When he made the announcement about thirty-six-year-old Walter Johnson starting his eighteenth season with the Senators, the fans cut loose with a lusty cheer.

Then came the arrival of Calvin Coolidge, the First Lady, and the rest of the president's party. As Secret Service and police officers escorted the president toward the flag-draped presidential box, a section composed of the first few rows from the field, located between home plate and the Senators dugout on the first base side, the fans cheered. Next was the march to the center field flagpole. Griffith and Secretary Wilbur led the band between a line of Athletics on one side and Senators lined up on the other. As the flag rose, the band began to play "The Star-Spangled Banner," causing the crowd to rise to their feet and remove their hats.

Following the playing of the national anthem, the crowd fell silent while the two teams returned to their dugouts. "Atta boy, Cal!" a fan shouted.[8] The president broke into a smile and the crowd cheered. Then Griffith, Johnson, and Harris, with a new official baseball in hand, emerged from the Senators' dugout and headed to the presidential box. Griffith introduced the president to his rookie manager, who shook the president's hand and gave him the baseball. Walter Johnson, ready to play his usual Opening Day role of catching the president's ceremonial throw, stood a few feet in front of the president's box. With the ball held high, Coolidge stood immobile for several seconds amid cries of "Throw the darn thing, Cal."[9] Coolidge finally tossed the ball into the air and Johnson made a barehanded catch. "His throw lacked zip and there was nothing on the ball but the cover," wrote a Philadelphia sportswriter.[10] "I never saw such a curve," said Senators coach Nick Altrock. "I thought it would break somebody's skull, too, unless it would be the umpire's. No ball is hard enough to do that."[11]

A Washington record home crowd of 25,581 cheered when the Senators took the field for the first inning. A louder cheer greeted Walter Johnson when he stepped onto the pitcher's mound to hurl his eleventh Washington home opener. Philadelphia's left-handed-hitting second baseman Max Bishop, playing in his first major-league game, stepped into the batter's box. Johnson then went into his windup and threw his first pitch of the season, a fastball that split the heart of the plate and hit Muddy Ruel's big catcher's mitt with a loud pop for strike one. The Athletics put two runners on base with two outs in the inning, but Johnson escaped the jam when rookie outfielder Al Simmons grounded out.

Philadelphia's starting pitcher was Slim Harriss, said to be a jinx to the Senators for his success against the Washington club in the past. He stood six feet six inches and had a sweeping side-arm cross-fire motion. "He's in the best shape of his career," A's manager Connie Mack said during the spring.[12] Harriss sent the Senators down in order in the first inning, but in the bottom of the second, Goslin singled, right fielder Showboat Fisher walked, and third baseman Doc Protho followed with a "well-placed" sacrifice bunt to move the runners along.[13] Roger Peckinpaugh made the second out of the inning, but Muddy Ruel, batting eighth in the Washington lineup, drilled a single to center to score the two runners. The Senators made it 3–0 an inning later when Rice walked and was said to look very fast when he stole second. He then scored on Goslin's second hit of the day.

A three-run lead appeared to be more than enough for the way Johnson was pitching. Following a shaky first inning, he sent the Athletics down in order in the next four innings. In the top of the sixth, with Washington now up, 4–0, following a triple by Judge and an RBI single by Rice, a Philadelphia batter finally reached base when Johnson issued a walk. In the top of the ninth, Johnson finished the game with his eighth strikeout of the day. The final score was 4–0, for the first Senators win of the season and the ninety-ninth shutout of Johnson's career. "All indications are his arm is as good as ever," a Philadelphia writer told the fans back home. "There was never a moment when Johnson was not the absolute master of the situation."[14]

The record crowd at Griffith Stadium was said to be orderly and impressed to the eighth precinct captain, Robert E. Doyle, who said there was never a more orderly crowd in all his years of policing Opening Day. Following the game's last out, fans immediately hurried out of the ballpark, but the street cars were unable to accommodate the many who sought to ride them. "For a few minutes, it looked as if the adage, 'There is always room for one more' was an exploded theory," quipped a local writer.[15] Finally, an expert streetcar packer arrived on the scene and every car carried fifteen to fifty over the labeled capacity.

The Washington Senators were 1–0 and in first place for a day. The party quickly ended when the Nats dropped their next two to the Athletics. The day after Johnson's five-hit shutout, George Mogridge took the mound for his first start of the season. At age thirty-five, he was starting his twelfth major-league season and his fourth with Washington. He was an eighteen-game winner for the Senators in 1921 and 1922, but his win total fell to thirteen in 1923, in what many believed to be a sign of age. In his first start of the new season, Mogridge was tagged for three runs on three hits and replaced after the first inning. The Athletics were ahead, 4–0, before the Senators finally got on the scoreboard. The A's went on to win, 6–1, with the Senators totaling just five hits off Athletics starting knuckleball pitcher, Eddie Rommel. "His knuckler was doing all sorts of things," according to John Dugan.[16]

The next day, before fifteen-hundred shivering fans, the Athletics once again struck early with a run in each of the first two innings against Senators starting pitcher Paul Zahniser. The Senators threatened in each of the first three innings but were unable to score. Down, 2–0, in the bottom of the fourth, the Senators got a gift when Athletics starting pitcher Fred Heimach walked four to give Washington a run. With the bases still loaded, Harris singled to score two more for a 3–2 Senators lead. An RBI single by Al Simmons in the sixth-inning tied the score, 3–3, and then the Athletics threatened in the top of the eighth when a walk and another single by Simmons put runners on first and third with two outs, which set the stage for a favorite play of A's manager Connie Mack— the double steal with runners on the corner bases. Mack also knew his favorite play might work against a young pitcher like Zahniser, and as Mack had hoped, the youngster went for the bait. Al Simmons broke for second base, and Zahniser, focusing on Simmons, ignored the runner on third, who broke for the plate. "Home! Throw home!"[17] his teammates hollered, but Zahniser threw to Harris, who tagged Simmons for an out after the runner on third had crossed home to give the A's a 4–3 lead. The Senators had a chance in the bottom of the ninth, when rookie Lance Richbourg socked a one-out pinch-hit double, but Judge and Harris grounded out to end the game.

The fourth and final scheduled game of the Athletics-Senators series was rained out. Later that evening, the New York Yankees came to town for a four-game series and checked into Washington's Raleigh Hotel. Like the Senators, the Yankees had lost two of their first three. At Boston, the Yanks won the opener by scoring two runs in the top of the ninth, thanks to two Red Sox errors, but then the New York pitching staff allowed nine runs in each of the next two games. Babe Ruth hit just two singles and did not homer in the series, although nobody worried. "I feel confident the Yankees will win another pennant," said

Yankees manager Miller Huggins. "My team this year is just as good as last year in every way, unless something unforeseen should happen." Huggins believed the biggest obstacle to surmount was overconfidence. "I must fight the feeling on my team that because they are champions they can go out and win anytime," Huggins said. When asked who he believed would be their greatest competition, the Yankees manager said Detroit. "I think the Tigers will get better pitching than Cleveland, also a dangerous club."[18]

A sportswriter from the *New York World* predicted the 1924 World Series would match the Yankees and Giants for the fourth straight year. "The New York Yankees and New York Giants should battle again in the World Series because the other teams have not improved enough to overcome the superiority shown by the two pennant winners of the 1923 races," he wrote.[19] The Yankees won ninety-eight games and finished sixteen full games ahead of the second-place Tigers in 1923. The Giants won ninety-five games and finished just four and a half games ahead of the next-best team, but they did spend every day in first-place during the 1923 season.

Most sportswriters were predicting the Yankees and Giants to repeat as pennant winners in 1924. The experts saw the Tigers and Indians as the next best in the American League. The St. Louis Browns and improving Philadelphia Athletics were expected to fight for fourth place, while the Red Sox, White Sox, and Senators were projected to fill the last three spots in the standings. Most writers were picking the Senators to finish sixth. The *Chicago Tribune* projected the Senators to finish last and a *New York Times* expert called the Senators one of the weakest teams in the league. "Stanley Harris has ambitions for a first division berth, but there is a rocky road ahead of him," penned a *New York Times* sports-writer.[20] *New York Sun* sportswriter Will Wedge agreed with most writers about a low finish in the standings for the Senators, but noted much interest in the Washington baseball club due to their new twenty-seven-year-old manager, "the youngest pilot in the Majors," wrote Wedge. "Many of the men Harris bosses are considerably older than himself, but this does not make for any unpleasant relationships, as Harris is extraordinarily popular and every man on his squad is working hard and pulling for him to succeed."[21]

The *Washington Post* had no comment about predictions and John Dugan of the *Washington Herald* backed out by writing, "It is a mystery where the Senators will finish this year."[22] Denman Thompson of the *Washington Star* stood alone among all writers when he forecasted a fourth-place finish for the Senators. "The 1924 edition of the Griffmen is a far more formidable combination than that of last year," wrote Thompson. "The spirit of hustle installed by Harris will pay off. The Nationals impress as a first-division club."[23]

When the Yankees arrived at Griffith Stadium to open the series, Babe Ruth immediately found that home runs would be harder to come by than in previous years in Washington. During batting practice, Ruth's long drives to right field hit high off the recently heightened right field wall and fell to the ground. The previous winter, Griffith had added six feet to the right field wall that was already over twenty feet tall. Finding right field too difficult, Ruth aimed for center field, and the last ball he hit during batting practice landed in the center field bleachers.

Griffith Stadium was the hardest park in Major League Baseball for home runs, not only due to the tall right field wall, but also because of the long out-field dimensions. The distances from home plate were 414 feet down the left field line, 421 from home to the center field wall, and 332 to the right field foul pole.[24] The stadium included a newly constructed set of left field bleachers, only opened to customers on Sundays, holidays, and Opening Day. Field-level and mezzanine seats extended from behind home plate to both foul poles, and there was an upper deck that ran from the third base side, behind home plate, and along the first-base side. In 1923, the upper-deck seating was extended on the third-base side to increase the capacity for baseball games and for more seating between the goalposts for college football games played at the stadium during the fall. There was also a two-foot section of seats in between the high right field wall and the right field foul pole.

Thirty-four-year-old Senators rookie Joe Martina took the mound for his first major-league career start. Known by his nickname, "Oyster Joe," because dealing oysters was his family's business, had spent his entire fourteen-year career pitching for minor league teams in the deep south.[25] He had won twenty or more games in four of his last five seasons and preferred to pitch in the Land of Dixie rather than in the majors. Now in his mid-thirties and a lifelong minor leaguer, many wondered if he could make the grade in the majors, but Senators scout Joe Engel was certain he would do well.

Yankees left-handed-hitting center fielder Whitey Witt was the first batter to step-in against Martina, and with a full count, the rookie pitcher elected to groove a fastball rather than go with his best pitch—the curveball—and Witt welcomed Martina to the American League by sending that fastball over the high right field wall with room to spare. After the rookie hurler retired the next batter, he pitched cautiously to Babe Ruth, who was greeted by a mix of boos and cheers before drawing a walk. Slugging Yankees outfielder Bob Meusel followed with a double to send Ruth to third, but Martina kept his poise and worked his way out of the jam. The Senators evened the score against Yankees starting pitcher Herb Pennock, who beat the Senators five times last season. Joe Judge greeted Pennock with a drive that hit ten feet up the center field wall for a triple and Harris followed with a single over second to score Judge. In the bottom of the fourth, Martina, who had singled in his first major-league at bat, singled again to drive in the go-ahead run. In the top of the fifth, Babe Ruth, at the plate for the third time in the game, took a strike, swung and missed for strike two, and then let a sharp curve go by for strike three. Unhappy with the called third strike by home plate umpire Billy Evans, Ruth tossed his bat high into the air, and when the bat landed, close to Martina on the pitcher's mound, Evans informed Ruth that he was out of the game. Ruth, who kept walking after tossing his bat and never turned around, responded to the boos from nine thousand fans by stopping and sarcastically doffing his cap. When play resumed, Martina struck out Wally Pipp on four pitches and ended the inning by striking out second baseman Aaron Ward for the second time. In the bottom of the fifth the Washington batsmen scored three, on a Yankees error, singles by Goslin and Fisher, and a triple by Protho for a 5–1 lead. In the top of the ninth, with the Senators now ahead, 7–2, Meusel whiffed to became Martina's seventh strikeout victim and Ward fouled out to end the game. "There's a pitcher who has wasted most of his time by remaining in the minors," Harris said about Martina following the game. "He's going to be a winner with Washington."[26]

The next day a Sunday crowd of twenty thousand came to Griffith Stadium and watched Walter Johnson beat the Yankees for his second win of the season. "Walter Johnson and that long, easy sweeping delivery of his are just as potent as ever," wrote Will Wedge. "He fanned six, which swelled his total all-time list of victims to 3,072. What a marvelous accomplishment."[27] In the top of the sixth of a scoreless game Babe Ruth stepped in against Johnson, with the great slugger still looking for his first homer of the 1924 season. "I thought about it and dreamed about it all winter," Ruth said. "Go get that homer out of your system, and maybe the boys will start hitting," Huggins told Ruth. Yankees trainer Doc Woods told Ruth that the cold weather was holding him up and he assured him that everything would turn out all right. "Wait'll you get back to New York," Woods told Ruth. "You'll be primed for a big opening there and I pity the pitcher you will bust out on."[28]

But Ruth walked in his first plate appearance when Walter Johnson, working the corners, missed on a 3–2 pitch, was retired in his second plate appearance, and worked the count to 3–0 the third time he came to the plate. Johnson then threw a fastball down the middle, and Ruth swung, connected, and sent a long fly ball to right-center, which would have been a home run in Washington in previous seasons, but now with the extension of the right field wall, Ruth's drive hit a sign on the top tier of advertisement boards and he settled for a triple. When Wally Pipp followed with a single, Ruth scored to give the Yankees a 1–0 lead, but the lead would be short-lived. Yankees starting pitcher Bob Shawkey, said to "look like a million dollars" through the first five innings, was kayoed by a four-run Washington rally in the bottom of the sixth.[29] One inning later, the Washington batters tagged Yankees relief pitchers Sam Jones and Ben Shields for six runs on six hits before a single Washington batter was retired. In the top of the eighth, with the Senators up, 10–1, Ruth finally found his stride by "lifting a beauty far and fast over the right-field fence," for his first homer of the season.[30] Washington scored two more in their half of the eighth en route to a 12–3 win.

"I'm pulling for Walter to hang up twenty-five victories this season," Harris said after the game, "and we'll do all in our power to help him do this. Then I want him to stay with the club. He knows we might cop a pennant before he hangs up the glove and forgets the game he has been a national figure for so long."[31] In today's win, Harris made three hits to lift his season average to .333; Goose Goslin added two hits, including a bases-loaded triple, to boost his season average to .438; and Walter Johnson also made two hits, including a double. But the star of the game was Showboat Fisher, who went four-for-five. Before the season, Fisher battled Lance Richbourg and Carr Smith for the Senators starting right field job until he won with a good spring and now owned a .353 season batting average while batting in the number five spot of the Washington lineup. "The Bucky Harris enthusiasm is beginning to catch," wrote *Washington Times* sportswriter Louis Dougher. "Joe Judge is willing to wager the Senators will finish at least in fourth place. Others say they have a winning germ or two within their system."[32]

"You can never tell about baseball," said Roger Peckinpaugh. "The club picked to win a pennant sometimes fizzles. The club picked for last sometimes steps up and breaks a record. Some of the writers have picked us for last place. Maybe they'll be fooled."[33]

The third game of the series was played before a good Monday-afternoon crowd of seven thousand on a cold and overcast day. In his second start of the season, George Mogridge once again allowed three runs on three hits in the first inning. When the first hit was in the air, a fan yelled, "Take him out!"[34] This time, however, Harris stuck with Mogridge and the veteran pitcher responded by allowing no runs and only four hits through the next six innings. "I'm not worrying about him at all," Harris said about Mogridge after the game. "He's going to win a lot of games before the season is gone."[35] The Senators fought back and cut the lead to 3–2, but an error by Harris in the top of the eighth led to another New York run in a 4–2 Yankees win.

For Harris, it was a tough day. He failed to come through with men on base on two occasions and made an error. After the game a fan suggested Harris "ought to bench himself," then growled a few other things.[36] Denman Thompson summed up the final game of the four-game set, writing, "The Yankees displayed more energy today since the season started."[37] The Senators scored two in the bottom of the first, when Judge tripled, Rice singled, and Goslin tripled, but the Yankees scored four in the top of the second and went on to win, 6–3.

CHAPTER 4

A Slow Start to the Season (April)

When the Senators arrived at the Aldine Hotel in Philadelphia before opening a four-game series against the Athletics, they were greeted by an old friend named Mike, an aged Irish hotel porter with well-nigh white hair. He took good care of all the visiting teams who quartered at the Aldine Hotel, and in return he attended most home games as a guest of the visiting teams. When talking about his favorite team—the Athletics—the fires of Celtic enthusiasm burned in his breast. "Let me tell you," the porter replied when *Washington Times* sportswriter Louis Dougher asked how he expected the Athletics would do. "Connie's goin' to win that pennant this year, or I know nothing about baseball." When asked why, the porter mentioned Philadelphia's highly touted rookie outfielders, Paul Strand and Al Simmons. The waitresses in the hotel's dining room agreed. "They know because Connie Mack says so, and that's good enough for them," wrote Dougher. According to the Washington sports scribe, Washington fans tended to be more cynical when talking about pennants. "Maybe because they never experienced a pennant-winner," guessed Dougher. "Second place stands as [Washington's] high-water mark and that was long ago."[1]

Once upon a time, Connie Mack's Philadelphia Athletics were the best team in baseball, winning four pennants and three world championships within a five-year span (1910–1914). Following the 1914 season, Mack lost a few stars to the lucrative contracts offered by the new Federal League, thus motivating the A's owner-manager to sell his remaining stars and build another winner from scratch, though this proved more difficult than expected. Seven consecutive last-place finishes followed the Athletics' half decade of dominance. In 1922, Mack's A's moved up a notch to a seventh-place finish, and in 1923, the A's finished sixth. Now in 1924, most writers expected Mack's team to climb another rung or two in the standings, and maybe post their first winning record since 1914.

Their gradual improvement helped the Athletics regain popularity in Philadelphia. All Opening Day box seats and grandstand tickets had been sold out for weeks. There was excitement over the promising rookies in the A's starting lineup joining holdovers Jimmy Dykes, Sam Hale, Bing Miller, and twenty-five-year-old Joe Hauser, who led the Athletics with a .307 batting average, sixteen homers, and ninety-four RBIs in 1923.

But most of the focus was on the newcomers, known as the Slugging Siamese and Sizzling Serpentine. "'S.S.' will be posted all over the bat bag and down the middle of the chest protector," a sportswriter quipped about the rookie outfielders.[2] With these two onboard, it was said that Mack finally got the hitters he had been looking for. In 1923, Paul Strand hit .394 with forty-three home runs and 187 RBIs in 194 games at Salt Lake City. Al Simmons hit .366 during his 1923 minor-league season in Milwaukee. "He looks to be a complete ballplayer in many ways," Mack said of Simmons. "He has no weaknesses. Naturally, he needs a little brushing up, but this ought to be easy."[3] Simmons had an unusual batting stance, described to be all wrong for a real hitter according to students of form. While standing in the batter's box, Simmons would point his left foot toward third base. "He not only 'sticks his foot in the bucket,' as players refer to this practice of pulling away from the plate," wrote Denman Thompson, "but he seems to have his entire leg immersed. Simmons has always batted that way, according to those who have followed his career, and has consistently murdered all sorts of pitching."[4]

Like the Washington home opener, the Athletics scheduled pregame entertainment. To add to the occasion, the A's were dressed in new white home uniforms that sported a white elephant emblem on the chest, the first time since 1914 that a white elephant had been worn by the A's. Mack's idea of this insignia came when New York Giants manager John McGraw referred to the American League as a White Elephant league, and Mack, finding humor in McGraw's comment, played along by turning the sarcastic remark into his team's logo.

Hard-throwing twenty-five-year-old right-handed rookie pitcher Fred Marberry, who went 4–0 after joining the Senators late in the 1923 season, made his first start of the season. He had arrived in Washington after a year and a half of mediocrity in the minor leagues and couldn't throw a curveball or any other pitches other than a fastball, but Senators scout Joe Engel didn't mind. It was the pitcher's physique that impressed Engel. Marberry stood six-feet-one, weighed 190 pounds, wore a size thirteen shoe, and was said to be built for hard work. His size and ability to throw hard were said to intimidate opposing batters, and his style of lifting his huge shoe high in the air during his "tremendous" high kick "would leave a picture of spikes in the batter's face," described a sportswriter.[5]

The Senators lost, 6–4, in typical Washington baseball fashion, beating themselves by failing to execute. Marberry was in trouble in each of the first five innings, although he managed to escape each jam. With still no score in the Philadelphia seventh, Jimmy Dykes lined one into the left field corner, and when Goslin was slow to get to the ball, Dykes made it all the way to third base. The next batter, Sam Hale, grounded to Peckinpaugh, who threw home. Senators catcher Muddy Ruel ran Dykes back to third base after receiving Peckinpaugh's heave, then threw the ball, intended for third baseman Doc Protho, but the throw hit Dykes and rolled into left field, allowing Dykes to score. Paul Strand followed with an RBI hit and Joe Hauser drove one that hit the top of the right field fence and bounced over for a two-run homer, pushing the A's lead to 4–0. Simmons extended the inning with an infield hit and the next batter, Bing Miller, lifted a fly ball into shallow left field, which Peckinpaugh dropped for an error. A sacrifice fly and a grounder that bounced over Protho for a hit scored two more for the A's. Down 6–0, the Senators kept fighting, just like Bucky Harris said his team would do in every game. The Senators did rally for four runs, but it wasn't enough.

The Nats won the next day, 4–3, though it wasn't easy. They squandered a 3–0 lead and missed on scoring opportunities, but according to *Washington Herald* sportswriter John Dugan, poor umpiring by home plate umpire Pants Rowland was the bigger obstacle. "Oyster Joe" Martina, making his second major-league start, allowed just three hits and struck out six in his second win of the season. He walked five, something that Dugan attributed to poor umpiring rather than the pitcher missing the strike zone. With the game tied, 3–3, in the top of the ninth, a single, error, and groundout put Washington runners on second and third with two outs. Athletics pitcher Curly Ogden was ready to work on the next batter, when Sam Rice, the Senators' crafty and fleet-footed baserunner on third base, began to walk toward the plate. Connie Mack and his players in the dugout shouted, "and this evidently caused our catcher to look at third," Mack said after the game. "Then Curly started to pitch, and before [catcher] Frank [Bruggy] could set himself for the ball, it was on top of him, hit his mitt, and went to the stand," and Rice easily scored to give Washington a 4–3 lead.[6] "Although this break gave Washington the battle, they had it coming to them," wrote Dugan, who believed the break made up for the Senators being victimized by the umpires.[7]

Walter Johnson started the third game of the series with hopes of winning his third straight start of the season. Like the day before, the Senators jumped out to a 3–0 lead, and like the day before, they blew their early lead, as errors pushed them to a 6–5 loss. They committed five misplays to give them fourteen in their last five games. "The Harris aggression is putting on a fine circus these days," wrote Louis Dougher. "No matter how powerful the hurling is, the Griffs are sure to lose."[8] Johnson struck out four and walked none in six innings, but the Senators' fielding, or the lack of it, sent him to his first defeat of the season.

The Senators managed to play an error-free game in the last match of the series; however, they made only five hits against Athletics knuckleballer Eddie Rommel in a 2–0 loss for Washington's fifth defeat in their last six games and dropped their season record to 4–7. But this didn't upset *Washington Herald* sportswriter John Dugan, who now believed that this year's Washington pitching staff was the team's best in ten years, "and first class pitching will win ball games in any league," he wrote. Dugan also wrote about the team's hitting, insisting that it has been as good as expected, "although they have not been hitting in the clutch lately." His only complaint was about the fielding, describing the Senators' defense as being "far off color." But Dugan was not too concerned. "Such a fielding combination of Peckinpaugh, Harris, and Judge cannot falter for long."[9]

In addition to the team's fielding woes and lack of timely hitting, right field was now a problem. During spring training, Harris talked about a battle between Showboat Fisher, Lance Richbourg, and Carr Smith for the position. Fisher won the job by hitting well throughout the spring, and he appeared to be heading for a good year when he went 4 for 5 against the Yankees on April 20; however, he then got only one hit in his next twenty at bats and lost his starting job to veteran Nemo Leibold. Harris decided that Fisher wouldn't do and sent the right fielder to Minneapolis in exchange for twenty-nine-year-old outfielder Carl East.

The Senators returned home and played before a Sunday home crowd of sixteen thousand disappointed fans. "They kicked, howled, and criticized," Dugan wrote about the home crowd, "but it was all uncalled for. Yesterday's victory over the Red Sox proves the fact that the team can win, and that it also has some punch in its make-up."[10] Harris had hoped to start George Mogridge, but when the left-handed veteran came down with a heavy cold, he turned to Tom Zachary, the forgotten man on the Washington pitching staff. Zachary, who disappointed with just ten wins in 1923, had a poor spring and was demoted to the bullpen. Asked why he would bother to keep him on the roster, Harris said the pitcher had value, because he consistently beat Chicago and Cleveland.

In the bottom of the third, Peckinpaugh came to the plate for his first at bat of the game. He was off to a slow start in 1924, hitting just .135 and had committed two errors in a 6–5 loss in Philadelphia a few days before. Now he struck out in his first plate appearance, and he heard about it from the home crowd. "Peck is a slow starter, but he'll be there before long," assured Harris. "You know we haven't had any baseball weather yet and Peck is a bit stiff after that warm weather we had in Florida before hitting the road."[11]

The Senators blew a 4–2 lead and were victimized by a triple play in the first inning when, with runners on first and second, Rice lined out to Boston first baseman Joe Harris, who threw to shortstop Dud Lee in time to nip the runner on second for the second out, and Lee threw back to Harris in time to complete the triple killing. With the score tied, 4–4, the Senators rallied for five in their half of the eighth inning: Goslin doubled; Judge and Ruel singled to score Goslin; Protho crushed a triple to deep center to score two more; Washington relief pitcher By Speece nailed a long drive to center field to score the inning's fourth run; and when the center fielder had trouble handling the drive, for an error, Speece completed the trip around the bases for the inning's fifth run.

Harris gave Fred Marberry the starting assignment the next day, and he kept the Red Sox off the board until he gave up two runs in the seventh inning for a 2–1 Boston lead. When the Senators came to bat in the bottom of the seventh, the skies darkened and a spring shower threatened. Peckinpaugh came through by leading off the inning with a long drive to the base of the left-center field stands for a triple. Two batters later, Peckinpaugh was still on third with two outs when Bucky Harris, who had two hits in this game to lift his season batting average to .290, showed why his teammates often referred to him as "Little Scrap Iron."[12] As Harris stood in the batter's box and waited for the pitch, the wind picked up and swept across the field. Red Sox pitcher Alex Ferguson, using the wind as an excuse to stall, rubbed his eye and called to home plate umpire Dick Nallin. He walked toward the Boston dugout and informed the umpire that something was in his eye. When Boston manager Lee Fohl stepped onto the field to attend to his pitcher, Nallin informed the Red Sox manager that either Ferguson or a relief pitcher needed to take the mound, or this game would be a forfeit. Ferguson slowly headed back to the mound, hoping for rain. Following a strike, a ball, and still no sign of rain, Harris hit a ground ball that looked as if it would roll into left field for an RBI single. Red Sox shortstop Dud Lee raced to his right, made a backhanded stop, and threw to first. Harris, knowing the play was going to be close, made a head-first slide and beat the throw while Peckinpaugh crossed home on the play to tie the score, 2–2.

Rice popped out to end the inning, and since the expected shower had yet to arrive, the game continued. But following the first pitch in the top of the eighth, the umpires decided that it was too dark and called the game with the tie score. The Senators did not win, but they didn't lose, thanks to their hustling, hard-nosed manager.

In the third game of the series, "Oyster Joe" Martina, the thirty-four-year-old Washington rookie pitcher who had done so well in his first two starts, gave up two hits, walked two, allowed three runs, and was out of the game after only one inning. The Senators fought back, but Boston scored six in the top of the sixth in a 15–6 Red Sox win.

When rain washed out the fourth game of the series the next day, the month of April ended with the Senators holding an unimpressive 5–8 record.

"Pilot Harris's club right now is in need of a winning streak," wrote Dugan, who reminded his readers about the team's good pitching and productive hitting.[13] He did admit that the batters were failing too often in the clutch and the fielding was subpar, but he was still convinced this was a good team. "I believe the club will find itself in each department on this voyage," Harris said.[14] The voyage he was talking about was a three-game series in New York followed by a home game versus the Athletics then four games at Boston.

CHAPTER 5

The Voyage (May)

Babe Ruth made a prediction during the Yankees-Senators series, about the Yankees catching fire before leaving Washington, and he was right. After winning the last two games in Washington, the Yanks reeled off six consecutive wins. Now riding an eight-game winning-streak, the red-hot Yankees faced Walter Johnson and the Senators at Yankee Stadium, and in the first game of the series, Johnson cooled off the Yankees with five strikeouts in six innings for his third win of the season. "He snapped them in fast and the Yankees couldn't see the ball," was how a New York sportswriter described it.[1] But the hero of the game was Fred Marberry. "[He] came through in great style, and the Nationals trounced the World Champion Yankees by a 3–2 count," wrote John Dugan.[2] Marberry replaced Johnson in the seventh inning and maintained Washington's lead.

"Washington is something of a puzzle to me," said Babe Ruth, who went 0–3 on the day. "The lineup was just as it was last year. The only important difference lies in the fact that the team has a new manager."[3]

Harris made two hits to help the Senators take a 3–0 lead after five innings, and Johnson kept New York hitless through the first four innings and scoreless through six. In the bottom of the seventh, Aaron Ward and Everett Scott hit back-to-back triples to score New York's first run. Then to everyone's surprise, Harris called on Marberry to replace Johnson. "Walter's hasty exit was a surprise, for the big fellow seemed to have his old-time stuff," commented one New York sportswriter.[4] Little did the writers know, it was a fatigued Walter Johnson who made the decision to remove himself.

With a runner on third and nobody out, Marberry retired the first batter he faced on a ground out, but the runner on third scored on the play to cut Washington's lead to 3–2. The next batter singled, then Yankees outfielder Whitey Witt exposed third baseman Doc Protho's inability to field bunts. Witt bunted toward third base and made it safely to first to put two men on base with only one out. The next batter, an overanxious Joe Dugan, swung and missed on a high Marberry fastball for strike three. Now with two outs and runners on first and second, the crowd became exhilarated when Babe Ruth stepped to the plate. Manager Harris ordered Marberry to purposely walk Ruth to load the bases. It was a wise decision because the threat ended when the next batter, Bob Meusel, fouled out to end the inning.

In the Yankees' half of the eighth, Pipp singled, stole second, and was sacrificed to third. Then Marberry buckled down and retired the next two batters. With one out in the bottom of the ninth, Witt singled and Joe Dugan followed by drilling a well-hit grounder that Harris couldn't glove, though the Washington second baseman managed to knock the hit to the ground to keep the ball in the infield and prevent Witt from advancing from first to third.

With one out and two runners on base, Babe Ruth came to the plate with a base opened, but the Washington manager had no intentions of purposely walking Ruth again and showed tremendous confidence in allowing Marberry to pitch to the Yankees slugger. The Bambino smacked a sizzling groundball, too hot for first baseman Joe Judge to handle. The hit bounced off Judge and trickled toward right field before Bucky Harris quickly retrieved the ball and threw it to Judge, who had hurried to cover first base. The throw barely beat Ruth for the second out of the inning. Then Meusel tipped a full-count pitch into Ruel's mitt for strike three to end the game.

Walter Johnson was now 3–1 with a 2.40 ERA, had struck out twenty-three and walked just six in thirty innings this season. Two days after beating the Yankees for the second time this season, he spoke to a host of sportswriters in the lobby of the new Concourse Plaza Hotel. They asked about his pitching arm. "It never felt better than it does right now," Johnson told the sportswriters before narrating the story about his sore arm of the previous four seasons:

> In 1920, while we were coming north from Florida, I caught a cold in my [pitching] arm and nearly ruined it. When the cold disappeared, it left a peculiar knot in the muscle of my upper arm. I was worried. Never before had my arm been sore. Never had my arm ever required any fancy treatments. A little rubbing alcohol after a hot game, that was all I ever done.
>
> Well, that knot stuck with me all of 1920, and I had my worst year, winning only eight games. I went to a specialist in Rochester, New York, who advised that all my arm needed was rest. I rested it during the winter, but the knot in my pitching muscle was still with me in 1921, 1922, and in 1923.
>
> This spring, for the first time in five years, that bothersome knot has entirely disappeared. I'm mighty glad. The old wing feels as

pliant and peaceful as it did ten years back. I have no idea of what caused it. I really haven't done anything for it. Of course, I've always taken good care of myself. In the off-season, I keep out in the open. This winter I trampled the Nevada mountains hunting deer. Funny thing is leg exercises restored my arm to normal. Maybe it didn't, but it might have helped. A pitching apparatus is too mysterious to dope out exactly.

"What's your secret of success and the reason to your long service?" a sportswriter asked.

"Temperate living, an easy delivery and a fastball," answered Johnson. "I never had a sore arm from pitching a game. The queer muscular knot I had came from a cold. I conserve my energies when I feel I have a game won. In the last four seasons, I have had to use curves more than ever before, and I am not a curve ball pitcher. If my fastball isn't good, I am no good. I feel I can employ my fast one this year like I used to. When my fast one is right, it has a little hop, usually upward."[5]

George Mogridge, back from his brief illness, took the mound the next day, and just like in his first two outings of the season, he got into trouble in the first inning. In fact, he was in trouble in every inning except when he retired the Yankees in order in the bottom of the sixth. With the score tied, 3–3, in the top of the seventh, Carl East, the right fielder recently acquired in exchange for Showboat Fisher, came through by grounding an RBI single into left field to give Washington a 4–3 lead. However, East's moment of glory was brief. In the bottom of the inning, he dropped a routine fly ball, and when third baseman Doc Protho followed by making his second error of the game, the Yankees tallied to retie the game.

With the count still knotted, 4–4, in the top of the ninth, Sam Rice hit one for what a New York sportswriter described as "one of those shots that could be heard around the world."[6] The shot landed in the right field bleachers for the first Washington home run of the season. Now trailing, 6–4, the Yankees had one last chance with their best hitters due up in the bottom of the ninth, but Mogridge preserved the lead for his first win of the season and the Senators' fourth win in six games over the Yankees in 1924.

In the final game of the three-game series, Washington rallied for three runs in the top of the seventh for a 4–2 lead and looked as if they might be heading for a series sweep. The Yankees reduced the margin with a run in the bottom of the seventh against Washington starting pitcher Joe Martina. Then with the score 4–3 in favor of the Senators in the bottom of the eighth, Meusel singled and Wally Pipp "swung sharply and hoisted a long, fast fly to left-center field."[7] The long drive landed, rolled up a bank, and hugged the wall at one of the deepest reaches of Yankee Stadium. As the crowd of twenty thousand went wild,

Meusel scored and Pipp rounded the bases for an inside-the-park homer, pushing the score to a 5–4 Yankees lead. "For a period of two minutes, you couldn't hear yourself think," reported a New York sportswriter. "Everybody just stood up and yelled."[8] Peckinpaugh led off the top of the ninth with a hit but was left on base, and the Yankees held on to salvage the last game of the series.

The Senators returned home for one game against the slumping Athletics before a Sunday afternoon crowd of nine thousand on an afternoon when dark clouds obscured the sun, making it difficult for the opposing batters to see Walter Johnson's blazing fastball. Connie Mack's team hadn't won since taking the last two games from Washington over a week ago, and they were about to face Johnson on an ideal day for him.

Bob Meeker, the A's starting pitcher making his first start of the season, got into trouble right away. After Johnson retired the A's in order in the top of the first, Meeker gave up a single, then "dealt out free transportation in the manner of John D. Rockefeller shelling out dimes," joked Washington sportswriter Bryan Morse.[9] He walked four consecutive batters to help Washington take a 2–0 lead. In the second inning, Johnson cracked a double off the concrete wall in left-center field and Harris singled to score Washington's great pitcher for a 3–0 lead. Mack responded by making a pitching change, and the Senators went scoreless for the rest of the afternoon. Johnson allowed just one hit through the first three innings, but then encountered trouble in the top of the fourth. Center fielder Sam Rice scampered into right field for a fly ball and muffed the attempt. Johnson followed Rice's error by walking a batter, then hitting a batsman to load the bases for A's shortstop Chick Galloway, who knocked a two-run single into left field to reduce the Washington lead to 3–2. Johnson handled the A's in the next three innings, but in the top of the ninth Joe Hauser walked and Al Simmons tagged Johnson for a single. With runners now on first and second with two outs, Harris walked to the pitcher's mound, turned to the Washington bullpen, and signaled by lifting his left leg high into the air, his way of communicating that he wanted Marberry, the pitcher with the high-kick during his windup. Marberry entered the game, struck out the next batter to end the inning, and retired the A's in the top of the ninth for a 3–2 Washington win.

The Senators, with an 8–9 season record, arrived in Boston for a four-game series with the Red Sox. They were seventh in the league in hitting, sixth in runs scored, and Sam Rice, hitting .333, was the only starter hitting over .300. In addition to the offense struggling, right field was still a problem. The Senators thought they had the problem solved when Carl East arrived from Minneapolis, but after going 2–6 with a double and two RBIs, the disgruntled newcomer walked out on the Senators. According to East, a clause in his contract with Minneapolis guaranteed him a share of the purchase price in any sale involving him, but East was traded, not sold, to Washington for Showboat Fisher. However, he still felt he was owed, and when he was told otherwise, he left the Senators and signed with a team in an outlaw league. The trade was nullified, due to East's decision to jump ship, and Fisher was returned to the Senators.

The cold snap that had been persistent since Opening Day continued into May and took its toll on the Senators. When the Nats arrived at Fenway Park, it was reported that five Washington players had the flu. If things weren't bad enough, Goslin was recovering from food poisoning, and Peckinpaugh was injured after Red Sox third baseman Danny Clark slid with his cleats in the air and barbed Peckinpaugh's right kneecap. Washington trainer Mike Martin applied two stitches to the wound and said the shortstop would be out a day or two.

The Senators lost the first two games of the series prior to eking out the third game in extra innings. "Minor league baseball was exhibited by the Washington Griffmen in the opening of the series at Fenway Park," wrote Louis Dougher.[10] Washington committed four errors and Tom Zachary, making his second start of the year, gave away five hits and walked four before being replaced after the third inning. "Zachary showed why he is on his way out of the big show," opined Dougher.[11] The next day the Senators gave up a nine-run Red Sox eighth-inning rally in a 14–4 loss. In the third game of the series the Nats jumped to a 3–0 lead. Mogridge, who was having trouble getting through the first inning this season, got through the first three before giving up two runs in the fourth, a run in the fifth, and one in the eighth for a 4–3 Red Sox lead. In the top of the ninth, with the Senators seemingly heading for their third straight defeat of the series, Judge doubled and moved to third on Ruel's sacrifice. Protho then made the second out of the inning, leaving Ossie Bluege as Washington's last hope.

The twenty-three-year-old Bluege, who had impatiently sat on the bench until Peckinpaugh's injury, was finally in the starting lineup. He had also begun the 1923 season on the bench, but when the hot corner became a troubled position, he became the starting third baseman until water on his right knee sent him to the injured list. This season, Bluege claimed his knees were fine and held up while spending the winter bowling back home in Chicago. In a March exhibition game in Tampa, though, he swung at a pitch and then hobbled back to the dugout with an injured left knee, the same knee he had injured a few years ago when playing in the minors. A few days later, he was back in uniform and pestered Harris for playing time.

Now with two outs and a runner on third in the top of the ninth, Bluege delivered a double to score Judge with the tying run. In the top of the eleventh, with the game still tied and with Judge, once again, on third, Bluege stepped to the plate. But it was a wild pitch that allowed the Senators' first baseman to score what proved to be the winning run.

In the final game of the series, Walter Johnson allowed only six hits and struck out eight to reach 3,100 career strikeouts; however, he was on the short-end of a 4–2 final, due to his rhythm being disrupted by two rain delays. "It was hard for Walter to break a sweat and stay warmed up," wrote Dugan.[12]

Johnson's defeat concluded what Harris had called the Voyage, and the Senators, who started the Voyage with three more losses than victories, were still three games under .500. But Harris had predicted they would find themselves during the Voyage. The question was: Did they?

CHAPTER 6

The Flood of 1924 (May)

Warmer weather had finally arrived in the District, and with it came a torrential downpour, resulting in the worst flood in Washington, D.C., since 1889. Rain, rain, and more rain reduced Washington's scheduled nineteen-game home stand to twelve games.

Ty Cobb's Detroit Tigers were a good team said to "have a snarly, snappy combination with many characters of the tiger, after which they are named," wrote *Washington Post* sportswriter Frank Young.[1] "Cobb, as a player-manager, always kept his players on their toes," recalled Bucky Harris. "He inspired them by his own deeds. He would never say quit."[2] Harris remembered a game in 1922, when the Senators had a 9–2 lead, only to watch Cobb and the Tigers rally for nine runs in the top of the ninth for an 11–9 win. Cobb became a player-manager in 1921, and the Tigers improved each season under his leadership.

The first game of the home stand, a Saturday afternoon on May 10, was Ty Cobb Day at Griffith Stadium. The occasion was arranged by a white-haired, youthful-looking Michigan congressman named Robert H. Clancy, who invited fifty representatives and twenty senators to help celebrate the occasion. Capitol Hill adjourned at three o'clock that afternoon to give the congressmen time to get to the ballpark before the game's 3:30 starting time. When Cobb came to the plate in the top of the first, time was called, and Clancy led his cohorts onto the field. As the lawmakers gathered around Cobb, seven or eight photographers rushed to the scene, and following a few minutes of deft maneuvering for position, photos were taken of Cobb surrounded by US senators and representatives. Congressman Clancy then presented Cobb with a few cartons containing books, each book telling a story about the life of a great man, including *The Life of Christ*; a book about P. T. Barnum; and books about Socrates, Plato, and American statesmen. There were twenty-one total books, one for each year Cobb played in the majors. When Cobb informed Clancy that 1924 was actually his twentieth season in the big leagues, the Michigan congressman removed a book from the collection.[3]

A crowd of five thousand braved the elements, for rain started falling before the game and dwindled to a drizzle for nine innings, muddying the baselines and chilling the air. Cobb, who went 3 for 5 in the game, crossed the plate in the top of the first and knocked in a run in the second inning to give the Tigers a 2–0 lead. In the bottom of the second, Goose Goslin tripled high off the right field wall and scored when Joe Judge singled. In the bottom of the eighth, Sam Rice and Judge doubled, and Doc Protho singled to claim the lead for the Senators. Washington starting pitcher Joe Martina then sent the Tigers down in order in the top of the ninth to seal the victory. "He did not win today over Detroit on speed and a dazzling curve," *Detroit News* sportswriter Harry Salsinger wrote about Washington's winning pitcher. "If you asked a ballplayer what he had he would answer, 'nothing.'" But the Detroit sportswriter believed the thirty-four-year-old rookie, who won his third game of the season, did have something. "He had control, for one thing," insisted Salsinger.[4]

Later that evening, Ty Cobb Day continued with a banquet at Washington's Hotel Roosevelt. "This is Cobb's night and nothing too good of him as an exponent of the national pastime and as a gentleman could be said," Massachusetts Senator David Walsh told the audience. Maine Senator Bert Fernald read his poem, titled, "To Ty Cobb," to the gathering. Also present and seated at the head table with Cobb were four senators, two representatives, Harry Heilmann, Clark Griffith, and Walter Johnson.

"The most remarkable player in the game," Johnson said about Cobb.

"No greater pitcher or greater sportsman ever graced baseball than Walter Johnson," Cobb said.[5]

Rain pelted D.C. for the next two days, forcing the second and third games of the series to be postponed. The entire region, from Cumberland, Maryland, to Harper's Ferry, West Virginia, to towns along the Shenandoah and Potomac rivers received warnings from the National Weather Bureau about flood-stage conditions. The Potomac was rising, due to both heavy rain and an onrush of water from Harper's Ferry, and homes along the river were evacuated. Finally, it overflowed, and the turbulent waters caused millions in damage. Hundreds of those who lived in the Georgetown district and along the Potomac became homeless. Small homes, tents, boat homes, canoes, and chicken coops by the river were swept away. Trees were submerged halfway to their topmost branches. At the Chain Bridge the water rose thirty-one feet, according to an actual measurement made by the bridge keeper. By noon, the water was reported to be just fourteen feet below the bridge floor, and its spray was dashing every now and then across the walk.

Following the two rainouts, the Tigers and Senators were back in action on a warm Tuesday afternoon. The game began as a good duel between Tigers pitcher Bert Cole and George Mogridge, who was trying for his third consecutive win. Each team made just one hit through the first five innings, the Tigers getting their lone hit when Cobb's routine grounder took a sudden skip over third baseman Doc Protho, a sign that the Griffith Stadium infield still needed work to complete the upgrade.

The batters eventually warmed up and each team scored two runs. With the game tied, 2–2, and with two Senators on base in the bottom of the seventh, Washington's right fielder Nemo Leibold came through with an RBI double to put Washington in front. Bucky Harris followed with a hit, and when the Detroit left fielder slipped and fell on the wet grass, two runs scored while Harris made it to third for a triple. Washington went on to win, 6–3, for Mogridge's third straight win. "Mogridge is one of the smartest and one of the most outstanding pitchers of the day," noted Salsinger. "He had little stuff, as pitching stuff is rated, but he knows what to use and when to use it."[6] Shortly after the game's last out, another downpour soaked the city and destroyed thousands of dollars' worth of residential furniture, though some quick-thinking citizens managed to save their furnishings by covering them with canvas. When water from the previous rain had begun to seep through roofs, walls, and doorways, residents had moved their furniture to their backyards, front lawns, and porches, hoping to save their belongings.

The flood was over, according to the Wednesday afternoon newspapers. High-standing water began to recede, and streets were reported to be passable. River residents began the task of cleanup by removing the layers of mud in their homes and boathouses and assessing their losses. The damage was crippling and left a sea of mud at every point where the river overflowed its banks. Some sections left deposits of thousands of gallons of water, now being pumped back into the river.

Later that day the Cleveland Indians arrived at Griffith Stadium to take on a banged-up Washington team. Sam Rice, who sustained a leg injury in the recent Detroit series, was sidelined; Joe Judge was out with a charley horse; and Goose Goslin said his sore tonsils were aching. Walter Johnson was the starting pitcher on his kind of day—dark and overcast—but he didn't have it on this day and was tagged for four runs on eight hits and removed after the fourth inning. In the bottom of the eighth the rain began to fall, and after a sixteen-minute delay, the umpires decided to rule a complete game with Cleveland ahead, 5–2.

The next day a five-run Cleveland eighth inning sent the Senators to another loss. "Only one run should have scored in that inning," wrote John Dugan, who also noted that Harris made a mistake by instructing his infielders to play in during the inning.[7] With one out and the bases loaded, the Washington manager positioned his infielders on the infield grass, and the strategy backfired when a ground ball caromed off Judge's leg and bounced into right field, resulting in two runs. With the infield still playing in, a pop fly eluded the infielders and dropped onto the outfield grass to score another run, and this was followed by a two-run triple for a 6–2 Cleveland lead. Washington did manage to rally for two in their half of the eighth inning; however, an inning-ending double play and another double play in the bottom of the ninth dashed Washington's victory hopes.

Following another rainout, the Senators and Indians engaged in the final game of the series, with Mogridge in line for his fourth win in a row. Washington was ahead, 6–4, in the top of the eighth, when Cleveland mounted a threat by putting runners on second and third with only one out. Harris replaced Mogridge with Zahniser, who retired a batter and walked a batter to load the bases. Then the two managers engaged in a cat-and-mouse game, with Cleveland's Tris Speaker sending a left-handed batter to face the right-handed-throwing Zahniser. After the pinch hitter was announced, Harris summoned left-hander Tom Zachary from the bullpen. Speaker then countered by sending up a right-handed pinch hitter, who was visibly nervous, and it took Zachary five pitches to strike out the scared batter to end the inning. Zachary also took care of business in the top of the ninth to earn a save and chalk up another win for Mogridge.

The St. Louis Browns were the next team to venture into town, and their two games in Washington sandwiched two more rainouts. The Browns won both games to drop the Senators to seventh place with a 12–16 record. Next came the fifth-place Chicago White Sox, projected by the experts to be one of the league's worst teams in 1924—along with the Red Sox and Senators. It wasn't so long ago when the White Sox were atop the baseball world. They had won the 1917 World Series and were heading back to the World Series in 1919 when Clark Griffith paid a compliment. "The White Sox have every essential of a championship baseball team," Griffith said. "They have a whirlwind attack, a wonderful defense and every move they can make is directed by keen baseball brains."[8] Griffith also predicted the White Sox to beat the Reds in the 1919 World Series. "What a team," recalled Washington outfielder Nemo Leibold, who was the starting right fielder for the White Sox from 1917 to 1920, "and we should have won the pennant in 1920."[9]

A few days before the start of the 1919 World Series, Senators first baseman Joe Judge was down by the rail at a New York racetrack with his friend, Dodgers pitcher Rube Marquard, when a fan approached with a red-hot tip. "If you'd like to make some money, bet everything you got on Cincinnati to win the first two games," the fan told them. "You're nuts," replied Marquard, "the White Sox are the best team in the country." When Judge and Marquard walked away, Judge inquired about the fan. "It's Arnold Rothstein, a gambler," replied Marquard.

"You realize what he was telling us?" Judge asked. "He was telling us the World Series is fixed."

"You're crazy, Joe," replied Marquard. "There is no way to fix a ballgame."

When Judge got back to Washington, he told Griffith what he had heard and said he thought the upcoming World Series was fixed. Griffith echoed Marquard's sentiment. A few days later, after the World Series had begun, Judge stopped by the Washington ballpark and was surprised to see Griffith. "I thought you were at the World Series," said Judge. "I was," replied Griffith. "I saw the first game. The whole White Sox club is throwing the World Series."

"The whole story didn't break until the following fall," Judge said in 1959, "but during the 1920 season, some of the White Sox spread stories that an oil well had come for them. 'You're not kidding me,'" Judge told them.[10] "It was a real blow to us when investigators, in September of 1920, proved the 1919 (World) Series had been fixed," said Leibold. "We couldn't believe that eight of our teammates let us down." Leibold roomed with Buck Weaver, the White Sox starting third baseman who was one of the eight. Although Weaver never took a dime and played to win, he sat in on meetings, and was banned along with the other seven for doing so. "I roomed with Buck through the 1919 and 1920 seasons and never had an inkling there was anything wrong," said Leibold. But according to Peckinpaugh, Leibold sang a different tune. In 1920, the White Sox continued to have lapses and mysteriously lost ballgames during a tight American League pennant race. "Something screwy is going on here," Leibold told Peckinpaugh. "I don't know what it is, but it's something screwy, all right."[11]

In the spring of 1921, Kid Gleason went to spring training without eight of his best players, who had been indicted and suspended and would be banned for life. However, he never lost his spirit. "If organized baseball or the courts tell me I must reinstate any of my White Sox who were indicted, I will tender my resignation immediately as manager of the Chicago club," Gleason said. "I am not going to win any pennants with this bunch," he said, pointing to his 1921 team, "but it is going to surprise whoever thinks that we are heading to the cellar. It is a young hustling club, full of vim and ambition and the determination to wipe out the effects of the blow that the indicted players handed the club."[12]

Gleason's White Sox didn't finish in the cellar and didn't post a winning record during his final three seasons as manager. Following the 1923 season, a worn-out Gleason retired and Frank Chance, who had managed the Cubs, Yankees, and the Red Sox, was hired to manage the 1924 White Sox. However, he was diagnosed with bronchial asthma before the season and ordered to rest. His replacement, Johnny Evers, was also ill, leaving Eddie Collins, the second baseman Griffith tried to obtain during the past winter, to fill in as manager.

On May 23, Walter Johnson never looked better—or not since winning sixteen straight in 1912 or when he posted a 36–7 record and pitched fifty-five and two-thirds scoreless innings in 1913. "Old Walter went back to his form of olden times, fanned 14, allowed only one hit, and shut out the White Sox, 4–0," reported *Chicago Tribune* sportswriter James Crusinberry.[13] The shutout was the hundredth of his career, and he tied an American League record by whiffing six in a row. After striking out Johnny Mostil for his sixth consecutive strikeout, Harry Hooper looped a single to right field for Chicago's only hit. Johnson proceeded to retire the next two batters, struck out the side in the top of the fifth, and retired the last seventeen batters he faced.

Following the sixth rainout of the home stand, the Senators rallied for four runs in the bottom of the fifth to take a 6–1 lead over the White Sox. In the four-run sixth, Harris reached base on an error; a now healthy Sam Rice singled; Goslin hit an RBI double; and Joe Judge, who went 4 for 5, hit a two-run triple and scored on Ruel's sacrifice fly. But just when it seemed like Washington was heading for an easy win, the White Sox scored six in the top of the sixth against Martina and Marberry to take a 7–6 lead. The Senators countered with three runs in the seventh to retake the lead, 9–7, but the White Sox fought back and loaded the bases with one out in the top of the eighth. Harris then called on Allen Russell, a key hurler with a team-leading fifty-two appearances in 1923. "The world's greatest little finisher," a Washington sportswriter called him,[14] was making just his third relief appearance of the 1924 season. He gave up a two-run single and a sacrifice fly for three runs in a 10–9 Washington loss.

The Senators took the last game of the series, with Joe Judge producing his second straight four-hit game to lift his season batting average to .356 in an 8–2 win.

What was wrong with the New York Yankees? Through the first thirty games in 1923, the World Champions owned a 22–8 record and were four full games ahead of the next-best team. But when they arrived for their second season series at Washington, they were 19–11 and tied for first with the surprising Red Sox. The third-place Browns were three games back, followed by the Tigers, then the Senators, who moved into fifth place after taking two of three from Chicago. A few Gotham City writers were impressed with the Browns' recent showing when taking two of three games at Yankee Stadium and believed St. Louis might be the team to dethrone the Yankees. "It's too early to pick the Browns to win the 1924 title," a Washington sportswriter warned, "but the Yankees have to get on their toes and play ball as if they want to win. The entire American League is out to spike their ambitions of a fourth consecutive pennant. The players on all of the clubs are tired of hearing about Ruth and the other Yankees."[15]

"I still figure the Yankees as almost sure winners," said Babe Ruth. "But we will, I think, have more trouble than last year. The reason for this is that the strength throughout the league is more evenly distributed and better balanced."[16]

The first game of the Yankees-Senators series was rained out and rescheduled to be played with the scheduled game the next day. With Babe Ruth and the Yankees in town, a big crowd was expected, but threatening weather kept the crowd down to four thousand when the first game began, but it grew to eight thousand on a cloudy day with light rain. "The games were long, drawn out and tiresome," wrote W. B. Hanna of the *New York Herald-Tribune*. "So much time was wasted by dilatory pitchers and this and that. The afternoon dragged inordinately."[17]

Walter Johnson, coming off one of the best games of his career, "was not himself," and his fastball, "was sadly lacking," according to John Dugan.[18] The Yankees scored three runs on four hits in the top of the second to send Johnson to the showers. The Senators fought back to tie the game, but the Yankees posted another three-run inning for a 6–3 lead in the fifth inning and went on to win, 7–4.

Before the nightcap, Harris sent Tom Zachary to the bullpen to warm up. The fans jeered him, and the boos continued until he retired the first twelve Yankees in order. Zachary also helped win the hometown fans' approval by pounding out two hits. The Senators took advantage of seven walks issued by the New York pitchers and won, 6–1, for Zachary's first win of the season. "When old Tom has his screwball in proper working order he is a pretty hard individual to beat," wrote Dugan. "His mound performance was one of the best of his career."[19]

The Senators-Yankees series and the Washington home stand concluded with a rainout. The Nats would now hit the road for the next twenty-three days, beginning with a series in Boston. When the Senators' road trip reached Detroit, Harris was greeted by his friend Frank Morse, the West Coast sportswriter who had assured Harris about Washington clubs generally playing the schedule out by mid-summer. "You're doing bully," Morse told Harris. "It doesn't look as if you'll finish in the cellar."

"We're just getting started," Harris declared. "We're going up, not down." The Senators were in fifth place with a 15–18 record, but in his heart, Harris believed he was managing a pennant contender. "The pennant bee was buzzing in my bonnet," Harris would later say. "And it made a pleasant sound."[20]

CHAPTER 7

Upgrading the Roster (May–June)

Back on May 22, following the Senators second consecutive loss to the Browns at Griffith Stadium to keep Washington in seventh place, Clark Griffith and Bucky Harris went to work on upgrading their roster. One month later, the Senators had a new starting pitcher, two new starters in the everyday lineup, and a new coach. Al Schacht, the victim of the practical joke in Tampa back in March and who made a valiant major-league comeback attempt during spring training, was added to the Washington coaching staff. He went from a promising prospect in 1919 to an arm injury in 1920 to barely being good enough to stick with the Senators in 1921, then spent the 1922 and 1923 seasons in the minor leagues before receiving an invitation from Clark Griffith to join the Senators in Tampa in 1924. Schacht, believing he was no longer useful as a major-league hurler, was surprised by Griffith's invite, but to Schacht's amazement, his arm felt great while in Tampa. "I couldn't believe it; I was pitching like my old self," said Schacht.

"Al, your arm looks as strong as when you first joined us," said Griffith, who had observed the pitcher throwing batting practice. "Keep up the good work. I'll be watching you."[1]

The Washington manager was also impressed and assigned him to work with Walter Johnson and the team's top pitchers. Harris also admired the pitcher's spirit and knowledge of the game. "If you ever decide to give up pitching, I'd like to have you as a coach," he told Schacht.[2]

During a morning practice session in Tampa, Griffith reminded Schacht about a Kiwanis Club luncheon they were to attend that afternoon at the Tampa Bay Hotel. "OK," said Schacht, "but first I want to hit against Johnson."

"I'll meet you at the hotel after practice," said Griffith.[3]

Johnson was the morning session batting practice pitcher, and Schacht, a big smile across his features, grabbed a bat, stepped up, and shouted, "I can hit you!" Johnson, also showing a broad smile, threw a fastball over the heart of the plate, and much to everyone's surprise, Schacht connected and lined a hit to right field. Astonished over his hit, Schacht literally jumped for joy, but when he came down, his right knee buckled. Johnson charged in from the pitcher's mound, and Mike Martin hurried to the scene. As Schacht lay on the ground, wincing in pain, Martin probed Schacht's right knee and said he believed there was torn cartilage. Schacht, who could hardly walk, was escorted to the locker room, where he slowly took off his uniform, showered, and dressed in his street clothes before heading to the hotel for the luncheon. He borrowed a bike from a Western Union messenger boy and inched his way to the hotel entrance while peddling with his left foot.

He saw Griffith waiting at the front porch, and when the Senators' president saw Schacht weaving and peddling only with his left foot, he laughed as he shook his head, thinking the comical pitcher was kidding. But when Griffith saw Schacht drop the bike and heavily limp toward him, his smile quickly disappeared. "What happened to you?" asked Griffith. The pitcher explained. "You just have too much hard luck, Al," said Griffith, who then advised the pitcher to retire. "If the knee doesn't come around, I might be looking for a coaching job," responded Schacht.[4]

One week later the Senators released Schacht, who was in no condition to pitch, to New Haven of the Eastern League. The swelling from the knee injury went down, but the knee didn't heal, and Schacht didn't pitch in a single game. In Mid-May, with his knee still hurting, New Haven team owner George Weiss spoke with Schacht. "Al, I'm sorry, but I have to suspend you," Weiss told him. "The club is losing money, and I simply can't afford to carry you like this, in the shape you are in. . . . Of course, when your knee comes around, I'll lift the suspension."

Schacht completely understood and knew his pitching days were over. But he wanted to stay in baseball, and Harris wanted him on his coaching staff. He was under contract with New Haven but could get out of it if he could buy his release. "How much would you want for my release?" asked Schacht.

"One thousand dollars," replied Weiss.

"I'll give you five hundred," offered Schacht.

Weiss thought for a minute before agreeing.[5]

"Griff," Schacht said into the phone after placing a collect call, "this is urgent. I am stranded in New Haven. I can buy my release for as little as five hundred but I've only got two hundred. Will you wire me three hundred dollars?"

"What are you going to do when you get your release?" asked Griffith.

"Why, I'm going to join your club," Schacht replied enthusiastically.

"You are, are you? How do you know I want you?" asked Griffith.

"Your manager wants me," said Schacht.

"That's nice, too," said Griffith, "but you can't pitch and I've got three coaches now and I'm in seventh place. What would I need you for?"

"A fourth coach won't hurt you," said Schacht, "and let's make this short as I'm on long distance and this is costing you money. Will you wire me the three hundred dollars?"[6]

Nick Altrock, Ben Egan, and Jack Chesbro comprised the current Washington coaching staff. Altrock, a Senators coach since 1912, served as the team's first base coach and worked with the pitchers. Egan and Chesbro, newcomers to the Washington coaching staff, were low key and lacked the pep Griffith wanted in his coaches. Schacht, on the other hand, was energetic, and Harris wanted him. Griffith decided to release Egan and Chesbro to make room for Schacht, and the new Senators coach immediately traveled to Washington to negotiate his contract. When he met with Griffith, he began to explain why he was a great addition to the coaching staff until he was interrupted. "Al, I'd like to make you my third base coach," said Griffith. "It's an important job. You have to handle signals and exercise sharp judgement in directing baserunners. I honestly think you'd be a good man for the position. Bucky wants you, too. So, if you think you can handle it, you've got the job."

"Boy, that's swell, Griff," replied Schacht, "now about—"

"I can't pay you much," Griffith said. "We're in seventh place; we're not pulling customers; and if we don't improve pretty soon, the sheriff probably will be gunning for me."

Schacht, wanting to get back into Major League Baseball and willing to work for almost nothing, signed a contract for only twenty-five hundred dollars. "Griff, about that three-hundred dollars I owe you—don't expect me to give any of it back to you on pay day, because I haven't gotten any pay in over three weeks now," said Schacht.

"OK," Griffith said while eyeing Schacht. "But you're not by any chance going to try to talk me out of that three hundred, are you?" asked Griffith.

"I'd like to meet the guy who could ever talk you out of three hundred bucks," Schacht said with a laugh.[7]

The Senators began their long road trip with a Memorial Day doubleheader in Boston in an era when the holiday was observed on May 30 rather than the last Monday in May. In 1924, it was a Friday, and the Senators–Red Sox scheduled holiday doubleheader drew a then Fenway Park record crowd of thirty-five thousand and was declared a sellout thirty minutes before the first game. Fans unable to buy a ticket entered the ballpark by crawling through holes or scaling fences. The Red Sox, who had finished last in 1922 and 1923, were currently 20–12 and tied for first with the Yankees. "These Red Hose men are not to be laughed at," John Dugan warned his readers. "[Manager Lee] Fohl has a pretty good ball club. The Bostonians can hit. With a little more pitching, they will not only be a hard club to beat, but may be among the contenders. Boston realizes this and the fans are flocking back to baseball here."[8]

A new era had begun in Boston last summer, when Harry Frazee, the despised former Red Sox owner who sent Babe Ruth to the Yankees in 1920, sold the Red Sox, a once-proud franchise that had followed the Philadelphia Athletics dynasty from the first half of the last decade by winning the 1915, 1916, and 1918 World Championships. Frazee became the team's owner in the fall of 1916, after the Red Sox had won two of their three championships. Then, due to personal financial trouble, the Red Sox owner sold Babe Ruth. The fans, fuming over the sale of Ruth, other unwise transactions, and the decline of the Red Sox, expressed their anger by continuously cursing Frazee and sarcastically cheering for the visiting teams at Fenway Park.

The Red Sox were now owned by a Columbus, Ohio, syndicate headed by Bob Quinn, the former successful St. Louis Browns business manager. Before the 1924 season, Quinn hired Lee Fohl—the former Browns manager who came within one game of winning the American League pennant while piloting the 1922 Browns to an amazing ninety-three-win season—to manage the Red Sox.

In the first game of the doubleheader, the Red Sox displayed the strong hitting attack that Dugan had warned about by scoring seven runs in the fourth inning. When outfielder Ike Boone capped the inning's scoring with a grand slam, Martina, who had allowed eight runs, was replaced. The Red Sox took the first game, 9–4, and took a 2–0 lead against Walter Johnson in the nightcap. When Johnson surrendered three more runs in the bottom of the sixth, he was replaced by Marberry. The Senators fought back with a run in the seventh, two in the eighth, and three in the ninth to win, 10–5. Late in the game, Harris, always aggressive on the base paths, slid into third base with so much gusto, he nearly tore the base from its moorings. His hard slide resulted in an ankle injury that would exclude him from the lineup for the next nine games.

The Senators' bats remained hot the following day for twelve runs on seventeen hits in a shutout win. Sam Rice led the attack with four hits to complete an 11-for-15 series in Boston, plus Peckinpaugh and Protho added three hits apiece. But the story of this game was the latest addition to the Washington starting rotation, who pitched a five-hit shutout for his second win since joining the Senators.

Twenty-three-year-old Warren Harvey Ogden went by his nickname, "Curly," which baffled baseball fans, for the pitcher's hirsute adornment was as unruffled as that of Rudy Valentino—but was not always so. As a kid, his classmates called him "Curly," because he had beautiful dark trusses that fell luxuriously about his shoulders, and the name stuck. He was inspired to become a pitcher by his older brother, Jack, also a pitcher and currently a member of the Baltimore Orioles' pitching staff, though it was former major-league star Frank

"Home Run" Baker to whom he attributed his success. When he had free time during his collegiate days, Ogden played for Baker's semipro team in Uplands, Pennsylvania, and learned the finer points about the game. After graduating with a degree in chemistry from Swarthmore College in 1922, he signed with the Athletics, his team until he was recently released.[9]

When the Senators heard about Ogden's release, "We sent Joe Engel to Philadelphia to look Ogden over, and when the scout reported him to be in good physical condition, the deal was closed," said Harris. "Ogden has much natural ability, and with proper handling, I believe he will make a valuable man for us."[10]

Ogden, who had good size—six foot one, 180 pounds—went directly from college to the Athletics and was projected to be a sensation until he suffered an arm injury late in the 1922 season. He expected the arm to recover, and he began to worry when it didn't. He pitched only forty-six innings in 1923, and his arm was still sore in 1924. With the Athletics off to a slow start and in need of more hitters, Mack made room on the roster by releasing Ogden, who was 0–3 with a 4.97 ERA.

When Ogden joined his new team, Harris gave the pitcher his first starting assignment on May 26, against the White Sox at Griffith Stadium, and Ogden did well, allowing two runs on seven hits in a complete-game win, which had the local sportswriters scribbling about Washington's fantastic transaction. "Like all Major-League managers and magnates, Connie Mack has made a number of mistakes," wrote Dugan. "From Ogden's performance, it appears that baseball must check another error against the lanky pilot of the A's. The hefty curly-locked flinger pitched well, extremely well."[11]

Connie Mack quietly sat in the shadow of the Athletics dugout as he watched his Athletics play the Senators at Shibe Park. Occasionally he flicked his score card. Every now and then he lifted his long, lean hand to signal to an outfielder or direct an infielder. His team had lost twelve straight during the first half of May and were last in games won, hitting, and runs scored. Al Simmons, one of his prize rookies, was doing well, but the rest of the team was not. Paul Strand was hitting just .245 and Joe Hauser, his best hitter in 1923, was batting .262. "My team simply must hit better," said Mack. "We can't go on much longer, making four, five, and six hits a game. I have hitters on my team. I am sure of it, for I have seen them hit."[12]

The Philadelphia fans, with high hopes heading into the season, began to express their frustration and disappointment. "I think the Philadelphia fans razz their players too much," said American League president Ban Johnson. "It seems that a condition exists here to a greater extent than in any other city that I have been in. It's bad for the players. The fans have a right to a certain extent in their criticism, but when they start really ill-natured booing, it will hurt a team a great deal."[13]

The last thing a team in a hitting slump needed was to oppose Walter Johnson, but after the first game of the two-game series was rained out, the Athletics faced Johnson, and Mack's team managed to score three runs on seven hits; however, the way the Senators had been hitting the previous few days, three runs weren't enough. The Senators scored eight runs on seventeen hits, with Goslin knocking out four hits and driving in three runs; Sam Rice continued his personal streak with two hits; and Peckinpaugh, Leibold, Protho, and Johnson also made two hits apiece.

Detroit was the next stop, for a four-game series against the Tigers, who entered the series riding a five-game winning streak and were atop the league standings with the Yankees and Red Sox. With Detroit on a tear and Washington arriving on the morning of the series opener following an all-night train trip from Philadelphia, the Tigers assumed they were in the driver's seat for an easy win. "Over-pressing your luck is one of the sins in sports," warned Detroit sportswriter Harry Salsinger. "Rain fell all morning and for two hours in the afternoon. It was chilly. Few clubs would ever attempt to play a ball game in weather like this, but Detroit insisted on playing."[14] Fatigue failed to cool off the red-hot Washington bats, as the Nats hitters wasted no time in scoring, held a 6–1 lead after four innings, and went on to pound out fourteen hits in an 11–1 win, as Sam Rice led the way with his fifth consecutive multi-hit game and Doc Protho added three hits to lift his season average to .311.

The star of the game was starting pitcher Tom Zachary, the hurler who was believed to be heading out of the league just a few weeks ago. "Zachary pitched the finest game witnessed here this season, allowing the Tigers but two singles, one in the fifth and one in the eighth," admitted Dugan.[15] "Zachary has been pitching a long time," wrote Salsinger. "He is a hard pitcher for Detroit to solve. He knows how to pitch. He knows weaknesses of the Detroit batsmen and he pitches to them."[16]

The Senators out-hit the Tigers, 15–9, the next day, but lost, 6–5 in ten innings. Rice, once again, had a multi-hit game, and Goslin got two hits to make eight for his last fourteen at bats, increasing his season batting average to .322. Ruel, also swinging a hot bat on the road trip, went 3 for 4 to up his batting average to .310. The Senators had their chances to win this game but were unable to get the big hit when needed. In the bottom of the tenth, with the game still tied, Goslin made what Dugan described as "an atrocious muff" on a fly ball that led to the Tigers' winning run.[17]

The Senators had a new face in their lineup for the third game of the series. Starting outfielder Nemo Leibold, said to have an uncanny ability to get on base, was currently hitting .289 and had an eleven-game hitting streak in mid-May, going 17 for 29 during that streak. He had started the 1924 season on the bench, while Showboat Fisher and Carl East were tried in right field. When

Fisher proved ineffective and East jumped ship, Leibold was inserted into the starting lineup. But he was believed to be slowing down at age thirty-two and Washington management viewed him as a good backup at best. Griffith and Harris also believed that Sam Rice, who had started the season as Washington's center fielder, was better suited for right field. The Senators had their eye on a former major-league starting center fielder who could cover ground and solidify the Washington outfield.

Washington sent Showboat Fisher to the Milwaukee Brewers for twenty-seven-year-old center fielder Wid Matthews, who was thrilled to be heading back to the major leagues. "Matthews is going to help Washington," insisted a Philadelphia sportswriter. "His radiant spirit will help any ball club. The westerner is one of those ball players who never stops trying, He has the will to win. He was a hit in Philly and it was surprising when he was benched for talking back to Mack."[18] Matthews was the Athletics starting center fielder before being dealt to Milwaukee in August of 1923. He was an aggressive player with a fighting spirit comparable to Cobb. It was said he became outspoken when the A's slumped in 1923, causing friction with his teammates and Connie Mack, resulting in his departure. Other teams were interested in his services but were turned off by his weak throwing arm and his desire for making breadbasket catches (a two-handed catch made belt-high and close to the body). More scouts became discouraged when an argument brewed between Matthews and Milwaukee ownership, resulting in suspension of the center fielder. "Much of what has been said about me has been exaggerated," said Matthews. "I have been accused of lying down, being an individual ballplayer, and that I refused to take an order from a manager. I never quit in a game, either."[19]

When Matthews reported to the Senators in Detroit, Harris sat down with his new center fielder and had a heart-to-heart talk. He told him he had to behave or he would lose his chance.

With Matthews batting second in the batting order, the Senators scored six in the top of the first. Rice began the rally by singling to extend his hitting streak to twelve straight games and Matthews, in his first at bat with his new team, sacrificed Rice to second. Goslin grounded out but Judge singled to score Rice. Ruel singled to put runners on first and third for Peckinpaugh, who hit an easy grounder that was fielded and thrown to first to apparently end the inning. The Tigers, thinking the inning was over, headed to their dugout. "Stay there!" home plate umpire George Moriarty told Tigers catcher Johnny Bassler.

"What for?" asked Bassler.

"You tipped his bat with your mitt, that's what for," replied Moriarty, and Peckinpaugh was awarded first base.[20]

Protho, and Bluege, filling in for the injured Harris at second base, followed with back-to-back singles to score three more. Then Ogden tripled in a pair to make it a 6–0 game.

After the Tigers fought back and cut the lead to 8–5, Matthews tripled and scored on Goslin's single to add one to the Washington lead. When the Tigers battled back and scored two, Harris called on Marberry, who pitched the last two and two-thirds innings without allowing a hit to finish off the Tigers. Ogden, who was replaced in the fifth inning, was credited with the win, his third in a row since joining the Nats.

Rice and Goslin went hitless the next day and the Senators scored just two runs on six hits, but it was enough for a 2–0 win. Walter Johnson, applauded throughout the game by the Detroit fans, pitched his 101st career shutout. He allowed just four hits and twice fanned the league's leading hitter, Harry Heilmann, for his seventh win of the season. The victory upped the Washington season record to 21–20, the first time the Senators had more wins than losses since they were 3–2 after their 12–3 win over New York on April 20. They were in fourth place and just four games behind the first-place Yankees.

The once slumping Washington batters were now leading the league in hitting and were the only American League club with a team batting average over .300. They were third in the league in runs scored and had scored sixty-one runs on 105 hits through the first eight games of this road trip. But when their road trip reached Cleveland for their next series, their bats cooled off and the Senators were swept. They made thirty-eight hits in their four games, but their inability to produce the clutch hit resulted in only seven total runs in the series. The Senators, venting their frustrations at the umpires during the series, received four ejections during the first two games. Nick Altrock, Bucky Harris, Tom Zachary, and George Mogridge were all banished for becoming too intense in their debates. In the fourth and final game of the series, the Senators owned a 3–2 lead in the bottom of the ninth when the Indians put runners on first and second with one out. Then Bucky Harris and Indians manager Tris Speaker renewed the cat and mouse game they had started the previous month in Washington. After Marberry pitched ball one to Cleveland left-handed-hitting Pat McNulty, Harris decided on better odds and called lefty Tom Zachary out of the bullpen. Speaker countered by sending a right-handed hitter to the plate to pinch-hit, and the pinch batter drilled one to left field that Goslin got his hands on but couldn't hold. The play, ruled a hit, scored a run and put runners on second and third. Then Charlie Jamieson, who didn't hit the ball out of the infield in his four previous at bats, singled to score the winning run to complete the series sweep.

The timely hitting and run production returned at St. Louis, with the Senators scoring twenty-five runs in a three-game sweep to even their season record at 24–24. They won the first game, 12–1, behind an eighteen-hit attack, led by

Peckinpaugh's three hits and Goslin's second homer of the season. In the second game of the series, a hot day combined with a cold limited Walter Johnson to less than five innings, but the official scorer credited him the win, his eighth of the season, in a 6–4 Washington victory. The Senators jumped to a 6–0 led and won, 7–3 in the final game of the series, with Goslin leading the attack by going 4 for 4 to improve his season average to .351. He also hit his third homer of the season.

The next stop was Chicago, a city in a state of shock as its citizenry tried to figure out why two well-educated and gifted young men committed "The Perfect Crime." Three weeks earlier, Leopold and Loeb confessed to the murder of schoolboy Bobby Franks, and in their attempt to conceal evidence, they dumped the typewriter they had used to type a phony ransom note into a lagoon located steps away from the Cooper-Carlton Hotel, where the Senators and other American League teams quartered when in town.

Two weeks earlier, New York sportswriter Ford Frick, who was in the Windy City to cover the Yankees–White Sox series and was staying at the Cooper-Carlton Hotel, stood at the bank and watched a group of serious-faced policemen probe the water of a shaded, ornamental lagoon, looking for the typewriter. He was soon joined by hundreds, including an unidentified Yankee, who watched the policemen go through the muddy, murky waters. "I may be wrong," the New York player quietly told Frick, "but it seems to me these two young fellows are the victims of a poor educational system. They are young fellows of high intellect and they were permitted to force that intellectual development. What I mean is these boys needed less intellectual development and more baseball, football, hunting, fishing and everything else that is part of an average boy. They needed to get away from Nietzsche and Freud and learn about Honus Wagner and Ty Cobb. Their development wasn't normal. It was biased."[21]

In the first game at Chicago, the Senators blew a 4–0 lead and lost, 6–4. "The Nats these days are emulating the Finnegan of the ancient song. It is 'In again, out again,' for them," wrote a disappointed Washington sportswriter.[22] The next day, the Senators built a 3–1 lead when Goslin homered in the top of the fourth. Washington was still up by two in the bottom of the seventh when a fatigued Walter Johnson walked two in a row. The White Sox then loaded the bases when the next batter bunted toward third, and third baseman Doc Protho, still having trouble handling bunts, failed to react in time to make a play. Then Harry Hooper followed with a long drive to right field that cleared the barrier for a grand slam to give the White Sox a 5–3 lead. "Not many men achieved fame by hitting a home run off Walter Johnson with the bases filled," commented Chicago sportswriter Irving Vaughan.[23]

In the top of the eighth, Harris, who had returned to the starting lineup a week ago, took one for the team by leaning in to a pitch with the bases loaded to score a run. Goslin and Protho followed with a pair of two-run singles to put Washington ahead, 8–5. But in the bottom of the inning, Allen Russell gave up a hit and walked two to load the bases. Harris called on Martina, who surrendered a pair of two-run hits in a 9–8 Senators loss.

Following the heartbreaking defeat, Harris decided on the last piece of the puzzle in the Washington lineup. The Senators had hired Schacht, claimed Ogden off waivers, and obtained Wid Matthews. Now it was time for a change at third base. The Washington manager spotted Ossie Bluege in the showers and told him, "You are playing third base tomorrow and from here on in, come hell or high water."[24] Protho had a .333 season batting average and was hitting .446 with ten RBIs on the current road trip, but his defense was another story. He had made four of his ten season errors during the current trip, including an error at a key moment in one of the setbacks at Cleveland and two errors (and botched the play on a bunt) in the 9–8 loss in Chicago. Harris said he could spare less hitting for better defense at third base. The Senators kept Protho on their roster for twelve more days before surprising their followers by sending the third baseman to Memphis of the Southern Association in exchange for infielder Tommy Taylor.

With Bluege in the starting lineup the next day, the Nats scored twelve runs on sixteen hits and made no errors. Sam Rice went 4 for 6 and scored three times and Matthews went 3 for 5 to increase his batting average to .364 since joining the Nats. Harris made two hits, and Bluege, currently hitting .274, also added a pair of hits. In the final game of the series, the Senators trailed, 4–3, in the top of the ninth and were down to their last two outs when Harris hit a 3–2 pitch into left field for a single. Goslin, who was red-hot on this road trip, fouled out; however, Ruel followed with a walk to put runners on first and second for Bluege, who grounded to shortstop Bill Barrett. Ruel ran as fast as he could, which wasn't very fast, and slid into second base. Second baseman Eddie Collins took Barrett's throw for what the White Sox thought was the game's last out. But umpire Pants Rowland called Ruel safe. The White Sox argued, especially Eddie Collins, who kept informing the umpire, "I got my man by a couple of steps."[25] Rowland, who once managed Collins and the White Sox before becoming an arbitrator, stood by his call, and Collins, who kept roaring his side of the story, was ejected for the first time in his career. When play resumed, Peckinpaugh singled to score Harris and Ruel for a 5–4 Washington lead.

In the bottom of the ninth, the White Sox quickly put two runners on base on a single and when Mogridge made a poor throw to first base after fielding a bunt. With a runner on first and second and nobody out, the next batter also bunted, and this time Mogridge made a good throw to first to retire the batter, the runners moving up to second and third on the play. After a walk followed to load the bases with only one out, Harris called on Fred Marberry to extinguish another fire, and the hard-throwing rookie came through by retiring the next two batters for a Washington victory.

The Senators would now head back east to conclude the road trip in Philadelphia. They were now 26–26 and just three and a half games behind the pace-setting Yankees and Tigers in a tight American League pennant race. They had posted an 8–7 record on their tour through the Midwest and an 11–8 record when adding the results from their games at Boston and Philadelphia at the beginning of the road trip. *Washington Star* sportswriter John Keller attributed the trip's success to out-hitting the opposition. "Well-pitched games were few," Keller noted. "The Nationals slabmen were prone to lose their magic after being handed a comfortable lead to work under." Keller also noted poor base running to be an enigma during the trip, and better base running could have swelled their run totals. "The matter of base running has been the real weakness of the club for some time," wrote Keller. The Washington sportswriter was pleased with the team's fielding. "Roger Peckinpaugh played as brilliantly at shortstop as at any other time in his career," opined Keller. He also complimented Bluege for doing a good job when filling in for Harris and becoming the team's starting third baseman, and Marberry for his late-game heroics. "He has developed into a steady relief pitcher," praised Keller.[26]

The Senators now had two games in Philadelphia before returning home to play a single game against the A's, and that would be followed by four games at Yankee Stadium, consisting of a doubleheader on June 23 and singles games on June 24 and 25.

At Philadelphia, the first game was tied, 2–2, with two outs in the top of the twelfth, when Bluege walked and scored on a double by Peckinpaugh to move Washington ahead by one run. In the bottom of the twelfth, Martina retired the first batter but then walked two. Marberry was called to the rescue and came through by whiffing Jimmy Dykes and ending the game when inducing the next hitter to fly out to right fielder Sam Rice. "Young Fred Marberry, from the wilds of Texas certainly is proving himself to be an iron man as a relief hurler, and a very dependable one, too," wrote Keller. "Now-a-days, whenever one of Bucky Harris's moundsmen begins to waver, and this has been happening all too frequently of late, Marberry is called to the rescue, and generally the war clubs of the enemy immediately become useless."[27]

Later that evening, Bucky Harris was relaxing while reading congratulatory telegrams when he began to talk with a reporter about the upcoming series at Yankee Stadium. "Can't promise anything," Harris told the reporter. "No, that's not so," he said after thinking for a minute. "I can promise one thing—We're going after every game, from now until the end of the season. It looks as if we might win some of them, too, doesn't it?"[28]

The road trip concluded with an 11–3 win at Philadelphia, the fourth win in a row for Washington. Walter Johnson, the winning pitcher, won his fifth consecutive game to make his season record 9–3. "That grand old wreck, Walter Johnson, twirling another one of his wonderful games" reported a Philadelphia sportswriter.[29]

CHAPTER 8

First Place (June–July)

> Something has got to be done about those Washington Griffmen. They're playing with fire, climbing up within touching distance of first place. The worst of it is not one so-called expert paid attention to them. They were just in the league, that's all, and while the Yanks, Tigers and Browns tore up all the space in the papers, the Griffs kept right on playing.[1]
>
> —Ford Frick, New York sportswriter

Nick Altrock was the most popular coach in the American League. Baseball's "Clown Prince" earned his nickname for amusing fans with his funny antics, such as appearing on the field with his big plug of tobacco popping his jaw and wearing his hat sideways while clowning around during infield practice. He also entertained by juggling baseballs, mimicking umpires, and performing other zany and silly skits. "His stuff never gets stale," admitted a New York sportswriter.[2] He had bolstered his comedy act when partnering with comical Washington teammate Germany Schaefer, and later teamed with another teammate, Carl Sawyer. When his sidekicks were no longer with the club, Altrock became a solo act—until Al Schacht arrived at the end of the 1919 season. "Wait'll you see this screwball!" Joe Judge told Altrock and his teammates, and when Schacht, a funny man in the minors, arrived in Washington, baseball's Clown Prince was unamused. "Some of the other players got Altrock and I together to gag for them, but Nick was anything but friendly," recalled Schacht.[3]

Altrock never did warm up to Schacht, though he was willing to ally with him, and their performances were a hit at the 1921, 1922, and 1923 World Series. On June 22, before the Senators hosted the Athletics, the two comedians were thunderously applauded by the Griffith Stadium crowd after staging pantomime spoofs of a slow movie, fishing from a boat, and a prize fight.

"The homecoming of the Griffs was awaited with keen interest by the fans and they crowded into the park at an early hour to watch the team at practice," a local sportswriter reported.[4] The home crowd paid most attention to newcomer Wid Matthews, making his first appearance in Washington as a member of the Senators. "It's said that 'Matty' has pepped up everyone," a sportswriter believed. "Everyone ran to their positions in the first inning, including Ogden."[5]

Ogden entered this game hoping for his fourth straight victory and the Senators were looking to add another win to their winning streak, but things didn't get off on the right foot. The Athletics, who came to town with a six-game losing streak, tagged their former teammate for two runs in the first inning, and led, 3–1, after three frames, which sent Ogden to the showers. Joe Martina came on to pitch in the top of the fourth on a day when the temperature reached eighty-seven degrees. "My weather is coming right along," Martina said with a smile before the game.[6] Pitching his entire career in the sweltering hot weather of the Deep South, the heat was his preference, and it was said that the cold early-season weather was hampering his pitching. But now pitching in his kind of weather, he struck out the first batter he faced on three pitches and threw two consecutive bull's-eyes past the next batter. The A's managed to score one against Martina for a 4–1 lead before the Washington bats came alive in the bottom half of the inning. A double by Ruel, a Texas-League single by Peckinpaugh, and a walk to Bluege loaded the bases. Martina then hit into a force out at home, but Rice cleared the bases with a triple to left field and scored when the Philadelphia shortstop made a poor relay throw to give Washington a 5–4 lead. Martina then held the A's scoreless for the remainder of the afternoon for Washington's fifth straight win, described by one local writer as "one of the best exhibitions put up by a local team."[7]

The Senators' fielding was flawless, and the spectators shouted with glee when Peckinpaugh and Bluege each made a one-handed stop and when Peckinpaugh made an off-balanced throw following another nifty stop to retire a batter. The sweet-fielding Washington shortstop also teamed with Joe Judge to execute a 3-6-3 double play that brought the crowd to its feet. But it was Wid Matthews who stole the show, with his breadbasket catches and running back into deep center field to make another grab. He also doubled to drive in the first Washington run and made another hit to boost his batting average to .375. Applauded after every catch and his two hits, Matthews beamed from ear to ear, "probably reflecting his satisfaction at being back in the big show," guessed a sportswriter.[8]

"It will be possible for the Nats to return home next Thursday in first place," warned a Washington sportswriter.[9] While the Senators were beating the A's, the Yankees lost and saw their lead fall to just two games over the fourth-place Senators in a very tight American League pennant race. The second-place Tigers were within a half game of the Yankees and the third-place Red Sox were only one percentage point ahead of Washington. On Monday, June 23, the Senators arrived at Yankee Stadium with a five-game winning streak and were playing their best baseball of the season. The Yankees were anything but hot, posting a 12–14 record since winning eighteen of their first twenty-seven games of the season. "The Yankees first western trip of the year was a bust," Babe Ruth said about their recent road trip. A sportswriter asked Ruth if the Yankees, after winning three consecutive pennants, were beginning to slip. "That's what happened to the old Giants and Athletics," answered Ruth, though the Athletics didn't win three in a row, but did win the American League flag in 1910, 1911, 1913, and 1914, while the old Giants won three straight, from 1910 to 1913. "It took McGraw some time to get the Giants up again; Connie Mack hasn't recovered yet," said Ruth. "But despite the fact that we played a lot of bad baseball in the west," Ruth continued, "we got back to New York in first place. There's a lot of comfort in that. It means that the other teams couldn't take advantage of our slump."[10]

Not only were the Yankees slumping, Bob Meusel would miss the June 23 doubleheader due to serving the last two games of a ten-game suspension for his part in a brawl when the Yankees were at Detroit; Earle Combs, who had replaced Meusel and was hitting .412, was out with a broken ankle; and Yankees starting second baseman Aaron Ward was also sidelined with an injury.

Thinking about Ruth and Pipp, the Yankees' two power-hitting left-handed hitters, Harris had saved his two starting left-handers, George Mobridge and Tom Zachary, for the twin bill. "Both twirled in excellent fashion; whereas their rivals on the mound were unable to prevent the Senators from bunching hits," was how *New York* sportswriter Ford Frick summarized Washington's doubleheader win.[11] The two crafty Washington veteran left-handers kept the Yankees guessing all afternoon by often throwing side-arm and change-ups and using other forms of trickery. "The objectionable part of their pitching was standing there, holding the ball while looking at the batter, carrying them to aggravable lengths until the umpire told them to speed things up," complained a New York sportswriter.[12] Mogridge and Zachary took care of New York's power hitters, limiting Ruth to three singles and Pipp to just one hit in the sweep to move the Senators to within one percentage point of the Yankees.

Washington leadoff man Sam Rice began the day by lining a hit to left field, and when Harvey Hendrick, filling in for the suspended Meusel, misplayed the hit, Rice circled the bases for the first run of the game. The Senators added another run in the inning when Matthews tripled to left field and scored on Goslin's single. In the top of the third, Matthews doubled to right-center field, moved to third on Harris's sacrifice, and scored on Judge's single to make it 3–0.

The Yankees finally got something going in the bottom of the fourth on three consecutive hits and a sacrifice fly to cut the lead to 3–2; however, Washington answered with a run in the fifth on a single by Rice, a throwing error, and a sacrifice fly by Harris. The Yankees added one in the bottom of the eighth, but in the top of the ninth, Goslin put the game away with his fifth homer of the season.

The nightcap began as a pitching duel between Zachary and Yankees starting pitcher Waite Hoyt. There was no score after five innings, and the Senators had yet to register a hit. In the top of the sixth, Ruth rushed in on a Rice drive that wasn't catchable and missed the ball, resulting in a triple for Washington's first hit. It appeared the Senators might fail to capitalize when Matthews popped out and Harris routinely grounded to Yankees shortstop Everett Scott, who noticed Rice with a big lead off the third base bag, and instead of going for the sure out at first base, Scott threw too late to catch Rice heading back to third. With runners on first and third, Goslin scored Rice on a long fly out and a double by Judge brought Harris home for a 2–0 lead. The lead held until the Yankees' seventh, when two singles, a sacrifice, and a pinch hit two-run single by Joe Bush tied the score, 2–2. As in the first game, the Senators answered in the next inning, when Matthews doubled and Goslin came through with an RBI single. Judge sent Goslin to third with a single, and Ruel hit a fly out deep enough to allow Goslin to score for a 4–2 lead, and that was how it ended.

The next morning, Washington awoke to the possibility of the Senators moving into first place by the end of the day. Throughout the morning and into the early-afternoon hours, Washingtonians talked about their team. "Just think, if we beat New York today, we will hold first place," they kept reminding family, friends, and coworkers.[13] But no one knew who the starting pitcher would be. Harris went with his two lefties in the doubleheader and slated Walter Johnson to go in the next game. However, that changed when Johnson got word his wife needed surgery. When Johnson arrived back home, he learned that his wife's appendicitis wasn't as bad as originally believed, surgery wouldn't be necessary, and Mrs. Johnson was resting comfortably at home. After he was assured his wife was OK, Johnson went to Griffith Stadium for a workout. He would miss the remainder of the New York series, but Harris announced that his pitching ace would be the starting pitcher in the first game of the scheduled June 26 doubleheader versus the Athletics, and Johnson wanted to make sure he was ready. "I expect to be there, myself, rooting for Washington to win," Mrs. Johnson cheerfully confirmed.[14]

Washington sportswriter John Keller called the third game of the series, "the most grueling contest the Nationals have engaged in this season."[15] Harris gave Paul Zahniser the starting assignment, "and he didn't have a thing to fool the slipping Yankees," according to a Washington sportswriter.[16] As in the first game of the series, Washington scored in their first at bat. Rice began the game by singling to center field and Matthews placed a beautiful bunt just out of the reach of New York starting pitcher Herb Pennock, and the bunt rolled through the area second baseman Ernie Johnson had vacated to cover first base on the play, allowing Rice to go from first to third. Harris followed with a sacrifice fly to score Rice, but the Yankees quickly tied the score with a run in their half of first. However, Washington reclaimed the lead in the top of the second when Peckinpaugh singled, advanced on a wild pitch, and scored on a hit by Bluege.

With two outs in the top of the fourth, Peckinpaugh lifted a routine foul ball between first and home. New York first baseman Wally Pipp and catcher Wally Schang shouted back and forth, both claiming the ball. Pipp had three-fourths of the ball in his mitt when the two fielders collided, resulting in a dropped ball error. Given another chance, Peckinpaugh pounded the next pitch into the gap in right-center field, and as the long hit rolled all the way to the Ever-Ready Blades sign on the outfield fence, Peckinpaugh rounded the bases for an inside-the-park homer to make it 3–1 in favor of Washington. In the Yankees' half of the inning the two guilty parties who had muffed the foul ball redeemed themselves when Pipp drilled an RBI triple and scored when Schang singled to tie the game. In the top of the tenth, with Washington pitcher Allen Russell on first with one out and the game still tied, Sam Rice doubled to put runners on second and third, and Matthews followed with a fly ball to left field. Russell, who had replaced Zahniser in the bottom of the fifth, raced for home after the left fielder's catch and slid across the plate to give Washington the lead. The Washington dugout went wild in celebrating the go-ahead run. Peckinpaugh, Judge, and Ruel hurled a fusillade of bats and gloves into the air that imperiled the life of Clark Griffith's twelve-year-old nephew, Calvin, who was serving as the Washington bat boy in this series. Harris, who was the on-deck hitter, and first base coach Nick Altrock, ran to home plate, hoisted Russell off the ground and carried the pitcher on their shoulders to the dugout. "It was the most genuine enthusiastic display of feeling ever seen at the Stadium," reported a New York sportswriter.[17] Harris, so excited about retaking the lead, forgot that he was the next batter and had to be reminded by home plate umpire Billy Evans.

Trailing by one in the bottom of the tenth, Ernie Johnson gave the Yankees hope with a leadoff single. The next batter lifted a routine fly ball to center field, allowing Matthews to display his famous breadbasket catch for the inning's first out. This set the stage for Babe Ruth to add to his legend of coming to the plate with his team down by a run in the final inning and belting a game-winning homer, but this time the Bambino swung and missed on a 2–2 pitch for out number two. Bob Meusel, his first game back after his suspension, followed with a pop fly to left field that looked certain to fall for a hit. Senators left fielder Goose Goslin, "came in at full speed and made a miraculous catch at his shoe tops," described a New York sportswriter.[18] The other two starting Washington outfielders, Wid Matthews and Sam Rice, slap-happy over the catch for the game's last out, sprinted to Goslin and began to playfully rough him up.

The Senators' third straight win in the series combined with Detroit's doubleheader loss in St. Louis elevated the Senators into sole possession of first place in the American League, and the Washington majority owners—Clark Griffith and William Richardson, who were in New York to watch their ball club, celebrated the occasion by throwing a dinner party. "This is the highest the Washington team has ever been in the league scramble this late in June," said Griffith, his husky eyebrows vibrating with the occasion. "Maybe I can be excused if I indulge in pennant dreams. I really feel we'll come out on top."[19]

The Yankees were plenty sore over losing three straight and with the jubilant antics of the Senators. It was bad enough to lose first place and three straight home games, but the sight of Harris and Altrock carrying Russell off the field, the Washington dugout celebration after Russell scored, and Matthews and Rice kiddingly battering Goslin was too much. The Yankees' dugout was between the visiting team's dugout and dressing room. When the Senators walked past before the fourth and final game of the series, a New York pitcher had a message: "You guys better stay loose. Every one of you is goin' down today!"[20] When Sam Rice stepped in the batter's box as the game's first batter, Yankees starting pitcher Joe Bush confirmed the message by sending him ducking for cover.

Rice finished the at bat with a base on balls and advanced to second when New York second baseman Ernie Johnson dropped Matthews's pop fly in shallow right field. Harris moved the runners along with a pretty sacrifice bunt that impressed even the Yankees, and Goslin singled to score the two runners to give the unfazed Senators a 2–0 lead.

In the bottom of the first, Yankees manager Miller Huggins, hoping to change his team's luck, made a rare appearance in the first base coach's box, his first time on the base paths in many a game. Washington starting pitcher Fred Marberry retired the first two batters and had a 3–2 count on Babe Ruth. He then heaved a fastball over the heart of the plate, and Ruth hit what some called the farthest home run at Yankee Stadium. "The ball, rising to a great height, landed about ten rows from the top of the right-field bleachers," described a New York sportswriter.[21] "At Griffith Stadium, the drive would have cleared the right field wall by many yards," journaled *Washington Star* sportswriter John Keller.[22] Following Ruth's eighteenth homer of the season, Meusel, Pipp, and Schang singled in succession to produce another run to tie the game.

In the top of the third, Bucky Harris singled then took off for second base on the first pitch to the next batter, Goose Goslin. Yankees shortstop Everett Scott covered the second base bag, took the catcher's throw, and leaned over to apply the tag, but then backed off when Harris raised his spikes high in the air in retaliation for the first-inning knockdown pitch. Goslin singled to score Harris to put the Senators ahead, 3–2, and after the inning, as the Yankee fielders headed to the dugout and the Senators took the field, Ruth and Harris engaged in a heated discussion regarding the slide at second base. With one out in the bottom of the inning, Ruth walked then barreled his way to second base after the next batter grounded to Peckinpaugh. The Washington shortstop fielded the ball and threw to Harris, who was covering second base. As Harris made the relay throw to complete a double play, Ruth launched himself in the air, and Harris, undeterred, gave the soaring Ruth a hip check, sending the Yankees slugger tumbling into center field. Everyone held their collective breath, sure Ruth would respond, but much to everyone's surprise, Ruth picked himself up and headed to his position without saying a word.

In the top of the fourth, the sun disappeared when dark clouds appeared over the Bronx, greatly reducing visibility. After Marberry retired the Yankees in order in the fourth and fifth innings to make this an official game, he stalled in the bottom of the sixth, hoping the clouds would bring rain and persuade the umpires to call it with his team holding a one-run lead. "Marberry went into epileptic trances before every pitch," protested a New York sportswriter.[23] To help extend the delay, Harris repeatedly walked to the pitcher's mound and held weighty conversations with his pitcher. When the sixth inning concluded, the skies grew even darker, and a ruling by the umpires to end the game seemed likely. Surprisingly, the umpires decided to allow the game to continue.

While the Senators went down in order in the top of the seventh, lights broke out at the elevated train station and in the apartment buildings beyond the outfield bleachers. In the Yankees' half of the seventh, Marberry struck out Wally Schang. Then amid the darkness and a crackle of thunder, Joe Dugan singled for the Yankees' first hit since the first inning. Marberry, certain that rain would begin falling any minute, restarted his tactic of taking extra time between pitches. "Why two such competent umpires as Evans and Ormsby didn't step in and stop the dawdling is still a mystery," wrote an irritated New York sportswriter.[24] When Whitey Witt flew out and Joe Bush grounded out to end the inning, the umpires decided to call the game complete. A few minutes later, the clouds finally broke and a torrential downpour soaked the spectators as they filed out of Yankee Stadium. As the fans passed the Washington clubhouse, they could hear loud, happy, joyous voices through the clubhouse windows.

"All of Washington has gone insane over the fine work of the team," wrote Louis Dougher of the *Washington Times*, "and scattered far and wide over this broad land, folks are rubbing their eyes and asking themselves if they really see what they are looking at, a Washington team in the pennant hunt."[25] The news about the amazing Senators was a hot topic from coast to coast and stole newspaper space from the current Democratic convention. Even President Coolidge, wanting to participate in the fun, reserved the presidential box at Griffith Stadium for the next day's doubleheader.

The Senators were brilliant in their series sweep against the Yankees. They made only one error while extending their winning streak to nine. They went directly from Yankee Stadium to Grand Central Station to board their train for their trip back to Washington. When their journey reached Baltimore, Harris was informed about a huge crowd awaiting the team's arrival. "Delay as little as possible in your departure at Union Station," Harris warned his players.[26]

"Hurray! Hurray!" By 10:15, thirty-five hundred fans awaited the arrival of their hometown heroes at Union Station. "It was a great spectacle, the mass of humanity, men, women, and children," wrote *Washington Post* reporter Arthur Knapp.[27] At 10:54, a train nosed its way around a curve and came to a halt at the platform on track 16. People began to yell, cheer, sing, and whistle. Every station policeman was lined up outside the gate, making every effort to control the mass of people. Children pleaded with policemen, hoping to be allowed to pass through the gate and greet the players at the platform, and some cried when they were denied. Men also asked to be permitted to enter to welcome the players as they disembarked, and they too were denied.

The players filed out of the car at the extreme end of the train, and team trainer Mike Martin, the first to step off the train, smiled when he saw the crowd behind the barred gate. One by one, each team member stepped off the train, the loudest cheer greeting Clark Griffith, who was dressed in a light Palm Beach suit, a Panama hat, and a bright necktie. As he walked down the concrete aisle leading to the depot's exit, with his wife on one side and his niece on the other side, he casually smiled. "It was a wonderful greeting accorded to the club and myself," said Griffith. "We had expected to sidestep such an ovation at this hour of night. Who would have believed such a gathering would have waited up for us. I appreciate it and I know the boys do."[28]

Players were mobbed and greeted with words of, "Atta boy!" and "keep up the good work." Some fans followed the players and tried to board their cabs. Goslin was swarmed to the point where he was unable to find a pathway to the street, but he managed to push through and find a cab. "Speech! Speech!" fans cried out. Goslin smiled, blushed, and said a hasty "thank you" before climbing into a cab.[29]

"We're happy and we're tough to beat," said Harris, who was amazed at the size of the crowd. "I cannot tell you how much I appreciate how my friends and the fans have stuck by the club when we were not doing so well. I do not want the credit for the showing the club has made. Give all the boys what's coming to them. They have been trying all season, and now that we're getting somewhere, all the credit should go to them." When asked to make a prediction on how the rest of the season would go, Harris declined. "Pennants are not won in June or

July," he said, "I still stick with my statement made early in the season when I said the club would get somewhere. I believe my club is as strong as any in the league." When asked about Johnson's absence, he admitted he was disappointed when his star pitcher had to go home. "I am sure glad to learn that Mrs. Johnson has recovered," he said.[30]

The Senators would be at home for the next four weeks, beginning with a doubleheader starting at 1:30 against the Athletics. Following the twin bill and two more games with Philadelphia, Washington would host Boston for six games, followed by a five-game series with New York and five with Detroit. The home stand would conclude with series against Cleveland, St. Louis, and Chicago.

Before seven o'clock on the morning of the Senators-Athletics scheduled doubleheader, queues of fans began lining up for tickets at the Griffith Stadium box office. At 8:00, a cheer went up when Senators secretary Ed Eynon arrived. He rushed up the steps to open the clubhouse, then reappeared with pasteboards and kept busy for an hour in handling customers. At 9:00, the fans lined up outside the gates began to entertain themselves by singing songs. At 11:00, with the line extending from the Georgia Avenue entrance to beyond Florida Avenue, customers became impatient and threatened to crash the gate. Perhaps fearing a riot, Washington management ordered the gates to be opened and fans quickly filed in. By 1:20, nearly every box, grandstand, and upper-deck seat was occupied by men, women, children, government officials, military dignitaries, congressmen, and ambassadors, while just seventeen people occupied the bleachers. However, another thousand joined them after the first game had begun. At game time, the presidential box, decorated with red, white, and blue bunting, remained unoccupied. The president and his party were running late but were expected to arrive before the end of the day.

The doubleheader had an Opening Day feel, with the Navy Band on hand along with other pregame entertainment, including the performance of the popular Washington coaches, Altrock and Schacht. And just as in the Opening Day pregame amusement back in April, Harris received a floral wreath, presented by Washington Police Commissioner James F. Oyster on behalf of the appreciative Washington baseball fans.

At one o'clock, as the Navy Band led the Washington Senators onto the field, twenty-three thousand fans applauded. Then seemingly out of nowhere came a sextet of beautiful, classical dancing girls from the Pomberton School of Dancing, "Wearing nothing you couldn't write home about on a postcard," joked a sportswriter, and performing the "Dance of the Seven Veils."[31] The crowd let out a long salvo of cheers when the dancers approached the Washington players and petted the players with flowers. Then the dancers disappeared as quickly and mysteriously as they came.

Just as in three of their four wins at New York, the Senators scored in their first at bat. With two outs in the bottom of the first, Harris doubled and scored when Goslin tripled. In the bottom of the sixth, Judge drove in two more with a double to put the Senators up by three. After Johnson retired the Athletics in the top of the seventh and the fans stood for the seventh-inning stretch, the band broke into "The Star-Spangled Banner," and the crowd cheered as the president, the First Lady, the two Coolidge boys, and four Secret Service men appeared. When the Navy Band concluded the National Anthem, a fan shouted, "What's the matter with Coolidge?" and the crowd responded with a thunderous unified roar of "He's All Right!"[32]

Following the president's arrival, the Senators went down in order in the bottom of the seventh, but in the eighth inning, Harris doubled, Goslin walked, and Judge and Ruel singled to score two runs for a 5–0 lead. In the top of the ninth, the Athletics put Johnson's shutout in jeopardy with back-to-back singles to start the inning. After the next batter lined out, a batter tagged a hard grounder that deflected off Johnson's shins and looked like it might result in another hit, until third baseman Ossie Bluege picked up the ball and threw to first in time to retire the batter. When Johnson struck out the next batter to end the game, he had recorded his tenth win and fourth shutout of the season, and his 102nd career shutout. In addition, the win was the tenth in a row for the Senators.

Before the start of the second game of the doubleheader, the president and his family laughed along with the crowd during another performance by Altrock and Schacht. The Navy Band then entertained by playing "Hail, Hail, the Gang's All Here" and "Linger Awhile," assumed to be an indication that the president was thinking about four more years in Washington.[33] While the band performed, thousands swarmed onto the field for a close-up of the First Family. The president concluded the festivities by throwing out a ceremonial pitch, just as he had on Opening Day, making an underhand toss "that probably comes from pitching horseshoes as a boy on his father's farm in Vermont," quipped a sportswriter.[34] Umpire Billy Evans caught the president's soft throw and handed the ball to umpire Red Ormsby, who pocketed it.

In the nightcap, the Senators made just two hits off Eddie Rommel, who snapped Washington's winning streak. Joe Judge got both Washington hits to give him four for the day to increase his season batting average to .325. Martina, the tough-luck losing pitcher, allowed just six hits.

It rained the next day, forcing another doubleheader to be played the following day. "Performing like real champions, as befits a pace-setting club, the Nationals cleaned up both ends of the doubleheader with the Philadelphia A's," wrote Denman Thompson.[35] In the first game Al Simmons gave the Athletics a 1–0 lead by becoming the first player to homer into the new left field bleachers at Griffith Stadium. With two outs in the bottom of the seventh, Ruel, Peckin-paugh, Bluege, Zahniser, and Rice all singled in succession to score three runs. The Nats added another run in the next inning for a 4–1 win. In the nightcap, George Mogridge hurled a six-hit shutout for his eighth win of the season before thirteen thousand fans.

Next in town were the Red Sox, who had come down to earth following their surprising start. After fooling people into thinking they might contend in 1924, they lost eleven of sixteen and were now 31–30. Before a Sunday after-noon crowd of eighteen thousand, the Senators scored five runs in the second inning, more than enough for starting pitcher Tom Zachary, who limited the Red Sox to just one hit in the first five innings. The Senators won, 6–2, with Ruel posting his second straight three-hit game. In attendance to witness the Washington win was American actor DeWolf Hopper, best known for his recitation of "Casey at the Bat." The actor was in town to perform the famous baseball poem at a dinner party that evening. "I'm going to be there tonight to hear Hopper give his recitation," said Griffith. "I have read the ballad and I've heard it recited, but this will be the first time I've ever heard Hopper do it, and I know he is the best of them all."[36]

One day later, while the Senators and Red Sox battled in a doubleheader at Griffith Stadium, the two Coolidge boys—John, who was almost eighteen, and Calvin, who was sixteen—engaged in a competitive tennis game on the White House tennis court. During their match, Calvin Jr. developed a blister on his right heel, thought to be nothing serious at the time. As the boys battled away, the commander-in-chief was immersed in his work inside the Oval Office. It had been a busy year for President Coolidge, from working on the tax bill, signing the Indian Citizen Bill into law, and recently accepting the Republican presi-dential nomination for the 1924 election. All this happened in less than a year since Coolidge had unexpectedly become the president of the United States after Warren G. Harding's death.

On the night of August 2, 1923, Vice President Coolidge was sleeping at his father's farmhouse in Plymouth, Vermont, when he was awakened by his father coming up the stairs calling his name. "I noticed his voice trembled," recalled Coolidge. "As the only times I ever observed that were when death visited our family, I knew that something of the gravest nature had occurred." His father placed a report in his hand and informed him that President Harding had died. In a tiny parlor inside the farmhouse by the dim-lighting of a small kerosene lamp, "the most modern form of lighting that had reached the neighborhood," Coolidge would later write, Calvin Coolidge was sworn in as the thirtieth presi-dent of the United States when his father, in his capacity as a notary public, administered the oath of office.[37]

The first-place Senators finished the month of June with a doubleheader split with the Red Sox but gained a half game to increase their league lead to two and a half games over the second-place Yankees and Tigers. In the first game, crafty veteran Howard Ehmke and the Red Sox snapped Johnson's six-game-winning streak in a hard-fought 2–1 decision in eleven innings. The Senators, nearly perfect in the field in recent games, committed three errors and made just six hits. Johnson was still in the game in the top of the eleventh, with the game tied, 1–1. There were two outs and a runner on first when Judge mishandled a grounder that should have been the third out of the inning. With runners now on first and third, the next batter grounded one over the second base bag. Harris, moving quickly to his right, got his hands on the ball but then he fumbled it, allowing the go-ahead run to score. Washington won the nightcap, 3–1, behind Marberry's five-hitter.

The Senators opened July with another doubleheader and won both games behind two brilliant pitching performances to increase their league lead to three full games. Martina, a tough-luck loser back on June 26 when his team made just two hits in a 1–0 loss, was once again victimized by lack of runs and hits. His team scored two runs, with Martina knocking in one of the runs, but that was all he needed in a 2–1 win. In the nightcap, Ogden pitched a three-hit shutout to improve his record 4–0 since becoming a member of the Senators. The Senators got another great performance the next day, with Paul Zahniser pitching a two-hit shutout in what one writer called, "The masterpiece of his career."[38] The first-place Senators were now 41–28 and were heading for a showdown with the Yankees and Tigers.

CHAPTER 9

Taking on the Contenders (July)

On July 3, the Senators gained on their two closest rivals without even playing. While the Nats were enjoying an off day in their schedule and resting before their upcoming five-game series with the third-place Yankees, New York lost in Philadelphia to fall four games behind the league leaders. The Tigers also lost and now trailed the Senators by three and a half games, the largest first-place lead the Senators enjoyed since taking the top spot in the American League. "Personally, I'm glad to see it," admitted Babe Ruth. "Most fans are, too. I guess fellows like Walter Johnson, Bucky Harris, Nick Altrock, and Roger Peckinpaugh deserve a few breaks, and so does Clark Griffith. I'm pulling for the Yankees to win the pennant, and I think they will, but if they don't there's no club in the league I'd rather see than Washington."[1]

Most were taking a wait-and-see approach with expectations of the Senators falling short, including Harry Cross of the *New York Evening Post*, who insisted that the Nats were playing above their heads and could not keep it up. "Manager Harris has had great luck with pitchers. Johnson, Mogridge, Martina, Zachary, and Ogden have been going great, but are due for a few setbacks," Cross wrote. "The Senators have lost only two of their last nineteen games, which is an accomplishment not realized by any other club this season."[2]

July 4, 1924, was America's 148th birthday and Calvin Coolidge's fifty-second birthday, but the president's birthday wouldn't be a happy one. Calvin Jr. was so ill that the president's physicians were summoned. Following an examination, the two doctors believed the boy was showing symptoms of appendicitis. However, a further examination revealed the blister Calvin Jr. had developed on his right heel when playing tennis with his older brother the previous Monday had ruptured, leaving a small hole and allowing an infection. Septic poisoning had developed before anyone realized the danger his entire biological system was in. A statement from the White House later that day reported the boy was very ill and getting along as well as he could.

The first game of the Yankees-Senators holiday doubleheader was set for a 10:30 morning game followed by a 3:30 game. Like in the doubleheader at New York back on June 23, Harris started his two veteran southpaws, Tom Zachary and George Mogridge, and just as in that doubleheader sweep, both pitchers threw well. But this time the Washington batters didn't back them, and by the end of the day New York was back in second place after splitting Washington's four game lead in half by taking both games.

Things started off well for Washington before twelve thousand fans in the morning game when a first-inning RBI double by Goslin gave them a 1–0 lead. The score became 2–0 in the bottom of the fifth when Bluege doubled, was sacrificed to third, and crossed home on Rice's sacrifice fly. Zachary had the Yankees in hand by yielding just three hits through the first five innings, but in the top of the sixth, Whitey Witt beat out a tapper in front of the plate, Ruth walked on four straight wide ones, and Bob Meusel singled sharply to left. Witt, who was on second base, rounded third and tried to score on the hit. Goslin fielded the ball and threw to the plate, but his throw took a bad bounce on the infield turf, skipped over catcher Muddy Ruel, and rolled to the backstop, allowing both Witt and Ruth to score and tie the game. Meusel, making it all the way to third on the play, scored when Wally Pipp singled for a 3–2 Yankees lead. Following New York's three-run rally, the Senators produced just one baserunner in the game's last four innings, while the Yankees added another run for a 4–2 win.

In the afternoon game, George Mogridge held the Yankees hitless—until Babe Ruth singled in the top of the seventh—and scoreless through eight innings. "His curve was breaking with a nice hook," said Ruth. "He had a hop on his fastball, and his change of pace was great. But a man can't go on forever without weakening."

When the Yankees came to the dugout after the eighth inning of a scoreless game, their manager gave a pep talk. "This is our inning," Huggins told his team. "If we can get one man on base, we can win." Witt became that one man when he grounded a single through the middle and scored on Joe Dugan's triple. Babe Ruth, with a chance to extend the lead, struck out, "and the fans gave me a laugh," said Ruth, "but I didn't mind. What mattered was the ball game."[3] Meusel followed with a single to score Dugan and cap the scoring in a 2–0 Yankees win.

On the evening following the doubleheader, Al Schacht had plans to celebrate the Fourth of July at a local dinner party hosted by the secretary of the Polish Legation, a baseball fanatic who idolized Babe Ruth and the Yankees and had a few favorites on the Senators, including Schacht. The Polish secretary invited Schacht and Goslin and Ruth, and a few other Yankees to his party, where libations would be served, despite Prohibition.

"I want you and Goose to be sure to attend this party tonight," Harris instructed Schacht. "I understand Ruth will be there. You guys stick with him."

"And—?" asked Schacht.

"You fellas do your damnedest to keep him out late—all night if you can," replied Harris. "If he's got a hangover tomorrow, we got the games half won."

Schacht and Goslin liked the idea but had doubts about being able to keep up with Ruth, who had a well-earned reputation for late evenings.

The party was a hit. Schacht drank beer and kept Ruth supplied with champagne, and he "swizzled it down like soda pop," Schacht said. The other Yankees players left the party early enough to get back to their hotel before curfew, but Ruth, who never paid attention to curfew, kept on going. At three o'clock in the morning, Ruth was still going strong.

"Al, I'm dead," moaned Goslin. "I got to get some sleep. We done our job. Whadya say we blow?"

"Yeah, that big guy is just getting warmed up," replied Schacht. "He'll never be able to play tomorrow."

Before leaving the party, Schacht reminded Ruth about a commitment to visit soldiers at Camp Meade, Maryland, later that morning. A few hours later, Schacht met Ruth in the lobby of the Wardman Park Hotel.

"Where the hell are you coming from?" asked Schacht.

"I just left the Legation," replied Ruth. "C'mon, let's get this over with."[4]

At Camp Meade, Ruth had a busy morning signing baseballs for the clustered personnel of citizen soldiers' summer encampment. "One fellow, who seemed to know a lot about the game, came to me with a lot of questions," said Ruth. "'Which league do you think plays the best baseball?' the citizen soldier asked. Being an American Leaguer, it's only natural that I should favor my own league."[5]

After spending time at Camp Meade, Ruth and Schacht taxied to Griffith Stadium for an afternoon of back-to-back games, and when they got to the ballpark, Schacht went directly to the Senators' clubhouse to give Harris his report, which brought a smile to the Washington manager's face.

Before a Saturday afternoon crowd of twenty-five thousand, the Yankees wasted no time against Washington's starting pitcher Walter Johnson. Witt hit a high hopper over Johnson for a single on the game's first pitch. After Joe Dugan popped out, Babe Ruth, assumed to be too hungover to play, slammed a double high off the tall right field wall. With runners on second and third, Meusel hit a sacrifice fly to score one. In the bottom of the fourth, Matthews singled and moved to third on a sacrifice and a groundout. Needing a hit to score Matthews, Joe Judge lifted a high fly ball down the right field line. Ruth hustled from his right field position by running toward the first-base pavilion in a "gallant effort" to make the catch,[6] crossed over the right field foul line, then lived one of his worst fears. "I've been afraid about bumping into that [pavilion] wall in the Washington Park ever since I began to play right field," Ruth confirmed a few days later.[7] There was very little ground between the right field foul line and the concrete first-base pavilion wall, so a fielder had to be careful. Ruth slammed into the pavilion parapet with full force and dropped, unconscious, to the grass as the ball fell into the stands for a foul ball. Policemen ran to the scene to control the fans, who seemed disposed to leave their seats and get a close-up view. Several photographers rushed to the injured ballplayer, as did Yankees trainer Doc Woods, holding a water bucket in one hand and a small black bag containing his first-aid kit in the other. A motionless Babe Ruth lay on the ground "for several anxious minutes," reported a New York sportswriter.[8] After Ruth regained consciousness, Huggins ordered him to quit for the day, but the Bambino insisted on remaining in the game. When Ruth came to the plate in the top of the sixth, he was roundly cheered and "swung in obvious pain," noted a sportswriter, though he did connect on a pitch and sent a long drive to left-center field.[9] The ball hit four-feet below the top of the fence and Ruth settled for a double for his third straight hit. Later in the inning, he was said to "look lame" when running the bases to score on a single for another Yankees run.[10] The Senators, totaling just six hits off Yankees starting pitcher Herb Pennock, were shutout for the second straight game in another 2–0 final score. Their first-place lead over the Yankees was down to one game, and if they dropped the second game of the twin ball, they'd fall two percentage points behind the Yankees.

In the nightcap, Yankees leadoff batter Whitey Witt greeted starting pitcher Fred Marberry with a single past Peckinpaugh. Dugan walked and Ruth successfully sacrificed to move up the runners. Then Meusel singled to score both runners.

When the Senators came to bat in the bottom of the first, they were trailing by two, and had gone twenty-three straight innings without scoring a run. In the inning, Matthews walked, Harris singled, and a sleep-deprived Goose Goslin singled past second base to score Matthews to snap the scoreless drought. Judge also singled to load the bases, and Peckinpaugh walked to force in another run to tie the game. Bluege hit into a force-out at second base, allowing Goslin to score from third base on the play, and Judge scored when backup catcher Bennie Tate singled to put Washington up, 4–2. In the bottom of the fourth, the Senators rallied for two more to extend their lead, highlighted by a well-executed squeeze play by Matthews to score Tate. An RBI single by Rice in the eighth inning finished the scoring in a 7–2 Washington win.

As the Senators-Yankees battled through a doubleheader for the second straight day, the devoted First Lady rode with her ailing son in an ordinary

Army ambulance from the White House to Walter Reed Hospital. Blood tests had disclosed poison mixed with Calvin Jr.'s blood, making surgery imperative. At eight o'clock, Calvin Jr. was administered gas anesthesia and taken to the operating room. As specialists worked to drain the poison and reduce the bacteria during the surgical procedure, they discovered that osteomyelitis, an infection of the bone, had developed in his left leg. Following the operation, they announced the patient was doing slightly better. At nine-thirty, the White House confirmed a successful operation, but Calvin Jr. was in critical condition.

Overcast skies and rain in the forecast limited Sunday's attendance to twelve thousand for the final game of the series. Behind the good pitching of Martina and two RBIs by Peckinpaugh, the Senators led, 4–2, after seven innings. In the top of the eighth, Babe Ruth, claiming to be sore from his collision with the wall from the day before, hit his twenty-second homer of the season, a tremendous blast ten rows into the left-center field bleachers to cut the Washington lead to one. With the Senators clinging to their one-run lead and three outs away from an important win that would increase their lead to three games over the Yankees, Wally Schang began the top of the ninth with an infield hit, and Aaron Ward followed by sending Matthews deep into center field to haul in his long drive for the first out of the inning. As Schang quickly scurried back to first base following the catch, the crowd stood and gave the popular Washington center fielder a cheer. "The Senators breathed easier, and the fans felt safer," a sportswriter noted.[11] After the next Yankees batter grounded into a force-out at second base, Yankees manager Miller Huggins made a surprise move by calling on Harvey Hendrick to pinch hit. "That was the wrong move," a New York sportswriter said in the press box,[12] but Hendrick, hitting just .237 this season, came through with a single down the right field line, then surprised everyone by attempting to stretch his hit. "We all held our breath when Harvey kept on going to second base," said Ruth. Washington right fielder Sam Rice made a snap throw to Roger Peckinpaugh, who was covering second base. "It looked as if he was out for sure," said Ruth. Umpire Red Ormsby signaled and called the runner out, then changed his call when the usually sure-handed Peckinpaugh dropped the ball for an error. The Yankees baserunner on first base completed the circuit around the bases on the play to tie the game, 4–4. "That was a real break," admitted Ruth.[13] No sooner than the tying run crossed the plate, rain began to fall.

When Martina walked the next batter to put Yankees baserunners on first and second, Harris called for Marberry, who induced the first batter he faced to hit a soft grounder to Washington's player-manager, "who allowed the ball to play him with the result that it rolled through his legs," described a Washington sportswriter. As the ball rolled into right field, Hendrick touched third and headed home. Sam Rice, backing up Harris on the play, picked up the ball and made a perfect throw to Senators catcher Muddy Ruel, who was five feet up the third base line in his effort to block the plate. Hendrick, a former collegiate football player at Vanderbilt, elected to plow into the Washington catcher rather than make a slide. "Bang, crash, the way they do it at college, and Hendrick piled into and over the catcher," explained *Washington Times* sportswriter Louis Dougher.[14] Ruel fell flat on his back, dropped the ball, and Hendrick touched the plate to give New York the lead. Whitey Witt, who was on first base, also rounded third and headed for the plate. Marberry retrieved the baseball and threw to Ruel, hoping to retire Witt in his effort to score, but Ruel, too dazed to react, remained on his back as the ball plopped onto his chest protector, and Witt easily scored. Following this incredible sequence, the injured Ruel was helped to his feet and escorted to the Washington dugout.

Ruth extended the inning with a hit to score the fourth run of the inning for a three-run Yankees lead, and when Ruth reached second base on his hit, the rain started to fall harder. "For a moment, it seemed that this shower might develop to such proportions as to end the game right then and there and deprive New York of their runs," a worried New York sportswriter commented.[15]

As disappointed fans staggered down the Griffith Stadium walkways and exited following the Senators 7–4 loss, a few claimed this to be the toughest setback in Washington baseball history. Others said they were fighting mad at the gridiron tactics employed by the Yankees to annex a victory. There were also words of praise for the spirit of the Senators, who were still one full game ahead of the Yankees and three ahead of the Tigers.

Around the time the disappointed Washington fans were heading home, a blood transfusion was performed and additional oxygen was provided for Calvin Jr. The president and First Lady stayed by his side, leaving only to eat their meals at the White House. During one of these short periods, the president nervously paced through each room, attempting to relieve his mind. At six o'clock the following evening, shortly after Calvin Jr. lapsed into unconsciousness, there was an announcement that the boy was clinging to life with tenacity. At ten thirty, though, it was over; Calvin Jr. died at the age of sixteen. "He suffered very little during the last three hours," someone close to the First Family wrote in a letter to a friend. "He was unconscious and entirely without suffering."[16] Fifteen minutes later, a tearful Mrs. Coolidge was seen leaning heavily on her husband for support while leaving the hospital. Two days later, during a Senators-Tigers doubleheader at Griffith Stadium, the fans stood and removed their hats to observe two minutes of silence in tribute to Calvin Coolidge Jr. Players from both teams lined up on the baselines and doffed their caps.

When the Tigers made their first visit to town back in May, a Washington scribe reported that the Tigers believed they would annex the American League pennant this season. "That's one of the best qualities about my team," said Tigers player-manager Ty Cobb. "That's the kind of talk a manager likes to hear."[17]

The Tigers had improved each year since Cobb was assigned the team's managerial duties in 1921, and in 1923, they had won eighty-three games, the most wins Detroit had since 1916. A strong-hitting attack, added pitching depth, and the belief that the odds were against the Yankees in winning a fourth consecutive pennant inflated the Tigers' hopes, but Cobb believed he had one important missing ingredient in his starting lineup—a reliable second baseman. "Nobody realizes more than I do the importance of second base to be a championship team," Cobb insisted. Back in December, Cobb attended the Baseball Winter Meetings in Chicago in search of a trade for a starting second baseman but came home empty handed. "I'll be everlasting doggoned, pewterized, and nickel-plated if I can get a darned man in baseball to give, sell or trade me a second baseman," said a frustrated Cobb.[18] Donie Bush, a former teammate of Cobb's, said, "Nobody liked Cobb and nobody gave him anything."[19]

At thirty-seven, Cobb was still in the Tigers' everyday starting lineup, was hitting .345, and became the first player during the 1924 major-league season to reach one hundred hits. He could still hit and inspire his players in leading by example, but Cobb did have one enigma: He was so tough on his players that his uptight team consistently made fielding and base-running mistakes.

The series with the Tigers was scheduled to begin with a July 8 doubleheader, and the Senators, eager to play after the tough setback in the last game with the Yankees, were reportedly disappointed when rain postponed the two games. When the two teams engaged in a doubleheader the next day, Cobb made it clear that he was going to do whatever he could to distract his counterpart. "He called him 'Baby Face,' 'Shnookums,' and anything that would imply Bucky was a boy among men," recalled longtime *Washington Post* columnist Shirley Povich. When a grounder was hit in Harris's direction, Cobb, who spent time in the third-base coaching box during the series, shouted, "Boot it! Boot it!"[20]

Cobb was also on his players during the series. When convinced that outfielder Heinie Manush was too unaggressive during an at bat, Cobb called time from the third-base coach's box, summoned Manush from the batter's box, and held a conference hallway between third and home.

As Cobb spent thirty seconds chewing out Manush, the Griffith Stadium fans began to boo. "Oh, you boll weevil!" a fan shouted at Cobb.[21]

"Come down into the clubhouse after the game and settle your argument with your bare fists," Cobb shouted to the fan.[22]

With the Senators trailing, 5–0 in the bottom of the eighth of the first game, newcomer Tommy Taylor, a thirty-one-year-old rookie infielder the Nats had acquired from Memphis in a trade for Doc Protho, made his major-league debut as a pinch-hitter. For more than a week he sat on the bench, watching other teammates step to the plate. "Why don't they send me up there?" Taylor often thought, "I'd get hold of one."[23] Finally, manager Harris sent him to the plate, and Taylor came through with a hit. Rice followed with a single, and Goslin tripled to score Taylor and Rice to put Washington on the board, but it was too little too late in a 5–2 Washington setback.

In the nightcap, the Tigers took the lead in the first inning when outfielder Heinie Manush, fired up following Cobb's heated lecture, circled the bases after tagging a long drive to center field. In the bottom of the inning, Washington took their first lead of the day when Goslin doubled home a pair. With runners on first and second in the bottom of the fourth, Ogden slammed one back at the opposing pitcher, and when the drive hit the opposing pitcher's arm and bounced into right field, the baserunners advanced and scored when right fielder Harry Heilmann missed the cutoff man. The Senators held on to win, 4–2, for Ogden's fifth straight win.

In the first game of the doubleheader the following day, "both teams managed to play some stupid baseball, and both made mechanical as well as mental errors," summarized Harry Salsinger of the *Detroit News*.[24] In a game that took four hours and eight minutes and thirteen innings, Washington was ahead, 7–5, before the Tigers scored five in the top of the eighth to take a 10–7 lead. In the bottom of the ninth the Senators cut the lead to 10–8, had runners on second and third with two outs, and Sam Rice due to bat. Before pitching to Rice, Cobb and the Tigers battery held a conference at the pitcher's mound. Rice, who was patiently waiting for Cobb to conclude his conference, assumed they were planning to purposely walk him since first base was unoccupied, but much to his surprise the first two pitches were over the plate. A bewildered Rice took both pitches for strikes, but he drove the next pitch for a two-run single to tie the game, 10–10. In the bottom of the tenth, Harris and Goslin singled to put the Senators in position to win the game. "Two on and nobody out, things looked pretty rosy for the Griffs," commented a Washington sportswriter.[25] But hopes of a win vanished when the next three batters grounded out.

With the game still tied in the top of the thirteenth, the Tigers finally got something going against Fred Marberry, the sixth Washington pitcher of the game, who "lost his stuff in the thirteenth inning," noted Washington sportswriter John Keller.[26] Manush walked and was propelled across the plate when Cobb and Heilmann singled. Cobb scored the final run later in the inning in a 12–10 Detroit win.

Because the first game lasted thirteen innings, the fans assumed there wouldn't be a second game. It was after 6:00 when one-armed Griffith Stadium megaphone announcer E. Lawrence Phillips broadcast that there wouldn't be a second game that day. The fans were walking across the field and heading to the exits when Phillips made another announcement: there would be a second game.

In the second game the Senators scored in the first inning but trailed, 3–1, after three, and the way Tigers left-handed starting pitcher Earl Whitehill was throwing, another setback seemed likely, until the Tigers became too confident. "The Tigers were satisfied that Washington could not score another run, so they bent all their efforts to hurrying as much as possible to get five innings in and make the game official in the book before the umpires called play," wrote Salsinger.[27]

In the bottom of the fourth, Harris and Goslin both walked after being down in the count. Judge moved the runners along with a sacrifice, and Ruel grounded to Tigers' shortstop Topper Rigney, who lunged for the ball rather than fielding it. The ball glanced off Rigney's glove and rolled into left field, allowing Harris and Goslin to score to tie the game. With the game still tied after the fifth inning, the umpires decided it was too dark to continue and started off the field. "Had the Tigers pressed their opponent at bat, they could have scored at least two more runs," wrote Salsinger, who believed the Tigers depended too much on Whitehill. "In these days, a two-run lead means nothing, no matter who is doing the pitching," Salsinger added.[28]

While the Senators were unable to salvage a win in their doubleheader, the Yankees swept two from the White Sox to put the Senators and Yankees in a first-place tie with identical 43–34 records. "Washington is cracking under the strain," said Giants manager John McGraw.

"McGraw, of course, has not seen the Griffs in action, being occupied with his own team in the National League," wrote Louis Dougher, "but some of us who have watched the Griffs since their return from four straight victories over the Yankees in New York last month are inclined to agree with the estimable leader of the NL champions. They had made their way by combining hard hitting, excellent fielding, and airtight pitching. They looked excellent when returning home versus Philadelphia and Boston, though it was noticeable that their hitting began to fall off. Then came their home series against the Yankees, and their hitting grew weaker."[29]

In late June, the Senators led the league in hitting with a team batting average over .300. They were now fifth in the league, with a .288 team average. Harris's and Peckinpaugh's season batting averages were down to .271; Bluege, who was hitting .274 when he became the starting third baseman, was now at .236; and Matthews, hitting .375 in late June, was now hitting .288. Rice, Goslin, and Judge were still hitting above .300, but even their batting averages had declined. Muddy Ruel was the one Washington player who was still hitting and had hit safely in fourteen straight games while going 19 for 47 since June 26 to boost his season batting average from .286 to .309. Though forced to leave the game after Harvey Hendrick bowled him over a few days earlier, he had started every game but one since and said he felt fine.

In the final game of the series with Detroit, the Senators lost a game they should have won and fell into second place. "Few times in the history of baseball has a team won a game in the manner that Detroit won yesterday," Salsinger wrote. "The Tigers literally blundered their way into a 4–3 victory over Washington." In the top of the eighth, with Washington ahead 3–1, Detroit second baseman Les Burke doubled off the right field wall and Manush walked to put runners on first and second. When Cobb hit a clean single to center field, Manush rounded second and headed to third, "the proper play since [Wid] Matthews is notorious for his weak throwing arm," noted Salsinger. Manush arrived at third base, and was surprised to find the lead runner, Les Burke, standing on the base. "Burke, for some reason unknown, pulled up to third and stayed there," commented Salsinger.[30] Matthews fielded the ball and made a throw, "one of his poorest since joining the Nats," according to John Dugan.[31] As Burke broke for home, third baseman Ossie Bluege retrieved the center fielder's underthrown heave, and amid the confusion, made an off-balanced throw without taking aim. His off-target throw allowed Burke and Manush to score and Cobb to move all the way to third base. Tigers first baseman Lu Blue followed with a hit to score Cobb for what proved to be the winning run.

On July 12, the Indians came to Washington to open a five-game series, beginning with a doubleheader, Washington's tenth twin bill in the previous twenty days. The Senators now trailed the Yankees by one game and were one game ahead of the third-place Tigers. Cleveland, expected to contend this season and picked by some to win the pennant, were a disappointing seventh place in the standings, though they were just six and a half games behind the Yankees in the cluttered American League pennant chase. Late in the first game of the doubleheader, with the Senators trailing and on their way to a 7–1 loss for their eighth defeat in their previous eleven games, the Washington fans soundly booed Harris when he made an error. "If the Nats had the pennant won and one player made an error, the fans would blaspheme the very players who gave them a winner," sarcastically commented Cleveland Plain-Dealer sportswriter Stuart Bell.[32] In the nightcap, the Senators rebounded for a 9–0 lead after seven innings and went on to win, 9–2, but lost a half game to the Yankees and Tigers, who both won that day.

The next day the Washington batters began the game where they had left off the day before, by scoring five runs on six hits to take a 5–0 lead after the second inning. The Indians fought back against Marberry, who struggled with his control, and when the Indians scored two in the top of the sixth, the game was tied, 7–7, though the game would not be deadlocked for long. In the bottom of the inning, the Senators sent twelve men to the plate and scored eight runs, with Joe Judge doubling in both of his at bats during the rally and Roger Peckinpaugh singling in his two turns at the plate in the inning. The Indians closed the gap to 15–11, with three runs in the seventh and one in the eighth. Paul Zahniser, who had replaced Marberry in the sixth, retired the first two batters in the top of the ninth, but then walked the bases loaded. "Take him out!" a fan shouted. Feeling he was being squeezed by home plate umpire Ducky Holmes, Zahniser looked back at Harris for support after each ball four. "Of the 15 walks handed out during the day, Holmes had a share of them," wrote Louis Dougher, who felt Holmes was missing low pitches in the strike zone.[33] When Tris Speaker trotted to first base after the third straight walk in the inning, Harris signaled to the bullpen for a new pitcher as he walked toward the plate. He then called to his catcher, Bennie Tate, asking him about the umpire's strike zone.

"The last one was through the groove," replied Tate.

"Say, Holmes, ain't this game bad enough without you making it worse?" Harris shouted to the umpire. "Come on, fat-head, call them right!"

"You will have to get a new second baseman to finish this game," Holmes informed Harris. As Harris walked to the Washington dugout, he made a parting shot. "The fat-head stands," he told Holmes.[34] Angered over Harris's ejection, the fans began riding the umpire, and a few pop bottles dropped onto the field, one landing in the grass within ten feet of home plate. Shortly after relief pitcher Allen Russell retired Joe Sewell on a fly out to end the game, a heavy-set man wearing a stiff straw hat emerged from the box seats and headed for Holmes. The irate fan spun the umpire around with one punch and wound up to throw another when Cleveland second baseman Chick Fewster grabbed the attacker's arm before he could swing. Umpire George Moriarty arrived on the scene and struck the spectator, and Cleveland catcher Luke Sewell intervened by grabbing the angry fan and held him until the police arrived. A few policemen escorted the furious fan off the field and to an area beneath the stands, where the fan managed to tug away from the grasp, then ran and disappeared with the departing crowd.

One day later, Harris watched the Senators-Indians game in his street clothes from a box seat behind the Washington dugout. He had a message from American League President Ban Johnson on a yellow slip of paper in his coat pocket that he had been suspended indefinitely. When asked by the press about his run-in with Ducky Holmes, Harris said he used no profanity and said nothing worse than "fat-head."[35] Joe Judge managed in Harris's absence, and the Senators responded by scoring twelve runs on eighteen hits in a 12–0 win. All nine Washington starters registered at least one hit and seven of the nine starters had a multiple-hit game. Starting pitcher Curly Ogden allowed just five hits and won his sixth in a row since joining the Senators. "Probably much of Ogden's troubles were mental," *Washington Evening Star* sportswriter John Keller wrote about Ogden's struggles prior to coming to Washington. "He may have actually believed that his wing was out of order and pitched accordingly. But it is certain that he believes his transfer to the Harrismen meant he 'must make good or pass out of the majors.'"[36]

It was hard to believe that Walter Johnson had not won a game since shutting out the Athletics back on June 26. Since then he had lost three in a row, but in the last game of the series with the Indians, he got back in the win column with a 4–2 victory to improve his season record to 11–6. The Senators were now back in a winning groove with four straight wins, but still trailed the first-place Yankees by one game.

CHAPTER 10

The American League Pennant Race Heats Up (July)

A young man dressed in a dapper gray suit and a brown hat atop his jet-black hair sat alone in the corner of a hotel lobby, reading a publication. Occasionally, he would break into a nice smile, an indication that he was amused by his reading material. "He has a smile that would win the hearts of his countrymen, if he were a public speaker," wrote *Washington Evening Star* sportswriter John Foster. Every now and then, a teammate would approach to tell a joke, and the seated gentleman would display his engaging smile as he listened to whatever joke each player had to tell. "Be merry while you can, because tomorrow the ax may fall," was a favorite adage of the young man, George Sisler, the player-manager of the St. Louis Browns.[1]

In 1923, Sisler was unable to see much of anything, let alone read. He had lost most of his eyesight rather suddenly, and carried himself like a man who was blind in one eye and had weak vision in the other. There were many who cast doubt about his future in Major League Baseball, until last March, when he confirmed his eyesight was fine and vowed to be back. "I'll be there this season—there is no doubt about it," he assured. "My eyes have not given me any trouble. There is no pain or strain or ill effects of any sort of my first three days of practice and I do not think there will be."[2]

Before his eyes went bad in the winter of 1923, George Sisler was arguably the best pure hitter in baseball. In 1920, he hit .407 while totaling a major-league record 257 hits. In 1922, he posted a .420 batting average with a league-leading 246 hits for a .360 lifetime average through his first eight major-league seasons. Led by Sisler's brilliance at the plate, the 1922 Browns won ninety-three games and finished one game behind the American League champion New York Yankees. Sisler and the Browns were looking forward to another great season in 1923, but that changed one morning in February, a week before Sisler would head to Mobile, Alabama, for spring training. "When I woke that morning, my

91

eyesight was gone," said Sisler. "Prior to that horrible awakening, I had always been in perfect health. My eyesight had always been perfect."[3] Sisler's temporary impaired vision was due to a severe sinus infection and a defective optic nerve. He sat out the entire 1923 season and the Browns plunged to a fifth-place finish. He returned as the Browns starting first baseman and assumed the team's managerial duties for the 1924 season. Under his leadership, the Browns got off to a good start and were in contention until their series at New York earlier in the week, where the Browns lost four of five games and slipped into fifth place with a 39–42 record. As for Sisler the player, who understandably needed time to regain his timing at the plate, he was currently hitting .308.

When the Senators and Browns began a five-game series with a Thursday afternoon doubleheader at Griffith Stadium, Harris was reinstated and in the starting lineup for both games. Griffith explained in a phone conversation with American League president Ban Johnson what had transpired in the Harris-Holmes incident and assured that Harris used no profanity. Ban Johnson also spoke with Cleveland player-manager Tris Speaker, who had been heading to first base after drawing a walk at the time when Harris called Holmes a fat-head, and he also confirmed that Harris used no obscenities.

The series began with the two teams splitting a doubleheader, the Browns winning the first game to snap Washington's four-game win streak. But Wid Matthews missing from the starting lineup for the fourth straight day bothered the Washington fans more than the loss. "Applesauce!" responded Harris when hearing rumors about benching Matthews due to his hitting slump.[4] Harris clarified that the only reason he wasn't playing the hardworking center fielder was to give him a rest.

In place of Matthews, Harris turned to Nemo Leibold. "I'm all for Wid Matthews, and I think it is a shame to attribute our failure to hold first-place to him," a woman fan wrote in her letter to *Washington Post* sportswriter Norman Baxter.[5] "We all know about Leibold. The team got nowhere with him. The team will get nowhere with him playing now," an angry fan stated in his note to *Washington Times* sportswriter Louis Dougher.[6] Harris also announced that third baseman Ossie Bluege would take a rest in favor of Tommy Taylor, who was said to be showing signs of becoming a good major-league hitter.

In the first game, Tom Zachary limited the Browns to six hits. Unfortunately, the Senators made only five against Browns starting pitcher Dixie Davis in a 3–0 loss. The game was scoreless until George Sisler, applauded by the Washington fans at every at bat, hit an RBI double in the sixth inning. In the second game, Nemo Leibold knocked out four hits while crossing home four times and Tommy Taylor made three hits and drove in three runs in a 12–7 Washington win. Maybe it did pay for the Washington manager to go with his gut in benching Matthews and Bluege. The Senators also made news off the field by sending three rarely used reserves and cash to the Kansas City Blues of the American Association for a twenty-five-year-old, hard-hitting, right-handed-batting outfielder named Pete Scott. "The Griffs need, and have needed all year, a slugging right-handed hitter, preferably an outfielder," Louis Dougher wrote.[7] "By securing Scott, Griffith is letting it be known that he intends to do everything humanly possible to win the pennant," commented John Foster.[8]

Shortly before the third game of the series with the Browns, the fans cheered when a Cleveland victory in the first game of a doubleheader at Yankee Stadium was posted on the out-of-town scoreboard. If the Senators won today, they'd be at least tied for first by the end of the day. If the Senators won and the Yankees lost the second game of their twin bill, the Nats would have sole possession of first, and with Curly Ogden, who was 6–0 since arriving in Washington, on the hill, the chances appeared good. But things didn't get off on the right foot for Ogden and the Senators. The Browns scored two in the top of the second; however, the Nats evened the score when Rice led off the bottom of the third with a double, the red-hot Leibold tripled to score Rice, and Goslin's sacrifice fly scored Leibold. In the bottom of the fourth, Leibold came through again, with a two-out, bases-loaded two-run single for a 4–2 Washington lead. The Browns rallied to tie the game, but the Senators retook the lead with two outs in the bottom of the fifth, when an error by Sisler led to a one-run Washington lead. In the top of the ninth, with the Senators still ahead by one, and one out away from a win, Roger Peckinpaugh mishandled a routine grounder that had all the looks of a game-ending out. Harris called on Marberry to get the last out of the game, but the first batter he faced, St. Louis outfielder Baby Doll Jacobson, smacked a fastball for a triple that led to a Browns win and sent Ogden to his first defeat since the Senators claimed him off waivers. "Had it not been for a most untimely error by Roger Peckinpaugh, the Nationals would have been in a tie for first-place," wrote a disappointed Washington reporter.[9]

In the fourth game of the series, the Senators kept battling back to stay in the ballgame, beginning with a rally to overcome a 5–0 deficit to tie the game, but trailed, 8–5, after the Browns scored three in the top of the eighth. With two outs in the bottom of the eighth, Rice and Leibold came through with extra-base hits to score two to reduce the deficit to one run. With two down in the bottom of the ninth, Taylor and Peckinpaugh produced in the clutch with back-to-back doubles to tie the game. The Browns scored in the top of the tenth to take a one-run lead, but the Senators answered in the bottom of the inning with the help of a St. Louis error to retie the game.

Then, with the score still even and with two outs in the bottom of the fourteenth, Harris hit what appeared to be a game-winning homer. His drive took a long bounce in deep left field, hopped into the bleachers, then bounced back onto the field. "Under the ground rule agreement, any ball hit into the stands, whether on the fly or bound, shall be ruled a home run," noted John Dugan.[10] Team secretary Ed Eynon and team employee Harold Johnson, both seated in the bleachers before performing the task of totaling the fan passage count of each ballpark turnstile, claimed the ball went into the bleachers before falling back onto the field. But umpire Dick Nallin ruled that the ball had bounced off the outfield wall and stayed in play. Harris settled for a triple and was left on base when Goose Goslin bounced back to the pitcher to end the inning. Neither team scored in the fifteenth inning, but the Browns added one in the sixteenth for a 10–9 win. And since the Yankees won, the Senators dropped two games behind the league leaders and fell behind the Tigers in the standings after Detroit swept a doubleheader in Boston.

When the game ended, Griffith immediately filed a protest, hoping to persuade league president Ban Johnson to change the game's outcome by ruling Harris's hit a home run. He also sent an affidavit to Johnson, signed by a prominent Washington banker, who had been seated in the bleachers during the game and affirmed he had witnessed Harris's drive bounce into the bleachers. "If Ban Johnson listens with reason, the Nationals will be credited with a 14-inning victory over the St. Louis Browns," wrote Frank Young.[11]

Walter Johnson was slated to pitch the final game of the series, and Sisler countered with Dixie Davis, the left-hander who had shut out the Senators on five hits in the series opener. The Browns wasted no time against Johnson, as Browns outfielder Jake Tobin started the game with a hit and scored on a Sisler double. After that, Johnson retired sixteen of the next eighteen Browns and the Senators led, 2–1, when Sisler came to the plate with two outs in the top of the sixth. The St. Louis player-manager tapped a Johnson fastball that died in the grass in front of the plate, and Senators catcher Muddy Ruel dashed from his position behind the plate, grabbed the baseball, and tagged Sisler for what appeared to be an out. The Senators, thinking the inning was over, began to head to their dugout until home plate umpire Bill Dinneen called a foul ball. Sisler then hit Johnson's next pitch, "which went like a cannon shot down the left field line," described Frank Young.[12] Assuming Sisler would stop at third base and settle for a triple, Peckinpaugh and Goslin took their time in relaying the ball back to the infield, but much to their surprise, Sisler kept running and crossed the plate for an inside-the-park home run to tie the score, 2–2. With the game still deadlocked in the top of the eighth, Jake Tobin and Herschel Bennett gave the Browns a one-run lead and ended Johnson's day by tagging back-to-back triples, and when Peckinpaugh made a throwing error later in the inning, Bennett scored from third to tack on another run for St. Louis. In the bottom of the inning, Goslin singled, Judge doubled, and a ground out by Ruel scored Goslin to pull Washington within a run. Then Peckinpaugh came to the plate and was "given an unmerciful booing," but he responded with an RBI single to retie the game.[13] In the bottom of the ninth, Rice singled, Leibold sacrificed, and Goslin singled to score Rice with the game-winning run.

On July 21, the Senators were in third place with a 49–39 record and trailed the first-place Yankees by two and a half games when they opened the next series against the White Sox. The second-place Tigers were one and a half games behind the Yankees and were in New York to play a four-game series. "Make no mistake about it—the Yankees have got to fight their heads off to win the pennant," Babe Ruth wrote in his syndicated sports column. "Frankly, I thought we would be quite a ways out in front by this time. I guess everybody thought so too—including most of the teams and players in the American League. But Washington has some different ideas about it and so has Detroit, and what do we have on our hands now but a lot of real battling to do." Were the Yankees too confident? "Down South this spring we were all pretty cocky," admitted Ruth.[14]

If the Yankees weren't focused earlier in the season, they sure were at the present. They had won sixteen of their past twenty-one, and leading the way was Babe Ruth, who had twenty-nine hits in his previous fifty-six at bats, with twenty-one runs, six homers, and twenty-two RBIs. He was currently leading the league in hitting (.384 batting average), runs scored (seventy-four), homers (twenty-eight), and RBIs (seventy-seven), and he was doing this while still hurting from his collision with the Griffith Stadium pavilion wall. "I haven't been able to sleep at night," Ruth said about the aftereffects of his injury, including a bruised solar plexus, left leg, and left hip.[15]

There had been bad blood between the Yankees and Tigers since the last time the two teams met in mid-June. The trouble in that series started during a Yankees blowout victory, when a Detroit pitcher plunked Ruth in retaliation for his homer earlier in the game. The next day, Ruth stiff-armed Tigers pitcher Bert Cole on a play at first base. While walking back to the dugout after that play, Ruth glanced at Ty Cobb in center field and saw the Tigers player-manager signal to Cole. Thinking Cobb was up to something, Ruth hollered a warning to the next batter, Bob Meusel. As Ruth had suspected, Cole hit the batter with a pitch between the shoulder blades, and Meusel reacted by charging the mound. Ruth headed for center field but was stopped before he could reach Cobb. After order was restored, Ruth and Meusel, who were ejected from the game, went toward the clubhouse, but the entrance was located inside the Detroit dugout, and that spelled trouble. An angry exchange between the two Yankees and the Tigers on the bench set off another brawl. In the New York clubhouse following the game, Meusel was approached by a Detroit grounds crew member with a message. "Cobb sent me," he said. "He told me that if you think he's the kind of manager who would tell a pitcher to dust a batter off, he'd be glad to meet you privately under the stands."

"Tell Cobb I will be right out," replied Meusel.

"No you don't!" said Yankees manager Huggins. "Let things stand as they are."[16]

The Tigers arrived with a six-game win streak a day before the first game of the series. Needing something to do on their day off, they headed to Yankee Stadium to watch the Yankees and Indians battle in a doubleheader. They snagged seats next to the New York dugout and fraternized with the Yankees between games, a sign that the two teams were at least on speaking terms. When the series began the following day, the Tigers took a 5–0 lead before the Yankees rallied for six in the bottom of the third to take a 6–5 lead. Detroit rebounded and pulled out a 9–7 win to cut the Yankees' first-place lead to one-half game. The following day, the Tigers took over the American League lead behind a wonderful pitching performance by Ed Wells, who held Ruth hitless in a 3–1 Tigers win.

While the Tigers and Yankees were battling, the Senators led, 12–0, after three innings against the White Sox. Before the game was over, Leibold and Taylor had made three hits apiece in a 16–2 win. Taylor now had a .364 batting average, Leibold was swinging a hot bat, and the fans were no longer yelling for Matthews.

The next day the Senators played their twelfth doubleheader in thirty days, and in the first game they were tamed by White Sox pitcher Sloppy Thurston, who limited the Senators to five hits in earning his tenth straight win. The Senators won the nightcap, thanks to another good pitching performance by Curly Ogden, who upped his season record with the Senators to 7–1. Starting pitcher Fred Marberry was in a jam in almost every inning in the fourth game of the series with Chicago, but escaped each, except when he yielded two runs in the top of the fifth. By that time, the Senators had four on the board, more than enough for a 4–2 win.

Meanwhile, at New York that day, the game was tied in the bottom of the eleventh, when Babe Ruth "slapped one into the old familiar spot in the right-field bleachers and knocked the Tigers into second place, where they belong," opined a New York sportswriter.[17] After the ball landed in the bleachers and while Ruth trotted around the bases, a wave of fans poured onto the field. When Ruth reached third base, a few of his teammates had to hold back the crowd so he could make it to home plate to register the winning run.

Before the fourth and final game of the Tigers-Yankees series, Yankee Stadium megaphone announcer Jack Lentz asked Ty Cobb for his lineup card for the press. "To hell with the press!" replied Cobb. "They don't pay my salary." Sportswriter Fred Lieb was insulted by Cobb's remark. "After twenty years of big league baseball, in which reams and reams of free advertisement have been given to Cobb, his expression of gratitude in his own words, 'To hell with the press!'" complained Lieb.[18] Why Cobb was angry wasn't known, but it may have been because he was thrown out on a play at the plate and picked off second base the day before, and words like "foolishly tried to score," and "Bush League," were used by the press to describe his two mistakes on the base paths.[19]

In the final series game, the Tigers took a 4–0 lead, but the Yankees came back to tie the game with two in the fifth and two in the seventh; however, the Tigers retook the lead with a run in the eighth inning. After the Yankees failed to score in their half of the eighth, the time was 5:15, and plenty of daylight remained before dusk. Babe Ruth was the fourth batter scheduled to bat in the bottom of the ninth, which must have had the hometown fans visualizing another game-winning homer. But then the unthinkable happened: The game was declared complete, because the Yankees had to catch a train for an exhibition game the next day in Indianapolis. "Shortening a game to allow a team to play an exhibition game is a new one, and if it costs the Yankees, they may be sorry for it," reported an appalled New York sportswriter.[20] "They are booked every off day of the season to play exhibition games in some tiny town," commented a reporter. "A team fighting for the pennant is under tremendous strain. The players have complained, but someone connected to the club pays no attention and keeps booking games."[21] As angry fans left the Stadium, many vowed to never attend another Yankees game, unless it was a World Series game.

"Every man on the Tigers believes Detroit will win," said a happy Ty Cobb, following Detroit's win to retake first place in the American League. He continued:

> I think we'll win the pennant. The remainder of the schedule favors us over the Yankees. We have almost completed our work against the Western teams (Chicago, Cleveland and St. Louis), but we have two more sets to play against with each of the Eastern teams (Boston, New York, Philadelphia and Washington). Now that Boston and Washington have cracked, they should be easier to beat in the future than they were in the past. The Yankees have a few games with them while we have many. The Western teams are getting stronger every day. We are practically through with them, while the Yankees have many contests to play with them.[22]

In the case of the Senators, they had seventeen games remaining against the three other Eastern teams, including four at Yankee Stadium at the end of August, and forty-four against the four Western teams.

The Senators had Walter Johnson on the hill for the final game of the series with the White Sox, but Johnson wasn't at his best. He was suffering from a summer cold and stomachaches, and it showed when he was tagged for five runs on seven hits and walked three before departing with his team trailing, 5–2, after the top of the fifth. In the bottom of the fifth, the Senators bailed Johnson out of a loss by scoring three to tie the game. Two walks, a single, a sacrifice fly, and a wild pitch scored two more for Washington in the next inning, and Allen Russell, who replaced Johnson in the top of the sixth, blanked the White Sox in the last four innings for a 7–5 Senators win.

Following the series with the White Sox to conclude their long home stand, the Senators headed west for a sixteen-day road trip, with series scheduled in Cleveland, Detroit, St. Louis, and Chicago. They currently owned a 53–40 record, were tied for second with the Yankees, and were just half a game behind the Tigers. Before traveling to Cleveland to begin the road trip, they received bad news. Pete Scott, the heavy-hitting right-handed outfielder they had acquired from Kansas City, who was expected to join the Senators in Cleveland, announced he wouldn't report to his new team unless either Kansas City or Washington paid him $2,500 for his share of the purchase price. Unwilling to appease the rookie, Griffith nullified the deal and instructed Kansas City owner George Muehlebach to return catcher Pinky Hargrave, one of the three reserves Washington had traded in the deal. Griffith permitted the Blues to keep the other two players in exchange for an undisclosed amount of cash. With the deal for Scott now dead, Griffith and Harris boarded a train bound for Buffalo to watch a right-handed-hitting outfielder Joe Engel had scouted and said he liked. On July 25, while the Senators were traveling to Cleveland, the Washington team president and manager watched minor-league outfielder Billy Zitzman go 1 for 3 with a single. Unimpressed, they headed for Cleveland after the game. During the series in Cleveland, Engel arrived and was chased out of town by Griffith following a two-hour meeting to discuss the topic of acquiring a right-handed-hitting outfielder. When asked about the meeting, Griffith said he had nothing to report.

In their first game of the road trip, the Senators made just three hits off Cleveland starting pitcher Sherry Smith in a 2–0 loss. "The Georgia peanut planter pitched the best ball at Dunn Field yesterday than any Cleveland pitcher has pitched this year," Cleveland sportswriter Stuart Bell wrote about Smith's great performance.[23] While Washington opened their series at Cleveland with a loss that dropped them back into third place, Babe Ruth homered in the top of the fourteenth, his thirtieth of the season, in a 5–4 win at Chicago. Meanwhile, the Tigers left nineteen on base but were aided by four Philadelphia errors in their 5–4 win.

The next day, the Senators scored a run in each of the first three innings and headed into the bottom of the ninth with a 4–3 lead behind the pitching of Curly Ogden, who gave up just six hits, but also walked six. In the bottom of the ninth, George Uhle made things nerve-racking when leading off with a single. Then the Nationals got a big break on a failed hit-and-run attempt. As Uhle ran for second, the batter missed Ogden's pitch and Ruel fired the ball to

Peckinpaugh, who tagged Uhle for the out, "probably saving the day for the Nationals right there," wrote Frank Young.[24] Ogden retired two batters to end the game for his fifth win in July. In addition to an important win, the Senators gained on the Yankees, who gave up four runs in the bottom of the ninth for a 7–6 loss at Chicago, and the Tigers, who lost, 4–2, to the A's.

Washington continued in their struggles with Cleveland by dropping the next two games to conclude the series. "Washington always finds some way to hand them [Cleveland] the verdict," wrote Frank Young.[25] In this verdict, the Senators handed Cleveland the two wins by totaling just three runs in the two games. While Washington was in the process of back-to-back losses, the Yankees took three in Chicago, including a win over White Sox star Sloppy Thurston, to snap the Chicago pitcher's ten-game winning streak.

"Tomorrow afternoon the Griffs are due to open one of their most important series of the year," wrote John Keller, "and it is to be hoped they will carry into the tussle with the Tigers in Detroit with better batting eyes and a more-keen appreciation of the art of base running than they have revealed thus far in the set of engagements with the Indians. The hitting and base running of the Cleveland series type is not calculated to get Bucky Harris his pennant."[26]

The Senators traveled from Cleveland to Detroit by boat rather than by train, and this proved to be a mistake. "Some players proved not to be sailors," wrote Keller.[27] In the first game at Detroit, Walter Johnson hit a two-run homer over the left field fence, "a real wallop," according to Keller,[28] to give his team a two-run lead in the top of the second. But in the bottom of the inning, Johnson gave up four singles, including one to his counterpart, Earl Whitehill, who had a .152 batting average, to give Detroit a 3–2 lead, and a triple by Heinie Manush added another run in the inning. In the top of the third, the Senators scored twice to even the score without getting a single hit. Two walks, a hit batsman, an error, and a ground out accounted for both runs. The Senators' bats then went to sleep for just two hits in the next four innings, but in the top of the ninth, Ossie Bluege, now back in the starting lineup after the honeymoon with Tommy Taylor ended when he went 2 for 12 in Cleveland, singled and Marberry, who did not allow a run after entering the game in the bottom of the third, surprised the Tigers by bunting with two strikes, resulting in another hit. Rice scored his two teammates with a triple down the right field line and scored when Harris singled for a 7–4 Washington win.

Washington won the next day to move into second place and to pull within one-half game of the Yankees. "From now on, watch our smoke," assured Harris, who sat out this game due to ptomaine poisoning.[29] The Senators got just four hits against Tigers starting pitcher Rip Collins, but scored the game's only run in the top of the fourth when Ralph Miller, a recently acquired minor-league infielder who took Harris's place in today's starting lineup, beat out a slow roller, moved to second on a wild pitch, went to third on a Texas-League single by Goslin, and scored when Judge hit into a fielder's choice. Zachary, a pitcher the Senators were willing to pass along to any club with a worthwhile offer after the 1923 season, was brilliant in allowing just three hits and pitching to only thirty-one batters for his eighth win of the season.

Harris came back with Walter Johnson in the third game of the series, even though he had pitched two days earlier. It was like a repeat of the game two days before: The Senators got the early lead for Johnson, who lost his lead during another tough second inning. Unlike the game from two days earlier, Harris elected to keep Johnson in the game, and the great pitcher responded by blanking the Tigers in the game's last seven innings in a 7–3 Washington victory for Johnson's twelfth win of the season. Sam Rice led the Washington attack with three hits, Peckinpaugh hit his second homer of the season, and Bluege added his second straight two-hit game, including an inside-the-park home run.

Curly Ogden was announced as Washington's starting pitcher for the final game of the series, but Harris elected to go with Mogridge, who was reportedly suffering from a flimsy shoulder. The Senators took a 2–0 lead in the top of the first on an RBI triple by Goslin and an RBI single by Judge, but the Tigers eventually kayoed Mogridge, who was clearly not at full strength, in an 8–3 setback for the Senators.

CHAPTER 11

Dog Days of Summer (August)

American League Standings on the Morning of August 3, 1924

Team	W–L	Games Back
Yankees	58–44	—
Senators	57–44	½
Tigers	56–44	1
Browns	50–48	6

At 10:45 on Friday night, August 1, the same day Walter Johnson and the Senators beat the Tigers, a Washington, D.C., resident running low on gas wheeled into a District gas station and pulled up to a gas pump. He then noticed a mob rushing onto the station's property in pursuit of a newspaper deliveryman carrying a stack of papers.

"What are they fighting for?" the resident asked the gas station attendant.

"It is the early edition of the *Washington Post*," replied the attendant. "From what I understand, it is all on the account of the Griffs."[1]

When the Senators were on the road, Washington baseball fans could catch the play-by-play results on the electronic scoreboard at the *Washington Herald* building or other Washington newspaper-sponsored scoreboards throughout the city, or they could hear the final score on the 7:25 evening radio broadcast of major-league baseball results. But the sports sections of the local newspapers served as the most popular source for day-to-day recaps.

Also on that day Johnson and the Senators won in Detroit, the Sacramento Saloons played at Portland in a Pacific Coast League contest. With a runner on first and one out in the bottom of the seventh of a close game, a Portland batter hit a fly ball to shallow center field. Saloons center fielder Earl McNeely charged forward, dived, turned a somersault, and felt a sharp pain in his right shoulder after making a spectacular catch. He then withdrew from the game.

McNeely was currently hitting .333 with ninety-three runs, was considered a good fielder with a strong throwing arm, and was acknowledged as the fastest man in the Pacific Coast League. "He gets down the first base line faster than [Sam] Rice," reported Senators scout Joe Engel, who had his eye on the twenty-six-year-old prospect and followed him for more than a week before deciding he was the Senators' missing link he had been searching for.[2] Prior to finalizing the deal, Engel warned Griffith about the high price tag placed on the right-handed-hitting center fielder and asked if he was serious about meeting it. Griffith didn't think a minor-league player was worth that kind of money, but now with his team fighting for a pennant he had a change of heart. "If it means a pennant, I am," answered Griffith.[3]

The Saloons wanted $35,000, an outfielder from the current Senators roster to immediately report to Sacramento, and two players to be named later. The deal included an option for Washington to pay $5,000 in lieu of each player, making the total value for McNeely $50,000. When Griffith closed the deal, he and Engel were unaware of McNeely's shoulder injury. Shortly after arriving in St. Louis on the morning of August 3, the Senators received a telegram advising that McNeely would join them in Chicago on Friday, August 8. "Yes, I do expect to play McNeely as soon as possible," Harris told the press. "We are getting him with the hopes of having right-handed punch in the outfield. If he can hit pitching in this league and can approach Joe Engel's description of his work on the coast, he will be needed now, not sometime in the future." Asked about the outfielder the Senators would immediately send to Sacramento to fulfill their obligation in the transaction, Harris refused to comment.[4]

The second-place Senators currently trailed New York by one-half game; however, they believed they were going to gain a game and move ahead of the Yankees as soon as American League president Ban Johnson ruled in favor of their July 19 game protest, the game in which Bucky Harris's hit was ruled a triple in a one-run loss to the Browns. "The fact that he [Ban Johnson] is willing to meet with Ed Eynon in Chicago satisfies me that we have a fine chance to have the verdict reversed," said Griffith.[5] Before meeting with the league president during the Senators–White Sox series at Chicago, Griffith and Eynon traveled to St. Louis, where the local sportswriters were praising the Browns for timely hitting, great pitching and defense, and for looking like champions while taking three of four games in their recent series with the Yankees.

At St. Louis, the Senators were counting on the absence of the customary summertime heat in the city on the western bank of the Mississippi River. This summer's average temperature was uncharacteristically cooler than the usual intense heat and high humidity during a River City summer solstice. Last month's temperature had averaged a mild seventy-five degrees, just one-tenth of a degree more than in July of 1891, the coolest July average temperature on record in city history. Unfortunately for the Senators, the intense heat of a typical St. Louis summer arrived in time for their series. When the Washington players stepped off the train on August 3, the morning temperature had spiked into the lower eighties, and at game time that afternoon, the mercury had reached a sweltering ninety-three. "Oh, this isn't hot," claimed the St. Louis citizens. "We don't take off our coats until the sun starts blistering the paint on our houses."[6] Being accustomed to this kind of mid-summer weather, more than twenty thousand local fans attended the first game of the series.

Riding the momentum of their impressive series win over the Yankees, the Browns knocked the Nats back into third place in a 3–1 win in the first series game. "Disappointing," was how *Washington Post* sportswriter Frank Young described the loss. "Disappointing because the scoreboard showed the Tigers beat New York, thus losing a chance to move into first place."[7] The Tigers' triumph before an overflow home crowd of forty-two thousand put Detroit a percentage point ahead of New York. The Tigers appeared to be heading for another win over their league rivals after scoring four in the first inning and led, 6–1, through four innings in the second game of the series; however, in the bottom of the fifth, Ruth blasted a three-run homer to spark a Yankees comeback, and following Bob Meusel's single to score the game-winning run in the eleventh inning for a 9–8 New York win, the Yankees were, once again, atop the American League standings. The next day Ruth's season batting average surpassed the .400 mark, as he punched out three more hits, including another three-run shot during a 9–2 Yankees win. "We're on our way," Ruth assured. "If the Yankees play ball like they did yesterday, the Tigers nor any other team in the league can stop us."[8]

The 1924 season was evolving into the best in Ruth's career. On August 8, he had the American League's highest batting average (.408) and led the league in several other offensive categories, and he was fielding his position. According to *Detroit News* sportswriter Harry Salsinger, "[Ruth's] throwing is remarkable for speed and accuracy, and he covers a great deal of ground." The Detroit scribe also noted that Ruth was heavier than he had been the previous season. "He is undeniably fat," wrote Salsinger. "He violates all dietary rules and keeps no regular hours."[9] New York sportswriter Ford Frick informed his readers how Ruth recently astonished his teammates by devouring twelve frankfurter sandwiches and drinking six bottles of soda at a single sitting. His daily diet also included fried potatoes for breakfast, a steak topped with gravy for dinner, and schooners upon schooners of ice cream for dessert.

The combination of the heat making it too difficult to sleep and the temperature climbing into the upper nineties the next day persuaded the Washington manager to cancel pregame batting and infield practice. In the game that day, the Senators lost again, 5–1, their third loss in a row, and they tacked on two more losses by dropping both ends of a doubleheader the next day. In the first game of the double feature, Paul Zahniser allowed just four hits, but the Senators got only three against Browns starting pitcher Urban Shocker in a 2–0 loss. In the second game, Harris put Matthews in the starting lineup, hoping the peppery little outfielder could fire up the team, and the energetic center fielder came through with three hits. Joe Judge also made three hits, but it was far from enough in a 4–2 loss.

Relief arrived the following day in St. Louis, thanks to a morning rain shower paving the way for cooler temperatures, and the extreme heat that had overwhelmed the Senators moved eastward and arrived in Washington. August 6, 1924, was the hottest day in the District since a record-high of 106 exactly six years earlier. As the temperature soared to a high of 101.6, seventeen people were treated at local hospitals and government departments closed early. On August 7, it was reported that two Washingtonians succumbed to excessive heat. Later that evening, a thunderstorm reached the District and dropped the temperature twenty degrees, and the start of cooler temperatures for the rest of the week.

In the final series game at St. Louis, Harris decided to shuffle his batting order by inserting Leibold into the leadoff spot, moving himself from the number three spot in the order to two, followed by Rice, Goslin, Judge, Bluege, Ruel, and Peckinpaugh. In the top of the first, Harris, Rice, and Goslin singled in succession to give Washington a 1–0 lead, their first lead in the series. In the bottom of the first, two walks issued by starting pitcher George Mogridge, an error by Harris, and two hits scored four for the Browns. Trailing 6–2 in the top of the eighth, Judge and Bluege hit back-to-back doubles to score one and a Browns error added another run to make it a 6–4 game. Washington scored again in the top of the ninth to cut the St. Louis lead to 6–5, as Matthews swatted a pinch-hit double and scored on a double by Leibold. Now with Leibold on second and nobody out, Harris sacrificed the potential tying run to third, but Washington's hopes plummeted when Leibold was run down between third and home during his attempt to score on Rice's grounder. Goslin followed with a game-ending ground out to conclude the series and a five-game sweep by the Browns The loss was the sixth straight for the Senators, who fell three full games behind the Yankees and two behind the Tigers and now had the Browns breathing down their necks. "Has the Washington club shot its bolt? The answer would be yes," Washington sportswriter John Dugan told his readers.[10] According to *Washington Times* sportswriter Louis Dougher, Washington baseball fans were ready for a pennant but were expecting this team to fall short. "If the players followed the same line of thought, the team would not be where it is today," wrote Dougher.[11] Washington sportswriter Heinie Miller knew how the fans were talking: "They have a fine chance to win the pennant," they said when the going was good, but they claimed, "Well, they were just a flash in the pan," or, "I knew they'd blow up," with the team now slumping. "Listen gang!" Miller advised, "When the going is rough is the time to stick by the team. Any sap can win while he's winning, but it takes a good one to win while he's losing, and baseball pennants are won by the fighting men on the diamond and by fighting fans in the bleachers and grandstand. Don't give up the ship!"[12]

While most Washington baseball fans and sportswriters were skeptical about the remaining eight weeks of the season, the Washington players were optimistic. "The team is confident they will break the streak and end the slump," wrote Dugan. "Harris doesn't like to talk about it. Neither does Griffith, who is confident. The fighting spirit that burns deep in those dark eyes of the boy pilot flashed when questioned on the subject tonight."[13] Harris and Griffith said they were unable to explain the slump but refused to blame the blistering heat, claiming they saw no advantage to the Browns in playing in the heat.

The first thing the Senators noticed upon arrival in Chicago at 7:00 the following morning was the temperature was a bearable seventy-four degrees, and they responded to the tolerable weather conditions that afternoon by scoring a run in the first inning. In the top of the sixth, the Nats added another run when Bluege, "who has been developing long-hitting proclivities since returning to the lineup," according to Frank Young, hit his second homer of the road trip.[14] Walter Johnson, kept idle by Harris in St. Louis for fear the heat might wear him out, kept Chicago scoreless through five innings, but in the bottom of the sixth the White Sox converted two doubles, a walk, and a triple into a 3–2 lead. In the top of the eighth, Bluege backed the Chicago left fielder to the wall for a long sacrifice fly to tie the game, and in the top of the tenth, the Senators were aided by two walks and two White Sox errors in a three-run rally for a 6–3 win to snap their six-game losing streak. The win was the thirteenth of the season for Walter Johnson.

Shortly after breakfast the next morning, rain began to fall. By early afternoon, the game was declared a rainout and rescheduled to be played with the game scheduled for the next day—another doubleheader on the Washington schedule.

Around the time the game was called, Washington's new outfielder arrived after spending the past five days traveling from the Pacific Coast to Chicago. He went directly to the Cooper-Carlton Hotel and knocked on Griffith's hotel room door. The moderately sized, sandy-blond young man entered and introduced himself. "I'm Earl McNeely," the young man said.

"So, you're the fellow who cost me a fortune," Griffith laughed. "Well glad to meet you." Griffith extended his hand.[15]

"Sorry, I can't raise my arm above my hip," replied McNeely. "Dislocated my shoulder last week."[16]

Griffith was stunned. He had agreed to pay $35,000 in cash and send three players in exchange for an injured ball player? He immediately wired the Sacramento Saloons to clarify that the injury occurred while McNeely was with Sacramento. The deal called for McNeely to report in playing condition, and if he did not round into shape shortly, the matter would be taken to Commissioner Landis. After Griffith settled down, he sat with Harris and McNeely to talk contract terms with the new outfielder. The rookie signed his new contract, checked in to his hotel room, and had dinner with his new manager later that evening. The next day, Mike Martin examined McNeely's injured shoulder and concluded that the injury would heal within a week or two, but to be sure, he wanted to take an X-ray when the team returned to Washington. McNeely, who said he felt pain in the shoulder every time he threw the ball, claimed an X-ray was taken on the coast and revealed nothing more than a bruise. When the Senators were back in Washington, Martin said the rookie's injured shoulder was rapidly improving and an X-ray wouldn't be necessary.

Now that McNeely had arrived, the Senators had to send an outfielder to Sacramento. The Washington fans thought and hoped it would be Leibold, but because baseball law prohibited the veteran outfielder from being that player on account of his age, the Nats had no choice but to send Matthews, who was reported to be heartbroken when hearing the news. "I don't know what a player has to do in this league to make good," said Matthews.[17] He said he was sorry he had to leave the Senators and was quick to praise his fair treatment by Griffith and Harris. "I am sorry to have to send Matthews to the coast," said Griffith, "but my hands are tied. I must have a right-handed hitter and Matthews is the only man I have for the deal. All my years in baseball I have never met a better player for a club than Matthews."[18]

Before the doubleheader the next day, Griffith and Eynon paid a visit to Ban Johnson at his Chicago office to discuss their protest. Later questioned about the meeting, Griffith unenthusiastically answered that the league president didn't render a decision. The next morning, Ban Johnson stopped by the Cooper-Carlton Hotel and had a long conversation with Harris. "[He] appeared to be handing out some fatherly advice," a Washington sportswriter reported.[19] The topic of conversation wasn't mentioned, but when Johnson left, his ruling on the protest was still unknown.

With the Senators down, 5–0, in the sixth inning of the first game of the doubleheader, Harris substituted McNeely into the game, and in the top of the seventh, the rookie outfielder singled down the third-base line to drive in a run in his first Major League at bat. Following an 8–2 loss in the first game, Goslin knocked out four hits, including his sixth homer of the season, plus Rice, Judge, Bluege, and Ruel made three hits apiece in an 8–5 Washington win in the nightcap. In the final game of the road trip, McNeely was in the starting lineup and batting fourth in place of Goslin, who sat out due to a knee bruise sustained when sliding into second base the day before. McNeely hit the ball hard in his first at-bat—but right at the first baseman. In his next plate appearance, he thumped a double to center field and scored on a single by Judge to give Washington a 2–1 lead. The Senators went on to win, 4–2. Later that evening, the Senators boarded a train at 6:00 and arrived back in Washington at 4:40 the following afternoon.

Walter Johnson began Washington's home stand by striking out eight in his fifth shutout and fourteenth win of the year. "His smokeball was working in great style," wrote Dugan.[20] Goose Goslin, who admitted his sore knee was a bit stiff but insisted on playing, went 2 for 3 and knocked in two runs, and McNeely, greeted with the loudest cheer of the day, continued to impress by adding a hit in Washington's 4–0 win over Cleveland. "McNeely will do; I'm sure of it," said Harris. "It isn't reasonable to judge a player's worth in only a game or two, but from what I have seen of McNeely, I believe he has the attributes of a winning player."[21]

In the top of the sixth the next day, Cleveland owned a 2–1 lead and had runners on the corners when Cleveland pitcher Stan Coveleski singled through the middle to score a run, and when center fielder Nemo Leibold overran the ball for an error, another run scored to give Cleveland a 4–1 lead. The error was Leibold's first of the season and the first in his last 127 fielding chances, but the fans, still sore that Matthews had to go, unmercifully booed Leibold for the rest of the afternoon in a 5–1 Senators loss.

In the final game of the series, Mogridge gave up a single in the top of the second and a double to Tris Speaker in the top of the fourth but retired seventeen of the next eighteen batters to complete a two-hit shutout in a 1–0 Washington win. "One could not ask to see a better pitched game than that turned in by George Mogridge," wrote Frank Young.[22] The game's only run was scored by Harris in the bottom of the sixth after the aggressive manager reached base on a single and advanced all the way to third on a sacrifice bunt by Rice. Goslin followed with a ground ball to the third baseman, who looked Harris back to the third-base bag before throwing to first to retire Goslin, but as soon as the fielder released the ball, Harris sprinted toward the plate and beat the first baseman's throw by a close margin.

Friday, August 15, the Senators finally had a day off in their schedule, until the manager ordered his team to report to the ballpark for batting practice. The players, looking forward to a day away, did some grumbling, but followed orders. On August 16, the Senators trailed New York by two games and Detroit by one and a half when the Tigers arrived at Griffith Stadium for the first game of a five-game series. A few days earlier, the Tigers received a huge blow to their pennant aspirations with the loss of their productive first baseman, Lu Blue, to a knee injury.

Before a Saturday home crowd of fifteen thousand, Harris elected to start Fred Marberry, a decision Frank Young called a mistake. "The Tigers are noted for their ability to hit 'hard ball' pitching, but manager Harris evidently did not believe this to be a fact," Young wrote.[23] Marberry was effective through the first five innings, but then the Tigers rallied for three in the top of the sixth for a 4–1 lead. The Tigers got a good pitching performance from left-handed rookie Earl Whitehill, played an errorless game, and rounded out the scoring on a triple by Cobb and an RBI single by Al Wingo for a 5–2 win.

Low clouds with flashes of lightning and rumbles of thunder threatened the second game of the series, but a postponement wasn't considered and the game began on time. In the bottom of the second, the Griffith Stadium grounds crew gathered by the tarpaulin in the left field corner in anticipation of a rainstorm. The Senators were ahead, 2–0, at the time and Walter Johnson was at the plate with runners on first and second. Detroit manager Ty Cobb, hoping for rain and postponement since his team was trailing, intentionally caused a delay by making a pitching change, and Johnson greeted the new pitcher by slamming his first offering into left-center field for an RBI double. Then the rain began to fall in torrents, and the grounds crew swung into action by dragging the tarpaulin along the outfield grass and toward the infield, until the wind and rain picked up to prevent them from moving a step closer. Aware that the downpour might make the infield unplayable and lead to a rainout, several Washington players darted from the dugout, ran through the rain, grabbed the tarp, and struggled with the grounds crew before finally getting the covering over the infield.

Thirty minutes later, the skies cleared, play resumed, and McNeely singled for his second hit of the game to score two more for a 5–0 Washington lead. The rookie sensation added two more hits before this game was over. "Griffith getting some of the interest back on his $50,000 investment when the Sacramento recruit came through with four hits out of five trips to the swinging block," praised Frank Young.[24] Washington was ahead, 8–0, in the top of the ninth, and Walter Johnson, on his way to his fifth straight and fifteenth win of the season, had faced just twenty-five batters and allowed only two hits. A Sunday crowd of more than sixteen thousand stuck around, hoping to witness the great pitcher complete his second straight shutout. He was one out away from the shutout, when "[Bob] Jones hit a fast hopper directly at Peckinpaugh, but just before reaching Roger, the ball hit an obstruction and bounced over his head," reported a Washington sportswriter.[25] The next batter, Frank O'Rourke, 0 for 3 with two strikeouts on the day, connected with a Johnson pitch and sent a drive to left-center field for an extra base hit. McNeely fetched the batted ball and threw it to Peckinpaugh, who had a play at the plate, but for whatever reason, the Washington shortstop didn't make a relay, and Jones crossed the plate for Detroit's first and only run.

On Monday, August 18, Goose Goslin was driving to Griffith Stadium for the third game of the Senators-Tigers series. At the intersection of 12th Street and S Street NW, his automobile collided with a truck, overturned, and pinned the ballplayer underneath. Miraculously, Goslin sustained only a scratched left ear, a bruised hip, and a few other minor scratches in the collision. Shortly after he arrived at the ballpark, Mike Martin examined Goslin and cleared him to play, and he played the entire game with a hunk of cotton covering the cut on his left ear, causing fans to think he was using his ear to hold his chewing gum. In the game that day, Harris went with Paul Zahniser. He retired the Tigers in the first two innings but then yielded three runs in the top of the third and was replaced by Marberry. The Senators fought back: Judge delivered a two-run single in the bottom of the third, and Peckinpaugh doubled and scored on an RBI single by McNeely to tie the game in the bottom of the fourth. With the game still knotted, 3–3, in the bottom of the eighth, Judge and Bluege doubled in succession, Ruel walked, and Leibold came through with a pinch-hit two-run single to cap a three-run rally for a 6–3 victory.

The Senators finished off the Tigers and moved back into second place by concluding the series with a doubleheader sweep in what *Washington Post* writer Frank Young called "a red-letter day in Washington baseball, and for Bucky Harris, too."[26] The bad news was Ban Johnson announced his decision regarding the Senators' July 19 game protest, and his verdict was to uphold the call by the umpires in ruling Harris's hit was a triple in the 6–5 loss to the Browns.

Following a day off in the schedule, the Senators went back to work before a Thursday afternoon home crowd of six thousand, who watched Walter Johnson retire the first nine White Sox batters. With Washington ahead, 2–0, Johnson, who had allowed just four hits in seven innings, was replaced by Fred Marberry, a move that baffled the Washington fans and sportswriters. Why would Harris remove Johnson during a well-pitched game? It was later reported that he was forced to withdraw due to acute indigestion. The first batter Marberry faced bounced one to Judge, who gloved the grounder, ran to first, and thought he had won the foot race to the base, but first-base umpire Ducky Holmes, who was anything but popular in Washington, ruled that the batter beat Judge to the bag. Judge didn't use any profanity in his argument, nor did he call the umpire a fat-head, but he slightly shoved Holmes, resulting in a game ejection. The White Sox went on to score one to cut the Washington lead to 2–1, but the Senators held on for another win.

The next day was another off day in the Washington schedule, and the manager, wanting to give his team a day to rest, didn't schedule a practice. Unlike the Yankees' commitment to play an out-of-town exhibition game on every off day in their schedule, the Senators had no intention to barnstorm, even though Bucky Harris, Walter Johnson, Goose Goslin, and the rest of the team were in high demand. In response to the many invites received by the Nationals, Griffith responded with a letter he kept on file: "In reply to your letter concerning an exhibition game, I beg to state that manager Harris does not feel as though he should book, at the present, as we figure in being in the pennant fight all the way, and he needs to preserve the strength of this club in every way possible."[27]

On his day off, Harris joined twenty-four other fans to watch a semipro game at Griffith Stadium. Zahniser, said to be a marksman, spent the day at the Washington gun club, and Goslin, preferring to drive than taking public transportation, took the time to buy a new automobile. He emptied his savings account to make his costly purchase. Now, because he would not receive a weekly paycheck following the season, Goslin needed the Senators to win the pennant so he could receive his cut of the players' share of the World Series gate receipts to give him the financial means to pay the bills during the winter months.

As the Senators enjoyed their day off, New York and Detroit battled at Yankee Stadium. With the game tied, 6–6, in the bottom of the ninth, the Yankees loaded the bases with only one out, and the fans, confident of victory, began to head to the exits. But Yankees catcher Wally Schang swung and missed three times, and the next batter also struck out to end the inning. The game was still tied in the top of the twelfth, until Harry Heilmann singled and Frank O'Rourke lifted a fly ball to center field, where Yankees center fielder Whitey Witt, after a long transverse run, got a hand on the ball, but couldn't hold it. "From where Witt was playing he had no license to catch the ball," wrote a baffled New York reporter.[28] The Yankees went on to lose, 8–6, to reduce their league lead to one game over the second-place Senators.

When the Senators–White Sox series resumed, the umpires appeared to be tempted to call the game when a heavy sprinkle began in the third inning but decided to let the game continue. In the bottom of the fifth, McNeely doubled and scored on a single by Rice to give the Nats a 2–1 lead. George Mogridge held the Washington lead into the ninth inning, but an infield hit by Eddie Collins put the tying run on base, and White Sox first baseman Earl Sheely followed by hitting a fast-dropping fly ball to center field. Earl McNeely sprinted toward the infield before making a diving attempt to catch the ball, and after he left his feet, the ball hit his mitt but was jarred loose when he heavily hit the ground and slid along the wet grass. Umpire Billy Evans called the batter out then immediately changed his call. But that initial call caused Collins to retreat to first base. McNeely got up from his dive, clutched the baseball, and threw it to Bucky Harris, who stepped on the second base sack. When Evans ruled Collins out at second base, White Sox manager Johnny Evers immediately charged from the third-base coach's box to protest and gave Evans a piece of his mind. He finished his argument by informing the umpire that he was going to continue the game under protest.

When play resumed, with one out and a runner on first, Mogridge retired the next batter, but White Sox third baseman Willie Kamm followed with a hard drive into center field that was too well hit for McNeely to handle, though the Washington center fielder managed to get his body in front of the drive. The ball bounced off McNeely's shins and rolled fifteen feet away. Maurice Archdeacon, the baserunner on first, rounded second and headed to third. McNeely hustled to the ball, but by the time he retrieved the baseball and threw it to Harris, Archdeacon had touched third and was heading for the plate. After receiving McNeely's throw, Harris wheeled around and uncorked a strike to catcher Muddy Ruel, who applied the tag on Archdeacon for the game's final out and for the second straight 2–1 Washington win over Chicago.

The Senators won their seventh in a row and completed a three-game sweep of the White Sox the next day when Tom Zachary won his eleventh of the season, and the Senators tied a then major-league record by turning five double plays. "Luck ought to give you guys the pennant if nothing else does," a Chicago sportswriter told a Washington sportswriter in the press box. "You ain't seen nothing yet," commented the Washington sportswriter.[29]

During the Senators' win over the White Sox, the crowd let out a lusty yell when the scoreboard operator posted the Tigers' win at New York. The Senators now trailed the first-place Yankees by a percentage point and were heading for a four-game series showdown in New York, beginning in five days. The Tigers were now two and a half games behind, and the Browns, who were 6–11 since sweeping the Senators, were seven games out. "We are still in the race," George Sisler told a group of sportswriters. "The long stretch of home games in September will help Detroit and St. Louis, while Washington and New York, playing on the road, will be at a disadvantage."[30]

August 25 was a dark, overcast day in Washington, the kind of day that makes it harder for opposing batters to see Walter Johnson's blazing fastball. Johnson, with a 16–6 season record and a current six-game winning-streak, was applauded by six thousand fans when he took the mound to start the game. Through the first three innings, he retired nine of the first ten St. Louis batters he faced, the one batter he failed to retire reached base on a walk. In the bottom of the third, Johnson singled past the third baseman, advanced to second on a passed ball, and made it to third on an infield hit. Two walks followed to score Johnson for a 1–0 lead, all the Nats would need on this day. Johnson retired the next eleven before giving up another walk in the top of the seventh. In the top of the eighth, with Washington now up, 2–0, rain began to fall, and after a thirty-minute delay, the umpires agreed to call the game. Johnson didn't allow a single hit, but because only seven innings were played, the game wouldn't go into the record books as a no-hitter. Meanwhile, the Yankees kept pace with the Senators, as Babe Ruth went 3 for 5 and hit his fortieth home run in a Yankees 8–3 win over Cleveland. Later that evening, Johnson received an ovation when attending a performance at B. F. Keith's Theater. Very few knew he was present until the director pointed him out, and applause quickly turned to cheers that lasted for six minutes. During the high-spirited moment, the theater host tossed a large bouquet of roses on behalf of the theater to the great pitcher.

Before more than twenty thousand at Griffith Stadium the next day, the Senators and Browns split a doubleheader, the Browns winning the first game behind a five-hit shutout by Urban Shocker, and the Senators taking the nightcap, 6–2, with Goslin leading the hitting attack by going 3 for 5 with a pair of doubles. "We can't be expected to win every game," Harris said after the doubleheader. "We don't feel that our showing—nine out of our last 10—is anything we have to apologize for."[31] Since the Yankees were rained out that day, New York remained a percentage point ahead of the Nats.

Before the Senators took the field to conclude their series with the Browns the following day, they were in first place. Cleveland Pitcher Stan Coveleski pitched a five-hit shutout at New York in the first game of a doubleheader. However, a few hours later, the Senators were back in second place. "This just goes to prove how fast things change these days," wrote Frank Young.[32] Against starting pitcher George Mogridge and reliever Allen Russell, the Browns took a 6–2 lead into the eighth inning. After two were out and nobody on base in the bottom of the eighth, the Washington batters went to work. Bluege and Ruel each singled to start the rally and Peckinpaugh walked to load the bases. Then Harris sent Pinky Hargrave, a rarely used catcher, to the plate and he launched a long drive to left field for a three-run triple to make it a 6–5 game. A shower of straw hats from the stands littered the field, causing a delay to allow the grounds crew to clear the diamond. With two outs, a runner on third, and the Browns clinging to a one-run lead, George Sisler called on Urban Shocker, the pitcher who had shut out the Senators in the first game of the doubleheader the day before, to get the last out of the inning. The first batter he faced was McNeely, and the rookie, who already had two hits in this game, sent the crowd into hysteria when he came through by doubling to score Hargrave to tie the game, 6–6. The game remained tied until the top of the eleventh, when the Browns broke through for two runs against Fred Marberry for an 8–6 win. "Heartbreaking," wrote a Washington sportswriter, made even more so by the Yankees taking the second game of the doubleheader to move a half-game ahead of the Senators.[33]

The stage was now set for a showdown between the Senators and Yankees in a four-game series at Yankee Stadium, beginning with a game the following day. Wanting to give his team as much rest as possible, Harris booked a 7:00 p.m. evening train trip. The team arrived in New York City at 12:30 a.m.

CHAPTER 12

Damn Yankees
(August–September)

American League Standings on the Morning of August 28, 1924		
Team	W–L	Games Back
Yankees	70–52	—
Senators	71–54	½
Tigers	67–56	3½
Browns	63–60	7½

As the Senators' New York City–bound train traveled through the night on the eve of the first game of the big series, *Washington Times* sportswriter Louis Dougher observed the ballplayers. Dougher, assigned to cover the series as a writer and broadcaster, noted that the younger players were bubbling over with confidence, some even confident enough to predict the Senators to take three games in the four-game series. A few veterans also surprised Dougher with their cockiness over the team's chances, like thirty-four-year-old mild-mannered Sam Rice, usually quiet, who talked about the Senators going all the way this season. Even Harris, Peckinpaugh, and Leibold smiled and exuded confidence, though Harris, who occupied the seat next to Dougher, wasn't about to predict a series win in New York. "Can't tell how things will turn out," he told Dougher. "But one thing is positively certain. We're confident, as a team, we are just as good as the Yankees. Take Babe Ruth from the New York lineup and I'd say we have an edge over the Yankees. There is only one Babe Ruth, thank heaven. He makes it an even thing between us. We have the pitchers and the Yankees have Babe Ruth." Harris assured Dougher that his pitching staff was the best in the American League. "Don't worry about them cracking," he said. "No, they can't win all their games, but they're going to win a large majority of the time, and the further the race goes, the more important is the pitching."[1]

Most experts gave Washington the edge over New York in the pitching department, but according to New York sportswriter Ford Frick, the Yankees had Herb Pennock, "the best left-hander in the league," in Frick's opinion.[2] Pennock, currently the hottest pitcher on the Yankees staff, with an 18–8 record and a 2.73 ERA this season, had allowed just one earned run in his previous twenty-nine innings, and was scheduled to pitch the first game of the series. He had lost three of his four decisions against Washington this season, but in his last start against the Senators back on July 5, he out-pitched Walter Johnson and surrendered only six hits in a 2–0 win.

When the train finally reached its destination and the players disembarked, Roger Peckinpaugh piloted a few teammates to a taxicab and instructed the driver to take his party to the Concourse Plaza, but when the cab reached the hotel, it dawned upon Peckinpaugh that the Washington baseball club had changed its New York City headquarters to the Hotel Almanac. At breakfast the following morning, Peckinpaugh and his party were still trying to decide how to divide the expensive $7.50 cab fare.

When the Senators finally arrived at their hotel, they were greeted by a lobby full of Washington baseball fans. "The Royal Rooting club from DC is here in full force," John Dugan commented about the large gathering. "Taking figures from hotel clerk Jimmy Monroe, over 200 Washingtonians are registered."[3]

Back in Washington, the fandom was ready. Before the 2:30 starting time in the first game of the series, a large crowd gathered at the Hearst Building to follow the play-by-play results by lightbulb signals on the *Washington Times* electronic scoreboard along with Louis Dougher's commentary from Yankee Stadium. Fans could also catch the game report on the *Washington Star* electronic scoreboard, located at the front of the *Star* building. In New York, twenty-five thousand filed into Yankee Stadium, including members of the New York Giants. Three weeks ago, the three-time National League defending champs had a nine-game lead and seemed destined for their fourth consecutive pennant; however, their once-comfortable league-lead was now down to four games. When asked whom they were pulling for in the American League, the New York National Leaguers said the Yankees, because they wanted to avenge last year's World Series setback.

Against the red-hot Herb Pennock, the Senators managed to put three runners on base in the first two innings but were unable to score. Senators starting pitcher Tom Zachary sent the Yankees down in order in the first inning and retired the first batter in the bottom of the second before Yankees first baseman Wally Pipp drove a hit into left-center field and made it all the way to third when center fielder Earl McNeely misplayed the hit. A fly out by Wally Schang was deep enough to score Pipp from third for the game's first run, though the Yankees first baseman barely beat Goslin's strong throw to the plate. In the top of the third, Harris, Rice, and Goslin singled in succession to tie the score, 1–1, and the game remained tied until Babe Ruth stepped in to lead off the bottom of the fourth. Ruth, who flew out in his first at bat, was currently slumping, hitting just .269 with two homers and nine RBIs since reaching .408 back on August 8. This time he tagged one and sent a high fly ball deep into the right-center field bleachers for his forty-first homer of the season. When Meusel followed with a drive into the left field seats, the Yankees had a 3–1 lead. After Zachary yielded two more hits in the inning, his afternoon was finished, and Allen Russell came on in relief.

In the top of the fifth, Harris drew a walk, and the Yankees were sure about the Washington manager's next move. Back on July 25, Harris stole second and scored what proved to be the winning run in a 3–2 Washington win at Yankee Stadium. This time Pennock stepped off the rubber and threw to first base just as Harris broke for second. As Harris slid into second base, spikes down this time, Everett Scott, who received the throw from first baseman Wally Pipp, applied the tag for the inning's second out. But Washington wasn't about to give up on the inning. Rice followed with a double and Goslin hit one far and deep into the left-center field power alley, and by the time the Yankees outfielders fetched the long drive, Rice and Goslin had crossed the plate to tie the game, 3–3. Back at the Hearst Building in Washington, when the electronic scoreboard lights noted Goslin's two-run homer, the crowd was so loud in its celebration that Dougher's voice coming through the amplifier was completely drowned out.

In the bottom of the sixth, a walk and Joe Dugan's double put Yankee runners on second and third with one out. With first base unoccupied, Harris ordered Russell to intentionally walk Ruth, and Bob Meusel followed by hitting a fly ball into right field, deep enough to allow the runner on third to tag up and score for a 4–3 Yankees lead. One inning later, with a runner on base, Ruth missed with a "gargantuan lunge at a curve ball," but got hold of the next pitch and sent it higher but not as far as his first homer to make it 6–3 in favor of New York.[4] "Up in the grand stand, blasé spectators figured they were through," Frick wrote of the Senators. "The Yankees thought they had the game in the basket. Everyone thought so except the Washington players themselves. They saw only the vision of victory and the sweetness of their first league pennant and battled on."[5]

Ossie Bluege started the top of the eighth with a base hit and moved to third base on a double by Ruel. The Senators were now threatening, the potential tying run was coming to the plate, and Yankees manager Miller Huggins, aware that his starting pitcher had given up eleven hits, opted for a pitching change, a decision that some did not agree with. "[Pennock] deserved more of an opportunity than he got," claimed a New York sportswriter.[6] Peckinpaugh followed by scoring Bluege on a ground out to cut the New York lead to 6–4. With one out and a runner on second, Leibold, pinch-hitting for Russell, walked and McNeely singled to load the bases. Then Harris tagged a hard grounder that third baseman Joe Dugan mishandled to allow another run and Harris to safely reach first base.

The New York lead was now down to a run with the bases still loaded. The Washington bench was encouraged. One New York writer credited the Senators for having a lot of college-like spirit, with a lot of back slapping, hand shaking, and cheering.

Huggins decided on another pitching change, and once again the strategy backfired. "It was out of the frying pan and into the fire," wrote a frustrated New York sportswriter.[7] After a grounder by Rice was converted into a force-out at the plate, Goslin lifted a high fly ball into left-center field. Yankees center fielder Whitey Witt made a sidelong chase while looking skyward, then lost sight of the ball in the bright summer sun. The ball dropped to the ground, rolled deeper into the outfield, and resulted in a three-run triple for an 8–6 Washington lead. Judge followed with a single to score Goslin for the sixth run of the inning, and Bluege, Ruel, and Peckinpaugh kept the inning alive with three consecutive singles to tack on two more runs. With the score now 11–6 in favor of Washington, manager Huggins opted to bring in the fourth Yankee pitcher of the inning. When Leibold lined out to right field the inning was over, after Washington sent thirteen men to the plate in an eight-run outburst. The stunned Yankees headed toward their dugout, heads down and beaten.

Washington relief specialist Fred Marberry entered the game in the bottom of the eighth and held the Yankees in check. The Senators didn't score in the top of the ninth, but Rice registered his fifth hit of the game and Goslin doubled to complete the cycle in a 4 for 5 day at the plate. Marberry finished the game by sending the Yankees down in order in the bottom of the ninth to put the Senators back on top in the American League.

"Watch us from now on," Harris warned the newspapermen after the game. He also reminded the press that he was going to start Walter Johnson in tomorrow's game, "and I don't think there is a team in the world who can beat him in the form he is in now," he added.[8]

"Walter Johnson got a 'big hand' from the Yankee Stadium crowd as he walked to the Senators bench before the start of the game," reported *New York Evening Journal* sportswriter Sam Crane. "He appeared some-what embarrassed, for he blushed like a school boy speaking his first piece."[9] Johnson reacted to the warm reception by retiring the first two batters and striking out Babe Ruth on three pitches. In the top of the second, Goslin looped one over the pitcher for an infield hit and Judge slammed a long hit for a triple to left-center field to score Goslin for a 1–0 lead. With Judge on third and Ruel at the plate, the Senators elected to try the squeeze play. Judge broke for home, and Yankees catcher Wally Schang, knowing what Washington was trying to do, signaled for a pitchout. Yankees pitcher Joe Bush obeyed the catcher's signal, but Ruel, the clever Washington catcher, leaned over the plate and put his bat on the ball to execute the bunt. With no play at the plate, Bush fielded the bunt and threw to first base for the sure out while Judge crossed home for another Washington run.

The Yankees threatened with two singles in the second and third innings but could not score. In the bottom of the fourth, Johnson walked the first two batters and gave up an infield hit to load the bases with nobody out. The crowd sensed a Yankees run when the next batter hit a fly ball to left field, but Goslin, after making the catch for the first out of the inning, "winged the ball into the plate like a shot," Sam Crane described, to hold the runner on third base. "That bird Goslin can surely peg," Crane added.[10] Johnson then recorded another strikeout and induced the next batter to fly out to end the threat. In the top of the sixth, Goslin swung at the first pitch and hit what a New York sportswriter described as a "slow, lazy fly that fell inside the bleachers." The home run gave the Senators a 3–0 lead.[11] In the top of the eighth, Rice hit a humpback grounder into right field for a double and scored on Goslin's hit, his seventh of the series. "If Johnson was a stone wall of defense, the Senators had a berserker on offense—Leon 'Goose' Goslin, who cut such a swath of terror on Thursday. Goslin continued his wonderful hitting streak and every one of his three hits he made counted in some kind of scoring," explained *Washington Evening Star* sportswriter John Keller.[12] Goslin stung the Yankees again in the top of the eighth with an RBI single. Then Judge lifted a high fly to right field, which Ruth gloved, juggled, and dropped for an error to allow Goslin to score the fifth Washington run of the day.

In the bottom of the eighth came a nervous moment for the Senators. With a runner on first, a Yankees batter hit a hard grounder that struck Johnson's pitching hand. Johnson completed the play to record the out, then clutched his hand and dropped to his knees in pain. Both team trainers immediately ran to the pitcher's mound and players from both teams also hurried to the injured pitcher. A few minutes later, the great pitcher came to his feet and threw a few practice pitches. He wanted to remain in the game, with hopes of adding another shutout to his record, but admitted he felt pain in his injured hand during each practice pitch. Harris, not wanting to extend the injury, called to the bullpen. Johnson yielded to the reliever and walked toward the Washington dugout. The crowd, "rose to its feet and gave what baseball reporters described as the greatest ovation a player ever received in this city," noted a *New York World* columnist.[13] It was revealed later that Johnson's injury wasn't serious, nothing more than a bruise just below his pinky.

Once again, Harris called on Marberry, and the first batter he faced came through with an RBI single to put the Yankees on the scoreboard, but any chance of a New York rally was extinguished when the next batter grounded into an inning-ending double play. In the bottom of the ninth, Marberry retired the Yankees to secure a 5–1 victory.

Was Washington on their way to the pennant? They had taken the first two games of the series, had now won eight out of nine games at Yankee Stadium this season, and were currently one and a half games ahead of the second-place Yankees.

"When would you be willing to admit to yourself that the Griffs are likely to win the pennant?" Dougher asked Johnson after the game.

"Well, that's a funny question," responded Johnson. "If you insist on some kind of answer I'd say that when we leave Chicago for the last four games of the season in Boston, if we're leading by enough games so that we can win by breaking even with the Red Sox, I'd begin thinking we are in."[14]

Harris sent Curly Ogden to the mound before forty thousand in the third game of the series. Ogden had won eight of his first nine decisions after the Senators claimed him off waivers in May, but then cooled off and had won just once after winning five times in July. In today's game, he retired nine of the first eleven Yankees he faced, but unfortunately for Ogden, his teammates were unable to break through against Yankees starting pitcher Waite Hoyt. In the bottom of the fourth, the Yankees put one on the board with the help of an incorrect call by Ducky Holmes, the umpire whom Harris had called "fat-head." The call was made when Ruth grounded to Bluege, who fielded the ball but made an off-target throw. First baseman Joe Judge made a fine effort by leaping high, catching the ball in mid-air, and tagging Ruth for what should have been an out. However, Holmes was looking down on the play, didn't see the tag, and called Ruth safe. Up in the press box *Washington Post* sportswriter Frank Young was fuming. "If Ban Johnson wants baseball games decided on their merits in his league he'll have to find some other job for Ducky Holmes," Young wrote.[15] A sacrifice, a groundout, and an infield hit scored Ruth with the game's first run. However, the Senators, unfazed, tied the game in the top of the sixth when Rice and Goslin singled and Judge grounded out to propel Rice across the plate. With the game still tied, 1–1, in the bottom of the ninth, Wally Pipp led off with a single for just the fourth hit off Ogden. A sacrifice and a single followed to score Pipp for a 2–1 Yankees win.

On Sunday, August 31, 1924, first place was on the line. Whoever won today would finish the series and head into the season's final month atop the American League standings. Forty thousand were at Yankee Stadium to see the all-important game, including an estimated two thousand Washingtonians who had traveled to New York during the wee hours. Clark Griffith, decked in a Panama hat and suit, and Joseph Patrick Judge, father of the Washington first baseman, were also on hand to cheer on the Senators. The bad news was Ducky Holmes was behind the plate, and that meant trouble. "Whenever Ducky Holmes is umpiring, the fans look for arguments—and they were not disappointed," according to Frank Young.[16]

Harris went with his veteran left-handed starting pitcher George Mogridge for the final game of the series. A finesse pitcher who specialized in breaking balls, the thirty-five-year-old Mogridge was 4–0 with a 1.50 ERA in his last four starts and 2–2 versus the Yankees this season. And he had a vendetta against his former manager Miller Huggins for trading him three years earlier. However, his chance for revenge and to extend his team's first-place lead may have been too much pressure. Mogridge got off to a slow start, and it was said that his breaking balls weren't moving properly, but the Yankees failed to capitalize before the veteran hurler settled down and kept them scoreless through the first six innings. In the top of the seventh, with Washington ahead, 1–0, Joe Judge, the five-foot-eight, thirty-year-old first baseman, was at the plate with a 3–1 count. He then took a pitch and, thinking it had missed the strike zone, dropped his bat and headed to first base. Halfway to first, he was surprised to learn that Ducky Holmes had called strike two. "Forget it," Griffith yelled out from his front row seat beside the Washington dugout. "Go hit again."[17]

Judge headed back to home plate, picked his bat up off the ground, and stepped into the batter's box. With the count now full, Yankees pitcher Sam Jones delivered his next pitch. Judge swung and lifted a long fly ball to right field. Babe Ruth stepped back to the barrier, looked up, and watched the ball fall into the bleachers to give Washington a 2–0 lead. As Judge trotted around the bases, the Washington fans seated behind their team's first base dugout and in the upper deck hooted and hollered. Straw hats sailed through the air and dropped onto the field, while other Washington fans celebrated by sounding their cowbells. Judge's father stood and called, "Didya see that?" to the people seated in his box seat section behind home plate. "That was Joe, my boy!"

"Down in front, you!" shouted an unamused Yankees fan. Mr. Judge responded by turning around and giving the heckler a broad smile.[18]

Down by two and in danger of losing the series, the Yankees fought back and managed to break through for a run in the bottom of the seventh, due to two fielding lapses by the Senators. A single and a misjudged fly ball by Leibold put Yankees runners on first and third with two outs. When the next batter hit a routine ground ball to Harris, it appeared as if the Senators might get out of the inning. But after fielding the grounder, Harris toyed with the ball before throwing it to first base, allowing the batter enough time to beat the throw and the runner on third to score to cut the Washington lead to 2–1. With the Nats still clinging to their one-run lead in the bottom of the eighth, the Yankees had a runner on base with one out and Babe Ruth at the plate. With a full count on the Yankees slugger, Mogridge made his next offering, and Ruth took the pitch.

"Outside! Outside!" called Ducky Holmes.

"It was right over the plate," protested Mogridge, who shrugged and walked toward the plate.

"Beat it!" Holmes told the pitcher.[19] When the pitcher refused to yield, Holmes banished him from the game.

Harris quickly ran in from his second base position and got involved in the discussion. Washington coach Al Schacht left the dugout and approached the umpire to voice his protest. George Moriarty and Dick Nallin, the other two umpires on duty, also arrived at the scene, hoping to quell the heated discussion. Despite the lack of profanity or insults before the argument concluded, Holmes had ejected Harris and Schacht. When order was restored, the Yankees had runners on first and second with one out, Fred Marberry was the new Washington pitcher, and hardly used infielder Ralph Miller replaced Harris at second base. After retiring the first batter he faced, Marberry walked a pair to force in the tying run.

With the game tied, 2–2, neither team scored in the ninth inning, though the Yankees threatened in their half. Two hits and an intentional walk to Ruth loaded the bases with two outs, but Marberry retired Pipp on a pop fly to end the threat. In the top of the tenth, Ruel singled and moved up a base on a sacrifice. With two outs, a runner on second, and the Senators a base hit away from retaking the lead, Nemo Leibold, hitless on the day, came to the plate, and much to everyone's surprise, Miller Huggins elected to intentionally walk Washington's little center fielder and take his chances with Ralph Miller, the infielder who had replaced Harris. Unfortunately for Huggins and the Yankees, Miller wouldn't have to take the bat off his shoulder, as Yankees pitcher Joe Bush missed on four consecutive pitches to load the bases for Sam Rice.

Though he had eight hits in the series, Rice was hitless today. This time he belted a long drive that sent Yankees left fielder Bob Meusel sprinting toward the left field fence. Meusel managed to get his glove on the ball but couldn't corral it for the putout. Ruel scored the go-ahead run and Leibold rounded third and crossed home to register another run. Miller touched second and third and attempted to score, but was thrown out in his attempt to add one more to the Washington lead. "By that time the beans were spilled, the hash was cooked, and the fat was in the fire," summarized a New York sportswriter.[20] The Senators were back on top, 4–2.

In the bottom of the tenth, Bob Meusel kept the New York hopes alive with a one-out single. Then to the plate came a pinch-hitter who had been called up from Hartford a few days ago. Young Lou Gehrig was overmatched by Marberry, who blew three pitches by the rookie. The game ended when Everett

Scott fouled out to Ruel. Washington had taken three of four and would leave town with a first-place lead of one and a half games.

Following the Washington victory approximately a thousand fans congregated outside the Yankee Stadium visiting team's clubhouse and patiently waited for the Washington ballplayers to appear. When they emerged from their dressing room and headed to the taxis lined up in the street, they were cheered and greeted by well-wishers. The Senators were in great spirits. Their laughter, cheering, and chanting from the taxis' backseats caught the attention of pedestrians on the streets. When the team arrived at Pennsylvania Station, Joe Judge's father, a New York City resident, was there to greet them. He shook Harris's hand and wished him luck then walked over to Griffith and extended his hand. "I wish you luck and the pennant," he told the Washington team president.[21]

On the train trip back to Washington, the Senators sang, told jokes, and played boyish pranks. The fans who had traveled to New York to cheer on the Nats and were on the same train joined the party in a special club car where they could mingle with the players. In Washington, players' wives were among the reception that awaited the team's return at Union Station. At 10:25, six hundred people were at the station. By 11:00, the crowd had expanded to five thousand. Shortly after, a station employee hung a huge sign with the word *Baseball* over track 3.[22] By 11:25, the crowd had ballooned to eight thousand frenzied fans of all ages, colors, and sizes, who nudged and pushed to get as close as possible to the exit where the players were expected to pass. Nearly every space of the west end of the concourse was occupied by overheated but happy fans. Those who were less anxious to greet the team sat in the main waiting area or in the plaza in front of the station.

When the team finally arrived, a cheer filled the air from one end of the plaza to the other. Harris led the players off the train and hurried them through a lane that was roped off for the team to pass through. As the players raced for the safety of taxis or their automobiles, they were patted, offered handshakes, and cheered. "It's good to be on top of the world again," Harris told a sportswriter.[23] A deafening cheer greeted Walter Johnson. "Walter, how is your hand?" they asked him repeatedly. "It's fine," he answered frequently while inching his way through the crowd.[24] Another loud cheer went up when Clark Griffith and his wife appeared. When asked about the crowd to greet his team, he replied, "it's fine."[25] He also said the size of this crowd made him wonder what the crowd size would be when they returned home after clinching the pennant. "Our team is up there now and no team is going to pass it," said Griffith, "I think my club is better than any in the league."[26]

The Senators wouldn't have time to savor their series win and rest before their next game. The day after their return from New York City, they were scheduled to play a morning–afternoon Labor Day doubleheader against the

Athletics at Griffith Stadium. This would be followed by two much-needed off days in the schedule, then three games in four days against the Red Sox to conclude their 1924 home season schedule. They would then finish their season with twenty road games in six different cities. The second-place Yankees, who played three fewer games than Washington, were slated to complete their home season schedule with five games against the Red Sox and three versus the Athletics. Like the Senators, they would play their final twenty games on the road. While the Senators and Yankees were battling in their recent series at Yankee Stadium, the Tigers lost three out of four to the Browns to fall five games behind the Nats. But there was still hope for the Tigers, since they were scheduled to play eighteen home games in September, including three each against the Senators and Yankees. Although they took three of four from Detroit, the fourth-place Browns were still seven games from the top. Like the Tigers, most of their remaining games would be at home.

The series win at New York set off baseball enthusiasm in a manner never experienced in Washington. Nearly forty thousand World Series ticket orders had been received by the Senators' front office and more applications were expected to pour in. To accommodate as many ticket applicants as possible, the Senators announced plans to expand the Griffith Stadium seating capacity to almost thirty-six thousand by adding more outfield bleachers and another tier of seats atop the upper-deck roof. On September 1, a total of forty thousand appeared at Griffith Stadium to set a city record for most fans to attend a morning–afternoon doubleheader. Before eighteen thousand at the morning game, Goose Goslin, who went 11 for 16 with nine RBIs in the four-game series at New York, singled in the game's first run in the bottom of the first. A sacrifice fly by Earl McNeely in the next inning and a two-out single by Harris in the bottom of the fourth added two more. And in the seventh inning, the Senators took a 5–0 lead when Judge hit an RBI double and scored on a single by Bluege. Through eight innings, starting pitcher Tom Zachary had allowed just four hits. But in the top of the ninth, the Athletics scored twice on a Washington error and four hits, three of which were deemed "lucky" due to a few bad bounces, including one on a routine grounder that skipped over the Washington third baseman. "Bluege had a made-to-order double play in front of him," described a Washington sportswriter. "The ball hopped over Oswald's shoulder and rolled into left field just as the third sacker was reaching for it."[27] With two runs home, nobody out, and runners on first and third, another Philadelphia run scored while the Washington infielders converted a grounder into a force-out. But then Zachary settled down and retired the next two batters to end the game.

With Miss District of Columbia among the twenty-two thousand on hand for the afternoon game, the Senators rallied in their final at bat for a 4–3 win. Trailing 3–2 and with two outs in the bottom of the ninth, the Senators had the potential tying run on first, but appeared to be heading for a loss when Roger Peckinpaugh lined one directly at Athletics shortstop John Chapman for what looked like the final out of the game. Then the unthinkable happened: Chapman dropped the line drive. With runners now on first and second, Harris called on backup first baseman Mule Shirley to pinch-hit, and Shirley, who had just forty-eight at bats this season, came through with an RBI single to tie the game. Then Earl McNeely ended the game with a drive down the left field line to score Peckinpaugh with the winning run. "They could never catch us now," Harris said in the locker room following the game.[28]

While the Nats were taking two from the Athletics, the Yankees kept pace by sweeping a doubleheader from the Red Sox and were scheduled to play three games in the next two days. The Senators would be idle but would be closely watching the results from Yankee Stadium. If the Yanks were to win all three, they would match Washington's win-loss record and tie with the Nats for the league lead. Although the Senators would be idle the next two days, their manager was going to grant only one off day. Harris scheduled a team practice at Griffith Stadium on the second day off. On September 2, the Yankees split a twin bill with the Red Sox to remain one and a half games behind the Senators. And to add injury to insult, they lost Babe Ruth. The damage occurred in the bottom of the sixth of the second game, when Ruth over-swung and strained his already sore left shoulder. He finished his at bat then withdrew from the game in the top of the seventh, but he intended to be in the starting lineup the next day.

On September 3, the Senators took batting practice and worked on their fielding before a few hundred fans and an army of reporters and photographers at Griffith Stadium. Walter Johnson, who had an 18–6 season record and had not lost a game since July 11, would be tomorrow's starting pitcher. During the team's practice session, he threw twenty fastballs and announced he was ready for the Red Sox. Following the workout, Harris held a team meeting. He talked to his team about hustle, spoke about "going at top speed from now until the end if they hope[d] to come out on top," and warned about taking the Red Sox too lightly.[29] In New York, the Yankees easily disposed of the Red Sox to reduce the Senators' league lead to one game. With the Yankees owning a 6–0 lead in the top of the seventh, Ruth, who went 2 for 4 while playing with a painful left shoulder, retired from the game.

On September 4, Walter Johnson took the mound for his last home start of the 1924 season. "Should Walter Johnson carry out his early spring intentions of retiring, Washington fans who love him like a brother saw him for the last time," wrote John Dugan. "If Harris and his fighting cast do not cop the American League bunting, few of the fans who cheered him to the echo when he advanced to the mound realized that Johnson was giving them his last performance."[30] Frank Young wrote about the Senators having an eye on the out-of-town scoreboard while battling the Red Sox in the first game of their series. "They appeared to be as much interested in what the scoreboard showed as they were in the battle at hand," observed Young.[31] In the top of the fourth the Griffith Stadium crowd let out a loud hurrah when the out-of-town scoreboard noted that the Athletics scored four in the top of the third for a 4–0 lead at New York, and they cheered again when two more were posted for Philadelphia later in the game. The Senators scored twelve runs on twenty hits in a 12–5 win over the Red Sox. Earl McNeely went 3 for 5 to boost his batting average to .330 since joining the Senators last month, and Bucky Harris and Walter Johnson each made three hits. Johnson hit one off the center field gate in what Frank Young described as "the longest of his proportion seen here this year."[32] Goose Goslin and Ossie Bluege also contributed to the hitting attack with two each, but the hitting star of the day was Sam Rice, who went 4 for 6 with five RBIs. Although not at his best, Johnson struck out seven in the seven innings he pitched for his nineteenth win of the season and his ninth win in a row.

"I think most people in the United States want to see Washington in the World Series," said President Coolidge. "I hope to attend the opening World Series game."[33] The Senators had accepted an invitation from the president and would visit the White House the next day, when the Senators had another break in their schedule. Although excited to meet the president, the Senators were more focused on the pennant race and their next game. Sportswriter John Dugan believed that the Nats would be "rarin' to go and ready for Howard Ehmke and the Red Sox." Ehmke was one of the league's best pitchers, with seventeen wins this season, including two wins and two saves against the Senators, but according to Dugan, the Senators had a "they all look the same to us," attitude.[34]

While Walter Johnson was potentially making his last mound appearance at Griffith Stadium, Babe Ruth's strained left shoulder was so painful, he was forced to make underhand throws from the outfield and withdrew from the game in the middle of the third inning. The Yankees went on to lose, 8–3, and fall two games behind the surging Senators. A week earlier, Ruth had referred to the Senators as a false alarm and labeled the Tigers and Browns the teams to worry about, but now Ruth was worried. The Yankees had lost three of four to the Senators, then dropped one at home to Boston and Philadelphia. "Not so good," Ruth told reporters. "But this race isn't over yet. Not by a long shot."[35]

President Coolidge was said to show little fondness for baseball in comparison to past presidents but was said to have the "welfare of the Nationals at heart."[36] The president shook hands with every player. He told them he was mighty proud of their showing and expressed his confidence in their ability to keep up the good work and to return to the capital with the pennant. Coolidge singled out Harris and Johnson for their great work, said he was very interested in the manner that Johnson pitches, and asked the great pitcher to show him how he threw a curveball. The president took the baseball from the pitcher and placed his fingers where Johnson instructed. Coolidge then showed Johnson how he held the ball when he played baseball during his childhood years in Plymouth, Vermont.

Before a Saturday afternoon crowd of twenty thousand, the Senators wasted no time in scoring against Ehmke and the Red Sox. Earl McNeely led off the bottom of the first with an infield hit and scored on Harris's triple to center field. Rice followed with a single to score Harris, and later in the inning, Bluege hit a two-run single for a 4–0 Washington lead. Singles by Goslin, Ruel, and Bluege scored another run in the fifth and a two-run triple by Harris followed by a sacrifice fly by Rice gave Washington an 8–0 lead after six innings. The Senators went on to win, 8–2, for George Mogridge's fifth straight win and thirteenth win of the season. At New York, the Yankees trailed, 4–1, but rallied for a 10–7 win over the Athletics. Babe Ruth, who played the entire game, went 3 for 4 and hit his forty-third home run of the season. Bob Meusel also went 3 for 4 with a homer and Joe Dugan added four hits.

The Yankees were still two games behind the Senators but expressed confidence in taking the pennant. They also conveyed fear about finishing behind the Nats and were worried about other teams supporting Washington in winning the pennant. "If they try to shoo-in that Washington club, there will be hell to pay," promised Yankees catcher Wally Schang. "All we ask on the western trip is an even break. Let them pitch the same way to us that they do against the Senators, and we'll win."[37]

When hearing this, the Senators laughed. "Maybe the Yankees, fearing we'll win, think we'll let down if we think the other clubs are going to help us win," said Harris. "If that's the case, they're in for a surprise. We're going to keep up our present pace until we win or lose. I am confident we are going to win, but even if we don't, we're going to stay in there."[38]

Sunday, September 7, a home record crowd of more than thirty thousand packed Griffith Stadium for the last Washington home game of the 1924 season. If the Senators were to play another game at home this year, it would be in the World Series. When the gates opened at noon, there were four thousand in line. One hour later, there were seven thousand on hand, and the fans were still pouring in after the game started. By three o'clock, all grandstand tickets were sold, leaving only bleachers seats and standing-room tickets.

Harris started Curly Ogden, the recent tough-luck loser at Yankee Stadium due to the lack of run support. Today his team failed to give him fielding support, and two errors led to a three-run first inning for the Red Sox. The Senators answered with a run in their half of the first, but Boston added two more in the top of the fourth, one in the seventh-inning, and went on to win, 6–2.

"Our pennant hopeful Nationals played bad baseball," Dugan wrote. He also noted that the crowd spirit was great and the attitude among the fans was "we cannot win all of them, and they will bring back the pennant."[39]

At New York, the Athletics scored two in the top of the ninth for a 2–1 win to keep the Yankees at two full games behind the Senators. When the final score was posted on the Griffith Stadium scoreboard, the fans responded by littering the field with more than a hundred straw hats, causing a five-minute delay.

CHAPTER 13

The Long Road to the Pennant (September)

I dreamed for years about bringing the first pennant to Washington. Some said it would never happen, but I knew it could and would if I could just get the right combination. I did my best to manage a winner in Washington, but I could not get the right combination. Then I tried other managers and still failed. Now I have the right combination and the best manager in the business.[1]

—Clark Griffith

American League Standings on the Morning of September 8, 1924

Team	W–L	Games Back
Senators	78–56	—
Yankees	76–58	2
Tigers	75–62	4½
Browns	70–65	8½

Walter Johnson had pitched his entire career for a franchise that had never won a pennant and had posted just six winning records since its founding in 1901. "In my opinion the greatest pitcher who ever lived was Walter Johnson," said former Red Sox standout pitcher Smokey Joe Wood. "If he ever had a good club behind him what records he would have set!"[2] But that didn't seem to bother the great pitcher. Not once did he ever complain or point the finger or talk about what could have been. Now, at age thirty-six, Johnson was having a great season pitching for a first-place team and was said to be in excellent physical condition.

When Washington pressman Lee Poe Hart and a host of reporters greeted Johnson when he emerged from the showers following the Senators' final home game, they were amazed by the veteran pitcher's body. "You could not have detected any deterioration in his physique," wrote Hart. "His erect stature, firm muscles, well-proportioned body, pink skin, and sparkling eyes reflected the splendid care he has taken of himself."

"What's your prediction on the 1924 pennant race?" a reporter asked.

Johnson responded with "a modest smile, characteristic of the 'prince of sportsmen,'" observed Hart.

"We have a good chance to win now," Johnson replied, looking at his pitching hand. "It looks like the last chance for me—and I would like to get in one of those games.

"Of course, we would like to see Joe [Judge] at his regular station. Some clubs would go to pieces if a man left the lineup. Our team isn't like that. It doesn't make any difference who is playing. The boys always work their hardest."[3]

On September 4, Joe Judge injured his left ankle and had been idle ever since. The extent of the injury was said to be minor—nothing more than a bruised tendon—but his absence from the starting lineup was a big one. Judge owned a .318 season batting average and was 12 for 27 with eight RBIs in his previous seven games. In addition to Judge's absence, Roger Peckinpaugh had only three hits in his previous twenty-four at bats and Muddy Ruel, who had started every game but one since July 20, was exhausted. The heavy workload of playing behind the plate every day had reduced Ruel's weight to thirteen pounds under his normal playing weight and made him weary, but the veteran catcher believed there was no time to rest during the pennant race and insisted on staying in the starting lineup. "I'll have plenty of time to rest after the season," Ruel said.[4]

The good news was that Judge was expected to return to the starting lineup during the team's first series on the road; Mike Martin reported that McNeely's shoulder was now 100 percent; and Ossie Bluege, said to be the weak link in Washington's lineup, had fourteen hits in his previous thirty-five at bats and had increased his batting average from .226 in early August to his current .260. Goose Goslin was also swinging a hot bat, going 24 for 66 with three homers and fourteen RBIs in his previous eighteen games, and Earl McNeely had eight hits in his previous eighteen at bats and was hitting .320 since debuting with the Senators on August 9. But the hottest hitter on the team was Sam Rice, who currently owned a fifteen-game hitting streak, with twenty-seven hits in his previous sixty-two at bats and a .332 season batting average.

With twenty road games remaining in the season, the Senators held a two-game lead over the Yankees, who were also scheduled to conclude the season with twenty road games. Washington's road trip would begin with four games in Philadelphia, followed by three each at Detroit, Cleveland, St. Louis, and Chicago. The team would then head back east to play their final four games of the 1924 regular season in Boston. In addition to playing twenty games in twenty-seven days, the Senators would play an exhibition game in Harris's hometown of Pittston, Pennsylvania, against a semipro team. Playing exhibition games in small towns during the season was common for major-league baseball teams, but with the Senators fighting for the pennant, Griffith and Harris felt it was best to let their team rest and focus on the pennant race rather than burn the energy. An exception was made for Pittston, however, and a game was scheduled for the day after the Senators concluded their series in Philadelphia.

Being in this year's pennant chase also persuaded Griffith and Harris to opt against the common practice of adding a few rookies to the team's late-season roster, although they were open to obtaining a hard-hitting minor-league veteran for pinch-hitting purposes. Clyde Milan, a former Senators star who was still active at age thirty-seven and currently hitting .316 for New Haven of the Eastern League, was a candidate for the position, but the Senators were more impressed with a scouting report about twenty-eight-year-old minor-league left-handed batter Wade Lefler, who was leading the Eastern League with a .369 batting average. The word was the Senators were closing a deal for Lefler, and he would join the team in Philadelphia.

The Senators began the road trip by scoring early and often and won, 8–4, at Philadelphia. Earl McNeely led the offense with three hits, Harris knocked in three runs, Sam Rice extended his hitting streak, and Goslin added two hits. In addition, Mule Shirley, batting eighth while filling in for Judge, drove in two runs on two hits. Walter Johnson pitched his twentieth win of the season and won his tenth consecutive game. "Philadelphia fans are pulling for the Nationals, make no mistake about it," noted Louis Dougher. "Here in Philadelphia, we don't want to see any New York clubs win pennants for a while," a Philadelphia fan said.[5]

In Boston, Joe Bush allowed just two hits and Babe Ruth hit a two-run homer in the top of the eighth for a 2–0 Yankees win. The homer, Ruth's forty-fourth of the season, landed in the left-center field bleachers and was said to be one of the farthest hit in Fenway Park history. "This town is pulling for the Nationals to win," a New York sportswriter wrote about the Boston fandom. "The feeling is that the Yankees have monopolized the spotlight long enough."[6] There was a similar feeling in the National League about the New York Giants. On August 9, the first-place Giants were ahead of the next best team by nine games and owned a twelve-game lead over fourth-place Brooklyn. But then the Giants slumped and finished August by dropping thirteen of twenty-one games while the Robins got red hot and concluded the month by sweeping a three-game series from the Giants to pull within two games of the league leaders. Brooklyn began September by extending their winning streak to fifteen and currently trailed New York by a half game. Leading the way for underdog Brooklyn was hard-throwing right-handed pitcher Dazzy Vance, who had a 25–4 season record, had not lost a game since July 6, and had baseball fans dreaming about a Walter Johnson versus Dazzy Vance Game 1 World Series matchup.

As rain fell during the morning prior to the second game of the series at Philadelphia, Clark Griffith, his eyes gleaming behind a pair of rubber-tired cheaters, talked to a group of sportswriters in the hotel lobby. "What about Walter Johnson?" inquired a sportswriter. "Stories are abroad that he is going to quit at the end of the season."

"All that is bunk," snapped Griffith as he chewed away at the butt of his cigar.

"No, it isn't," the writer shot back.

"All right," said Griffith, "I'll bet you anything that Johnson is back with our club next year."[7]

The rain continued into the afternoon and the Washington players were reported to be disappointed when the game was declared a rainout. It was rescheduled for the following day and would be played with the next day's scheduled game for the Senators' nineteenth doubleheader of the season. Meanwhile, a walk, two Red Sox errors, and a two-run pinch-hit double by Joe Bush in the top of the ninth gave the Yankees a 5–4 win in Boston and cut Washington's league lead to one and a half games.

In the first game of a doubleheader the next day, Senators starting pitcher Tom Zachary was in trouble in every inning but one and was said to be lucky to be down by just one run. The Senators were unable to produce the big hit with baserunners in scoring position and lost, 2–1. In the nightcap, the Nats scored five runs on six hits in the top of the second, and when Mule Shirley singled to drive in his third run of the game, the Senators led, 6–1. In the bottom of the ninth the Nationals led, 6–3, and starting pitcher George Mogridge looked good for his sixth straight win and his fourteenth of the season. But when the Athletics began the inning with three consecutive singles and a sacrifice to cut the Washington lead to 6–4, the sure win was in jeopardy. With the bases loaded, only one out, and hard-hitting rookie Al Simmons heading to the plate, Harris looked to his bullpen and waved to Fred Marberry to let the Washington relief specialist know that he was needed, and Marberry came through. "The Senators had a close call from a total disaster" wrote Stephen Grauley of the *Philadelphia Inquirer*. "Had it not been for the effective ninth-inning pinch-pitching of Fred Marberry the probabilities are that the A's would have won two for the day."[8] The Yankees, who were rained out in Boston, remained one and a half games behind Washington.

For the final game of the series at Philadelphia, Harris bypassed Curly Ogden, Joe Martina, and Paul Zahniser for Fred Marberry, who had pitched in seven of the team's previous thirteen games. In his thirteenth starting assignment of the season, Marberry got off to a shaky start but managed to allow only one run during a tough first inning. The rookie then settled down and kept the A's scoreless for the next six innings. In the top of the eighth, with the Nats clinging to a 2–1 lead, Joe Judge, now back in the starting lineup, drilled an RBI double down the right field line and Ruel followed with an RBI single for a 4–1 Washington lead. One inning later, Harris put the game out of reach by slapping a three-run homer into the left field bleachers, his first round-tripper of the season, much to the delight of eight thousand fans who had cheered the Senators throughout the game. As Harris rounded first base, A's first baseman Joe Hauser congratulated the Washington player-manager with a handshake, and when Harris approached third base during his home run trot, he received a pat on the back from Philadelphia third baseman Jimmy Dykes.

At Boston, the Red Sox were four outs away from defeating the Yankees in the first game of a doubleheader and appeared to have the game in good hands with Howard Ehmke on the mound, but then the roof caved in. Joe Dugan doubled, and Babe Ruth followed with his forty-fifth home run to tie the game. The Yanks scored again in the top of the ninth and hung on for a 4–3 win. In the nightcap, the Yankees totaled sixteen hits in an 8–3 win to gain a half game on the Senators.

The next day the Senators traveled to Bucky Harris's hometown for an exhibition game against the Pittston Craftsmen. The team took a train to Wilkes-Barre, were trooped into private cars adorned with banners, and wheeled nine miles over the fine roads to Pittston. "Bucky's old home is pretty much like every Pennsylvania mining town; not so good to look at, but breeding men for all that," explained Louis Dougher.[9] When the private cars entered Pittston, the Washington ballplayers saw children playing and shouting in front yards and small houses containing window boxes filled with flowers in full bloom. A large, florid man with a firm handshake led a warm reception by the Pittston citizens' committee, and the local Rotary Club held a luncheon in honor of the Senators—minus Bucky Harris, who had traveled to Jersey City the night before to see the Firpo-Willis fight and missed his train connection to Pittston. He arrived in time for the game and received a loud ovation from more than three thousand in attendance. The Senators won, 15–5, and Merle Harris, Bucky's older brother who played for the Craftsmen, got a hit and was said to look a lot better than his Pittston teammates.

On the morning of the series opener at Detroit, Walter Johnson received great news: He had been voted the American League's most valuable player. It was the second time in his career that the eight sportswriters who comprised the voting committee selected him as the league's best player of the season. When told that the highest honor that could be paid to a player had been bestowed upon him, he was so moved, he was unable to speak. When his teammates heard the news, they rushed to congratulate him. "I never dreamed of such a thing," he kept repeating. His teammates assured him he "had it coming." "The writers have selected me and that is wonderful to me and I greatly appreciate their consideration," Johnson said. "Believe me, whatever I have done this year I have done for the good of the club to which I belong and this action of the sportswriters' committee almost overwhelms me. I feel that the greatest reward that could come my way this year would be in sharing in the glory of earning for Washington its first pennant."[10]

The third-place Detroit Tigers were five games behind the Senators and four behind the Yankees with fifteen games left in their season. If they had any hope of winning the pennant, they would have to sweep their three-game series with the Senators and their three-game series next week against the Yankees. Before twenty-thousand wearing overcoats on a cold day at Navin Field, a nervous Detroit team aided the Senators by committing five errors in a 6–4 loss. The setback was the Tigers' fourteenth in twenty games against the Senators this season. "If all the Nats had to do was play the Tigers this season, they would have had the flag sewed up weeks ago," quipped Frank Young.[11] The batting star of the day was Roger Peckinpaugh, who broke out of his hitting slump by going 4 for 5 with a double and two RBIs. Harris added to the attack with three hits, and Sam Rice got a hit to extend his hitting-streak to twenty consecutive games. Walter Johnson, "who was cheered to the echo" when he walked to the mound to pitch the bottom of the first, won his twenty-first of the season and his eleventh in a row, but it didn't come easy.[12] With the Senators ahead, 5–2, and with one out in the bottom of the eighth, the 1924 American League MVP gave up a single, a walk, and an RBI single. Harris then called on Marberry, and once again the star relief pitcher extinguished the fire. While the Senators were winning at Detroit, the Yankees scored sixteen runs on seventeen hits, and Babe Ruth went 3 for 4 and hit his forty-sixth homer in a 16–1 New York win at Chicago to stay within a game of the Senators.

One day later, the Senators took a 1–0 first-inning lead when Sam Rice chalked up another game to his hitting streak with an RBI single. Before the Tigers came to bat in the bottom of the inning, there was a ten-minute delay while Ty Cobb protested to home-plate umpire Bill Dineen about an adhesive bandage worn by Washington starting pitcher Tom Zachary on a finger of his pitching hand. Harris explained that Zachary needed the bandage to protect the cuticle at the base of his fingernail when he pitched his knuckleball to prevent a blister. According to Cobb the tape allowed Zachary to put a spin on the ball that he wouldn't get with a bare knuckle. Dineen denied Cobb's request and ordered the first Detroit batter to step-in, but Cobb wouldn't yield. Dineen then asked the Tigers manager if he was willing to play the game under protest and deal with the issue later. Once again, Cobb refused.

Unable to get the home plate umpire to uphold his complaint, Cobb took his argument to first base umpire Tommy Connolly, who said he was aware of the bandage worn by Zachary and had written to league president Ban Johnson about it but never heard back. While Cobb and the umpires debated, a restless fan shouted, "Play ball!" Some of the other fans also grew impatient and lashed insults at both managers.[13]

Dineen, who had a change of heart, spoke with Harris and told him his pitcher had to remove the bandage or the game would be forfeited to Detroit. Harris told the umpire that his pitcher was not in violation of the rules. The Washington player-manager then turned his attention to the spectators and took a moment to survey the crowd before telling Zachary to remove the bandage. Visibly upset by the delay and Cobb's protest, Zachary began the inning by allowing a run on three hits and a walk. Harris then called on a relief pitcher to replace the distressed Zachary. The Tigers went on to win, 5–2, but the good news for the Nats was the Yankees lost. During the Senators-Tigers game the Navin Field crowd applauded when the final score of the Yankees' loss at Chicago was posted on the out-of-town scoreboard. "There is no friendship here for the Yanks," Dougher wrote.[14]

The next day, the Senators made only four hits and lost, 2–0, at Detroit. At Chicago, the Yankees also made only four hits, but Yankees pitcher Sam Jones blanked the White Sox in a 2–0 New York win. The Senators and Yankees were now tied for first place with identical 82–59 records and with thirteen games to play in the season.

Next on the schedule for the Yankees was a three-game series at St. Louis followed by three games at Detroit. The Senators were scheduled to play their next two series in Cleveland and St. Louis, two cities where they had struggled this season. Fortunately for the Nats, Cleveland's twenty-game winner Joe Shaute, who had three wins against the Senators this season, was injured and out for the season. "All I can say is Washington will not get anything soft," assured Cleveland manager Tris Speaker. "I am using young pitchers from day to day but not against contenders. If Washington can win the pennant, all right with me, but they will have to win it against the best I have to offer."[15]

"We're going to win, even if we have to fight it out to the final game of the season," insisted Harris. "We have the right spirit for this pennant victory."[16] But would the Senators wear out? Harris made it clear that he would only use his four top pitchers—Johnson, Mogridge, Zachary, and Marberry—during the pennant drive. Catcher Muddy Ruel, who had played in all but four games this season, was exhausted and had just one hit in the previous three games, prompting

Harris to drop the tired catcher from seventh to eighth in the batting order. "Don't worry about my feelings," Ruel answered when questioned by a sportswriter about his manager's decision. "If we can win games with me in the eighth place, or even ninth, go ahead."[17]

As promised, Speaker started his regulars and veteran spitball pitching ace Stan Coveleski in the series opener. In the top of the first, Harris, who was applauded by the small turnout, doubled off the center field wall, moved to third when Sam Rice extended his hitting streak to twenty-three with an infield hit, and scored on Goose Goslin's ground out. Washington starting pitcher Tom Zachary, who didn't retire a single batter at Detroit two days earlier, maintained the 1–0 lead through seven innings. In the top of the eighth, the Senators scored five runs on five hits, with a two-run double by Peckinpaugh highlighting the rally. Washington went on to win, 6–2, and moved back into sole possession of first place by a half game since the Yankees were rained out at St. Louis.

In the second game of the series the score was tied, 2–2, in the top of the seventh, when Ruel singled then lumbered all the way to third base on an errant pickoff attempt. Earl McNeely came through with a hit to score Ruel for a 3–2 Washington lead. After that, the Senators relied on starting pitcher Walter Johnson, who retired nine of the next ten Cleveland batters for his twenty-second season win and his twelfth consecutive win. "You can't blame baseball fans of the country for loving Walter Johnson," Harris told a Cleveland sportswriter after the game. "Nobody knows his worth as much as we do and we want to close his Major-League baseball career on a championship team."[18]

At St. Louis, the Yankees swept a doubleheader to gain a half game in the standings. Once again, the two top teams in the American League shared the league lead.

Harris had stated that he would use only his four best pitchers for the rest of the season, but that changed after starting pitcher Fred Marberry gave up three runs in the first two innings during the final game of the series in Cleveland. In the bottom of the third, Harris sent Allen Russell to the mound. Shortly after entering the game, Russell allowed a run to increase the Cleveland lead to 4–0. In the top of the fourth, Peckinpaugh singled, Ruel doubled, and Wade Lefler came through in his first pinch-hitting assignment since joining the Nats with a single to center field to score Peckinpaugh and Ruel to cut the deficit to 4–2. In the bottom of the fourth, Harris went with By Speece, Washington's submarine-style pitcher who had appeared in fewer than twenty games and pitched only forty-two innings this season. Cleveland proceeded to load the bases against the third Washington pitcher of the game, but Speece managed to escape the jam without allowing a run. In the top of the eighth, Goslin singled, Judge doubled, and Bluege delivered a two-run single to tie the game, 4–4. After Speece hurled his fifth straight scoreless inning, the Senators sent ten men to the plate during a five-run rally in the top of the ninth in a 9–5 win.

At St. Louis, the Yankees trailed by a run after eight innings, but in the top of the ninth, Joe Bush cracked a pinch-hit homer to tie the game, and in the top of the tenth, the Yankees scored again for a 2–1 win to keep the Yankees in a first-place tie with Washington. "If these Browns play as hard and as good against Washington as they have against us, we'll win the pennant," assured Yankees manager Miller Huggins.[19]

When the Senators arrived at Sportsman's Park in St. Louis to begin their next series, the Tigers, who had suffered a severe blow to their pennant aspirations when swept by the Athletics in their previous series, owned a 3–0 lead over the Yankees. But by the time the Senators-Browns game began under an overcast sky, the Yankees had rallied to tie the game, 3–3. In the top of the sixth, the Yankees added two more for a 5–3 lead.

In the top of the first at St. Louis, the Senators sent fourteen to the plate and kayoed two pitchers in a nine-run rally. In the third inning, with Washington still up by nine, the Nats began to worry when light rain began to fall. If this game was rained out and the Yankees hung on to win at Detroit, the Nats would be in second place by the end of the day. Luckily for Washington, the rain let up and the Senators breathed a little easier when the fifth inning concluded to make it an official game.

At Detroit, the Tigers scored two in the bottom of the eighth to tie the game, 5–5. In the bottom of the ninth, Cobb hit a slow roller toward third base, and Yankees third baseman Joe Dugan, rushed in, arms extended to field the ball, and made a throw that was "very, very wild and went several yards past Pipp's outstretched arm," according to a New York sportswriter.[20] Cobb made it all the way to third on the throwing error and scored on a single for a 6–5 Tigers win. When the final score was posted at Sportsman's Park, several fans stood and roared their approval.

The Senators managed to outscore the Browns in an unimpressive 15–9 win to gain a full game on the Yankees. "To have won a full game advantage over New York on the result of such an exhibition can hardly be satisfying to Washington supporters," wrote a St. Louis newspaperman.[21] The Senators gave up nine runs on ten hits and committed four errors, but on the bright side, Earl McNeely and Goose Goslin made four hits apiece, Sam Rice went 4 for 4 to extend his hitting streak to twenty-six, and the Senators were back in sole possession of first place.

The following morning in St. Louis, Al Schacht and Walter Johnson were seated on the porch of the Kingsway Hotel when Griffith approached. Schacht, who had asked Griffith for a $300 loan to buy his release from New Haven and for a job on the Washington coaching staff back in May, whispered to Johnson about talking finances with Griffith. He knew with the Senators winning the day before, the team president would be in great spirits. "Griff," Schacht said after inviting Griffith to sit down, "if we win this pennant, and we both know we will, you should be ashamed to take the three hundred bucks from me."

"I knew you would try to talk me out of that money from the moment you joined the club," replied Griffith.

"All I know is you were in seventh place when I joined you, and afraid the sheriff would run you in, and now you are in first place. I don't say I personally put the club in first place, but my finger is in the pie somewhere."

"Griff, I'll bet he talks you out of the three hundred," Walter Johnson said with a laugh.

"Well, let's see how we make out with the pennant," Griffith said.[22]

Walter Johnson, vying for his twenty-third win of the season and thirteenth consecutive win, was on the mound for the second game of the series. However, today wouldn't be his day. He served up four runs on four hits, walked a batter, uncorked a wild pitch, and was replaced after the first inning. Harris was forced to dip into his bullpen and fared no better with Martina, Zahniser, and Russell, who combined to allow nine more runs. Led by Bluege's three hits, Ruel's four RBIs, Peckinpaugh's three doubles and five RBIs, and Goslin's four hits—including his tenth homer of the season—the Senators rallied and scored two more in the top of the ninth to tie the game, 13–13. Then in the top of the tenth, Goslin hit his second home run of the day to give Washington their first lead in the game.

It looked good for the Nats when they took the field in the bottom of the tenth. They were leading, 14–13, Fred Marberry was in the game, and the Tigers had scored a run in the bottom of the ninth to knock off the Yankees for the second straight day. If Marberry could get three outs, the Senators would have a two-game lead over the Yankees and would move one step closer to winning the pennant. But the usually reliable Marberry was touched for two hits and was instructed to intentionally walk a batter to load the bases with only one out. A single could potentially score two runs and win the game for the Browns, but the next batter tapped a grounder back to the mound to set up a possible game-ending double play. Marberry fielded the ball, looked toward second base, then made a hurried throw that sailed into center field to allow two runs to score for a heartbreaking 15–14 Senators loss. "The Nationals made a terrible showing, especially for a team with pennant aspirations," wrote a disappointed Frank Young.[23] It was a tough loss and missed opportunity, and nobody felt worse than Marberry. After the game, the sensitive rookie avoided reporters and teammates and took a quick shower and a solo cab ride back to the hotel. He played and replayed the throwing miscue in his mind and visualized the Senators finishing the season one game behind the Yankees.

Heavy rain greeted the Senators when they arrived at Sportsman's Park and delayed the start of the final game of the series. While waiting out the storm, the Nats watched the out-of-town scoreboard and noted that the Yankees had a 1–0 lead after five innings at Detroit. One inning later, a four-spot was posted in the Tigers' half of the sixth inning. At 4:00 in St. Louis, one hour after the game's scheduled starting time, the rain let up and the grounds crew began to peel the tarp off the infield. Tom Zachary, who had complained about a sore arm the previous morning and insisted he wouldn't be able to pitch until the next series, said his arm was OK today. He blanked the Browns through the first three innings. When Zachary took the mound in the bottom of the fourth, the Senators led, 3–0, but the Browns rallied to take a 4–3 lead.

With the skies dimming and the game in danger of being called because of darkness, the Senators tied the game in the top of the fifth when Goslin blasted a home run over the right field fence, his third round-tripper in the previous two games. In the top of the sixth, McNeely was on first base with one out when Harris grounded to the third baseman, who threw to first baseman George Sisler to retire Harris, but on the play, McNeely rounded second and kept running. Surprised by McNeely's aggressive base running, Sisler made a hasty throw that soared over the third baseman to permit McNeely to score for a 5–4 Washington lead. In the top of the seventh, Judge doubled, moved to third on a sacrifice, and scored on Peckinpaugh's well-executed suicide squeeze bunt for a 6–4 Washington lead. After Zachary retired the Browns in the seventh inning, the umpires ruled that it was too dark to continue and called the game complete. The Senators' win along with another Yankees loss at Detroit increased Washington's league lead to two games with seven games remaining, but Harris wasn't taking anything for granted. "I feel we must keep going. There mustn't be any slip between the cup and the lip," Harris said.[24]

At 9:00 on Monday morning, September 22, the 1924–1925 school year officially began in Washington, D.C. This year's public school enrollment was said to be more than sixty-two thousand and expected to exceed seventy-one thousand the following week, a problem for the unprepared and overcrowded school system. Shortly after the children were dismissed from their first day of school, the Senators were underway at Chicago. Walter Johnson, who had not lost since July 11, started slowly and allowed two runs in the first inning. After six innings, the Senators trailed, 3–1, but in the top of the seventh, the Nats struck for another big inning, much to the delight of the Comiskey Park fans who cheered when the Senators sent eleven to the plate and scored six runs on six hits. "It was probably the first time in history that the South Side crowd turned against the Sox and rooted for the visitors," wrote *Chicago Tribune* reporter James Crusinberry. "It was the first time in 12 years of covering baseball games on the South Side that this writer witnessed the spectacle of the White Sox fans rooting for the other team," reported *Chicago Herald and Examiner* sportswriter Larry Woltz.[25] The Senators went on to win, 8–3, for Johnson's twenty-third of the season and his thirteenth in a row. The Washington league lead remained at two games, as the Yankees won at Cleveland, but with only six games remaining in the season, time was running out on the Yankees.

George Mogridge was 3–1 against the White Sox in 1924, but the White Sox got to him for three runs in the first two innings on a cold day that was said to be more suitable for a football game. However, as at St. Louis, the Senators fought back, and in the top of the third, consecutive singles by Harris, Rice, and Goslin and a two-run double by Bluege propelled the Nats into a 4–3 lead. In the top of the fourth, Mogridge, McNeely, and Harris teamed up for three straight singles, and Goslin socked a two-run double in a three-run inning to increase the margin to 7–3. When the White Sox scored in the bottom of the sixth to cut the lead to 7–4, Harris called on Marberry, who didn't have it on this day. The Washington relief ace walked two and gave up a two-run double to cut the lead to 7–6. The White Sox loaded the bases in the bottom of the eighth and put runners in scoring position in the bottom of the ninth, but Marberry managed to snuff both threats and preserved the one-run lead for another Washington victory. Meanwhile, the Yankees won again at Cleveland to remain two games behind Washington with five games left in the season.

"We have to win the final game of this series here today," Harris insisted the following morning. "The Yankees should make a clean sweep of the Indians, just as we did." Harris also mentioned the Senators' next series against the last-place Red Sox in Boston and said he wasn't counting on a sure win. He knew the Red Sox had two solid veteran pitchers in Howard Ehmke and Alex Ferguson and expected to see them in the upcoming series. "Two tough eggs for us to face," said Harris.[26] The Senators had another rough one in White Sox pitching star Sloppy Thurston, a twenty-game winner who had defeated the Yankees a week earlier and shutout the Senators in Washington back on July 22. In addition to Thurston, Harris was concerned about four tough left-handed batters in the White Sox lineup: Maurice Archdeacon, Harry Hooper, Eddie Collins, and Bibb Falk, who were hitting .320 or higher this season. Harris knew that if he started a right-handed pitcher, those four would be in the White Sox starting lineup, and if he started a left-handed pitcher, White Sox manager Johnny Evers would stack his lineup with right-handed batters and would have those left-handers available for pinch-hitting duty. But what if those left-handed sluggers weren't in the lineup and were unavailable to pinch-hit during the game? Harris had an idea on how to make that happen.

In the top of the first, Harris walked, Rice singled to extend his hitting streak to thirty-one consecutive games, and—with the baserunners running on the pitch—Goslin delivered a hit for a 2–0 lead. In the bottom of the first,

Harris put his plan into action. Right-hander Curly Ogden, reported to have a sore arm and who had not pitched in more than two weeks, took the mound while left-hander Tom Zachary began to throw in the bullpen. Knowing that Ogden was Washington's starting pitcher, the White Sox manager wrote the names of Archdeacon, Hooper, and Falk (but not Eddie Collins, who did not play in this game) on his lineup card. After Ogden walked Archdeacon to lead off the bottom of the first, Harris called Zachary into the game. The first batter Zachary faced was Harry Hooper, and the lefty-versus-lefty matchup worked in Washington's favor when Hooper grounded into a double play. Zachary then retired Bibb Falk to end the inning. In the bottom of the third, Evers sent up a right-handed batter to pinch-hit for Archdeacon, and in the top of the fourth, the Chicago manager removed Hooper for another pinch-hitter. Harris's strategy had worked like a charm.

Zachary retired all but one batter through the first four innings, but in the bottom of the fifth, a few right-handed batters in the Chicago lineup managed to tie the game, 2–2. In the top of the sixth the Senators reclaimed the lead when Judge, Bluege, Peckinpaugh, and Zachary singled. The Senators went on to win, 6–3, to complete the series sweep and remain two games ahead of the Yankees, who won to complete their series sweep at Cleveland. The Senators would now travel to Boston for the final four games of the 1924 season with a magic number of three, meaning any combination of Washington wins and Yankees losses equaling three would give Washington the pennant.

A few hours after the completion of the series sweep over the White Sox, the Senators boarded an east-bound train for the long trip from Chicago to Boston. For a team that had a two-game lead with four games to go and were within grasp of winning the first pennant in franchise history, a twenty-six-hour train trip seemed like an eternity. Card games held the limelight, but most engaged in fanning bees to help pass the time. At 8:00 the following evening, the Senators arrived in Boston. The team, tired after their long journey, said very little as they walked the few blocks from the train station to the Brunswick Hotel. Walter Johnson said he was tired and wanted to hit the hay rather than talk baseball but took a few minutes to speak to the press. "We have gone so far, and done so well," said Johnson. "It would be a terrible thing to disappoint our friends at this stage."[27]

"Three wins and the flag," Harris said at the team's pregame meeting in the Washington clubhouse at Fenway Park "We'll win our games and let the Yankees take care of themselves. Don't expect them to waver. Just see to it that we don't and we'll take the championship back to Washington."[28]

Thirteen thousand at Fenway Park rooted for the Senators throughout the game and cheered for five minutes for Harris when he stepped in for his first at bat. When starting pitcher Walter Johnson took the mound in the bottom of the first, the Boston fans got on their feet and cheered. Johnson, who appreciated the ovation, touched his cap to acknowledge the fans. "No visiting ball club ever was given more encouragement to go in and win," claimed *Boston Globe* sportswriter James O'Leary.[29]

The game began as a pitcher's battle. Johnson struck out three and limited the Red Sox to one hit through the first three innings, while Red Sox starting pitcher Alex Ferguson, who had three wins against Washington this season, retired the Senators in order in three of the first four innings. In the top of the fifth, Johnson stepped in for his turn at bat and was hit by a pitch. "The ball caught Walter on the elbow, on what they call the crazy bone," Harris explained after the game. "Naturally, the pain at the time was excruciating."[30] According to O'Leary, a hush came over the crowd, thinking the pitcher might be seriously injured and the crowd hardly breathed as Johnson, with much difficulty, slipped into a sweater and walked to first base.

The Red Sox scored two in the fourth inning and still led by two when the Boston fans stood and cheered for a Washington rally in the top of the seventh. "It was not because the fans detested the Red Sox that they yelled for a Washington victory. It was not because they so dearly loved the Senators, with their youthful manager and the revered and universally respected veteran pitcher Walter Johnson. It was because of the desire for the Yankees to be humbled," reported *Boston Herald* sportswriter Burton Whitman.[31]

In the top of the eighth, with one out, a man on base, and the Nats still down, 2–0, Harris sent Wade Lefler to the plate for another pinch-hitting assignment, and the newcomer came through by placing an RBI double into the gap in left-center field to put the Senators on the board. With Harris due up and Rice, who was hitless on the day, to follow, Washington appeared to be in good shape to score again, but Harris grounded out and Rice popped out to end the inning.

There was hope in the top of the ninth with Goslin and Judge leading off the inning, but the two heavy hitters were retired. Down 2–1, nobody on base and down to the last out, Bluege kept the inning alive with a single, and Peckinpaugh dropped a Texas-League single into right field to advance Bluege to third base.

With runners on first and third, Muddy Ruel, batting .283 for the season including a hit in this game, was at the plate. As Boston pitcher Alex Ferguson went into his stretch, Peckinpaugh broke for second, hesitated, got caught in a rundown, and was tagged for the game's final out. In addition to the 2–1 defeat, Walter Johnson's thirteen-game winning streak and Sam Rice's thirty-one-game hitting streak were snapped. "It simply was not the Senators' day," wrote Whitman.[32] To add to a tough day, the Yankees won, 7–1, to pick up a full game and were just one game behind the first-place Senators.

The next day the Senators wasted no time and took a 2–0 first inning lead when Rice and Goslin tagged Red Sox pitcher Howard Ehmke for back-to-back doubles and Judge followed with an RBI triple. In the bottom of the first, the Red Sox rallied for four against starting pitcher George Mogridge and held a 4–2 lead until Harris sent Lefler to the plate to pinch-hit with two outs and the bases loaded in the top of the fifth. The team's newest addition got hold of one and sent a long drive to deep right field. "It was a real low blow, but [Red Sox right fielder] Ike Boone might have caught it and should have," wrote Whitman. "Boone, however, got a slow start, and then the ball broke through his hands. It was recorded as a two-base hit and all the runners scored with Lefler being cut off and rundown between second and third when he tried to stretch.

"It is not often that a player like Lefler gets a chance to shine like this—two doubles in successive days as a pinch hitter in a red-hot pennant race."[33] The three-run double gave the Senators the lead; however, in the bottom of the inning the Red Sox tallied to even the score, 5–5.

Nemo Leibold, now riding the bench while McNeely handled center field, was in Washington's starting lineup today and drew a walk to open the top of the sixth. He then completed the circuit around the bases when Harris followed with a sacrifice bunt that the Red Sox misplayed into a three-base error. The Senators added another run in the inning when Goslin singled to score Harris for a 7–5 Washington lead.

Allen Russell, the third Washington pitcher of the day, retired the Red Sox in order in the sixth and seventh innings, but then lost his control and walked three in the bottom of the eighth. The bases were loaded, and the Senators needed four more outs for an important win. Harris made another call to his bullpen; however, the call couldn't go to his closer. The Washington manager had summoned Marberry in the bottom of the second and removed him when Lefler was called to bat for the pitcher with bases filled in the top of the fifth. Harris turned to Zachary, who had pitched sixteen innings since complaining about a sore arm last week, and the veteran left-hander came through by getting the last four outs for a Washington win, much to the delight of the Boston fans who cheered for a Senators victory. "The cheering made one think he was in Washington today, and especially when the scoreboard showed that the Athletics had beaten the Yankees in Philadelphia," wrote Frank Young.[34] The Senators were now a win away from clinching the pennant with two games left on the schedule.

On September 28, 1924, the day after Washington moved another step closer to their first pennant by beating the Red Sox, the Senators were idle due to Sunday baseball games being prohibited at Fenway Park. Likewise, the Yankees would have the day off because of the Blue Laws outlawing Sunday baseball in Philadelphia. Bright and early that morning, Walter Kerr, a red-hot Senators fan who visited the team every spring in Tampa, pulled up at the Brunswick Hotel entrance. Bucky Harris, Walter Johnson, and Roger Peckinpaugh climbed into his automobile. Kerr had invited the Washington trio to get away from the mental strain of the battle for the pennant and spend the day at his large stock farm, located twenty-five miles southeast of Boston in the coastal town of Cohasset, Massachusetts. While they rested at Kerr's residence, the other Washington ballplayers spent a quiet day at the hotel or visited Boston's historical sites. Later that evening, Kerr drove his guests back to the hotel. "Kerr took us all around his farm, showed us the prize cattle, hogs and chickens," Harris said shortly after returning to the Brunswick Hotel. "Johnson ate it up, being a farmer. I've never seen him so interested in anything before. Roger and I, not being farmers, saw a lot we didn't understand, but the three of us sure did benefit from the salt air and the fine dinner we had. I feel like a new man right now.

"I have been thinking about baseball twenty-four hours a day for so long that it is beginning to get to me. All day long it has been baseball, baseball, baseball. Down at Kerr's place there was no baseball. It was just a lovely, quiet day on a farm near the ocean."[35]

When asked about the two remaining games in the season, Harris said that he believed the Senators would win. "I feel positive that we will experience little difficulty in disposing of the Red Sox in one of the remaining two games," said Harris.[36] Tom Zachary was slated to be the starting pitcher in tomorrow's game, and just in case the season came down to the final day, Walter Johnson was tapped to start the last game of the season. But according to Zachary, he was going to pitch the game that would clinch the pennant. "I will beat them," said Zachary. "Tell the folks back home I can beat them and I will. It will all be over tomorrow night. And just as a side note, I will beat those Giants when I pitch against them in the World Series."[37]

In the National League, the Giants managed to survive the late season surge by Brooklyn and clinched their fourth consecutive pennant. "We will beat the tar out of Washington," Giants outfielder Irish Meusel, older brother of Yankees outfielder Bob Meusel, assured with a sublime air of confidence. "They will not give us the trouble the Yankees would. We have the pitchers, and when Nehf, McQuillan, and Barnes get through with Washington, there will not be much of the series. It will be the Giants in a walk."[38]

Before heading to his room for the evening, Harris expressed his appreciation to the sportswriters. "I want to thank you fellows for all the good things you have said about my club."[39]

CHAPTER 14

Clinching the Pennant (September–October)

A new king sits on the American League throne. The old passed into the shadows and the new came into being on Fenway field today.[1]

—Irving Vaughan, *Chicago Tribune* sportswriter

On Monday morning, Washington, D.C., awoke to the possibility of a historic day—a day when a dream could come true for three generations of Washington baseball fans. Since major league baseball first came to the District with the Washington Olympics of the National Association in 1871, followed by other major-league franchises in the nineteenth century, including the Washington Senators of the National League in the 1890s, and the birth of the Washington American League franchise in 1901, Washington had yet to experience the honor of finishing on top in a major-league baseball pennant race.

As Washingtonians went about their business under dark skies and during rain showers with heavy wind gusts, the citizenry engaged in discussions about baseball, winning the pennant, and today's Senators game scheduled to begin at 3:00. In Boston, Bucky Harris began his day the same way he had ended it the night before: by talking to the press. "We are going out today to clinch this thing," he told the sportswriters at the Brunswick Hotel. "Never mind those Yankees. I don't care what happens in Philadelphia. We've got to win our own pennant, not have Philadelphia do it for us."[2] At Fenway Park, clouds were overhead on a warm day with the high expected to reach the low seventies. By game time, fifteen thousand were inside the ballpark, including Clark Griffith, who made the trip to Boston with his nephew Calvin and took his seat beside the Washington dugout on the third-base side. E. Lawrence Phillips, the one-armed Griffith Stadium megaphone announcer, was also present with hopes of watching the Senators clinch the pennant.

In the top of the first, Sam Rice stroked a two-out single to become the Senators first baserunner, and on the first pitch to the next batter, he was off and running. Knowing there would be a play in his attempt to steal second, Rice hit the dirt, and while sliding into the base, the catcher's throw caromed off his leg and bounced into the outfield. As the ball rolled across left field and into foul territory, Rice got up from his slide, continued his route around the bases and crossed the plate without a play for a 1–0 Washington lead.

Scoring the game's first run fired up the American League frontrunners. According to *Washington Post* sportswriter Frank Young, the Senators "took the field with blood in their eyes."[3] In the bottom of the first, starting pitcher Tom Zachary, who assured everyone he would pitch the pennant clincher, had the luxury of a one-run lead when he took the mound, but he immediately squandered it by yielding three consecutive singles to tie the game. He then got into deeper trouble by walking the fourth batter of the inning to load the bases; however, he escaped the jam with a strikeout and with help from Peckinpaugh, who made a brilliant one-hand stop on a bad-hop grounder and turned it into an inning-ending double play—Peckinpaugh to Harris to Judge. With two outs in the top of the second, Peckinpaugh, Ruel, Zachary, and Leibold teamed up for four consecutive singles to score a pair for a 3–1 Washington lead. In the Boston half of the second, a single, a walk, and an error filled the bases with nobody out and put Zachary on the ropes, but once again the left-handed-pitching veteran halted the Red Sox threat by gloving a line drive for one out, then throwing the ball to third baseman Ossie Bluege in time to retire the Boston baserunner on third base to complete the double play. A grounder to Peckinpaugh by the next batter resulted in the inning's last out with Washington's 3–1 lead still intact.

The Senators failed to score in the top of the third, and when they took the field in the bottom half of the inning, "Much to everyone's surprise, Zachary took the hill," wrote Frank Young.[4] Zachary's shakiness through the first two innings was enough to convince Young that a pitching change was in order, but Harris elected to stick with his starting pitcher, who began the bottom of the third by surrendering a single and hitting a batter. After a sacrifice followed to move the runners to second and third with only one out, the next Red Sox batter drilled a liner back to the mound, which Zachary knocked down, recovered, and threw to first base for an out, but the runner on third scored on the play to cut the Washington lead to 3–2.

When Harris entered the Washington dugout after the inning, he didn't hesitate to call for a new pitcher. "Get Ready to relieve Zachary," he told Marberry, an order that made the Washington rookie relief pitcher very happy. The twenty-five-year-old reliever had been praying for an opportunity for redemption ever since his throwing error resulted in a 15–14 Washington loss at St.

Louis. As Bluege headed to the batter's box to lead off the fourth inning, Marberry hurried to the bullpen to warm up.

After Leibold fouled out with two teammates on base to end the top of the fourth, a fired-up Marberry, who said he was determined to stop the Red Sox and felt strong enough to stop any team in the world, trotted to the pitcher's mound and retired the next five Red Sox batters in order.[5] He got into a tight spot when the next two batters singled to put runners on the corners, but the rookie hurler kept his cool and handled the next batter to end the inning. Marberry then proceeded to send the Red Sox down in order in the bottom of the sixth.

With six innings now in the books, Washington was still clinging to a one-run lead, and the Fenway fans loved it. When the Senators headed from the field to the dugout to bat in the top of the seventh, the home crowd cheered for a rally. "I never saw anything like that before," said Walter Johnson. "Even in Detroit and St. Louis the crowd pulled hard for Washington, and in Chicago and in Cleveland, a stranger would have thought we were the home team."[6] After the Senators were blanked in their half of the seventh, Denny Williams began the Boston seventh with a single, advanced to second on a sacrifice, and moved to third on a ground out. The Red Sox were once again a hit away from tying the game, and Ike Boone, the Boston cleanup hitter who was 4 for 9 in this series and had hit a grand slam against the Senators four months ago, was at the plate, thus creating a very tense moment for the Senators and their fans.

Back in Washington, thousands of nervous baseball fans braved the rain and high winds to make delirious shouts while standing before newspaper buildings to watch the game results noted on electronic scoreboards throughout the District. According to a *Washington Post* account, "the water poured in torrents off dripping umbrellas, coursed along the folds of raincoats and penetrated to the skins of those without protections against the weather."[7] Those who preferred to be indoors tracked the play-by-play announcements through their radios from a sometimes lucid, sometimes fading radio voice. Others besieged newspaper and telegraph offices and bugged radio headquarter corporations with constant requests for updates. At the Dominican Monastery in the Brookland section of the District, a visitor being escorted through the premises was baffled by a group of friars circled around someone who was reading something from a scrap of paper. "Boone out to Judge. No runs, one hit, one left," the reader announced.[8] The confused visitor was unsure why the group cheered the announcement and why a learned friar excitedly slapped another on the back.

Bucky Harris began the top of the eighth by launching a long drive to left field. If the drive cleared the fence, the Senators would be two runs ahead, but it hit the outfield fence and Harris settled for a double. Sam Rice followed by knocking a hit into center field to score Harris for a 4–2 lead. In the bottom of the eighth, Marberry retired three in a row to reduce the countdown to the pennant.

The Senators went quietly in the top of the ninth. With only three outs to go, Harris decided there was no tomorrow. He instructed Walter Johnson to go to the bullpen to warm up. If the Red Sox mounted a threat in the inning, Harris would have Johnson ready to put out the fire.

The first batter in the Red Sox ninth grounded to Harris, who fielded the ball and threw it to first baseman Joe Judge. "Two more to go, Bucky!" a few fans yelled from the box seats along the first base side.[9] The next batter singled for just the fourth hit since Marberry had entered the game in the bottom of the fourth. With a runner on first, Denny Williams, who was 2 for 4 today and representing the tying run, came to the plate. In the bullpen Walter Johnson halted his warmup and looked toward the infield, wondering if he would be summoned. When Harris didn't look his way, he went back to his warmup, and Marberry got ready to pitch to the next batter.

Marberry made his pitch. Denny Williams swung and hit a grounder toward Harris. "Bucky was on it like a terrier on a released rat," was how *Boston Herald* sportswriter Burton Whitman described the play. The Washington player-manager fielded the ball, scooted to the second base bag, touched it for the inning's second out, then made a pivot in mid-air that was "a rare gem of acrobatic art, and streamed the ball to Judge," wrote Whitman.[10] Harris's relay throw plunged into the webbing of Judge's mitt for the final out of the game.

The moment had finally arrived. Washington won the pennant!

The Washington reserves in the dugout celebrated by throwing all the bats and mitts onto the field and smashing the water buckets to pieces. The starters on the field enthusiastically shook hands and patted one another on the back. A few hundred fans spilled onto the field to join the jubilation. Several young fans, including Calvin Griffith, surrounded Joe Judge, hoping the Washington first baseman would hand over the ball he caught to end the game. Judge responded by joyfully motioning for the children to step aside so he could join his teammates in their dash for the Washington clubhouse.

When Harris entered the clubhouse, he encountered John Dugan and embraced the *Washington Herald* sportswriter. "We won!" Harris shouted.[11] Griffith exited his box and headed to his team's clubhouse. On his way, he was congratulated by E. Lawrence Phillips and headed off by Nick Flaherty, a sportswriter for the *Boston American*. "It is great to get a winner," he told Flaherty, "and I wish that you and the rest of the news boys give credit to Harris for the success of the team. I have nothing else to say." Then the Washington team president continued his hurried route to the clubhouse.[12]

Back in Washington, when a flash notified the fans that it was all over, there was "a wild outburst of cheering and shouting that told of Washington's victory in Boston," the *Associated Press* reported. Several frenzied fans celebrated by tossing their umbrellas, hats, and canes into the air.[13] "Well George, we lived to see the day," a grizzled old man said to his elderly friend.[14] When the White House received word of the victory, Mrs. Coolidge headed to the West Wing and delivered the news to the president.

Back in Boston, all the Washington ballplayers were inside the clubhouse—except for Walter Johnson, who slowly walked from the bullpen, across the infield, and toward the clubhouse entrance, clearly not in a hurry. A few fans rushed to him and extended a hand to congratulate the great pitcher, but Johnson, who had his head down because he was crying, didn't respond. As he moved closer to the stands, fifteen thousand fans came to their feet and gave the great pitcher an ovation.

In Philadelphia, the Yankees heard the news while waiting out a rain delay. Babe Ruth murmured something about being happy for Harris but sorry that the Yankees would not play in this year's World Series.[15]

Inside the Washington clubhouse, Walter Johnson and Nick Altrock each grabbed one of Harris's legs, and with help from Allen Russell and a teary-eyed Roger Peckinpaugh, Harris was hoisted into the air. Griffith, who watched his team rejoice over the victory, removed his hat and brushed his tears away with his other hand.

"How about that three hundred?" someone shouted.

Griffith turned and saw Al Schacht. "It's off, isn't it?" asked Schacht.

"Al, you're the most persistent mercenary cuss I have ever seen," answered Griffith. "Let's see how we make out in the Series before we cancel any debts."

"I don't know, Griff," complained Schacht. "I don't claim anything, but we were in seventh place when I joined the club. What do I have to do, win the Series too?"[16]

"I'm really too happy to talk," Harris told the sportswriters. "All I can say is we did what I expected we would and we will do the same thing in the World Series."[17]

"We have a great little ball club," said Walter Johnson. "Winning a pennant is a wonderful thing. If we can take the World Series it will be worth a great deal more to me now than it would have been years ago." A sportswriter asked Johnson if he still planned to retire. "When the season started, I had fully made up my mind to retire at the end of the year," answered Johnson. "Now it all depends on what comes up this winter."[18]

"I'll tell you frankly that I am the happiest of all the fellows on the team," said Marberry. He reminded the press about his throwing error at St. Louis and how he constantly worried that the error would cost his team the pennant. "Bucky kept perking me up," he said. "He'd tell me not to worry, that we were going to win anyway. But, always I kept thinking of that terrible throw I made in St. Louis, taking away a victory from us that might be necessary at the very end."[19]

Harris announced that there would be no curfew this evening. "The sky's the limit, boys. Go to it," he told his team.[20] The players quickly peeled off their uniforms, showered, dressed in their street clothes, and headed out for an evening to celebrate. The Washington clubhouse emptied in a hurry, and soon all the Washington ballplayers were gone, except for Walter Johnson, who mingled with fans outside the Fenway Park main gate, thanked well-wishers, and signed autograph books into the evening.

"Wonderful! Exquisite De lux!" Harris hollered in the Brunswick Hotel lobby. "I attribute our success to the fighting spirit of the club. We have taken our bumps, but the boys never let themselves get in the habit of getting licked and always came back. When we lost five straight to St. Louis almost everyone except members of our club figured we had cracked. I knew we hadn't."[21] With the pennant now in hand, Griffith, Harris, Johnson, Goslin, Rice, and Judge boarded a train and headed back to Washington. The rest of the Washington team would head back home after Tuesday's nearly meaningless final game of the season. On Wednesday, the team would hold its first practice at Griffith Stadium in preparation for the World Series, scheduled to begin in Washington on Saturday. Arrangements were being made for a pennant victory parade and banquet. The parade was arranged to progress down Pennsylvania Avenue and proceed to the Ellipse, where the president would greet the victorious Washington baseball team. The banquet was scheduled for later that evening at the Occidental Hotel.

At 7:30 the next morning a crowd met Griffith, Harris, and the others when their train arrived at Union Station. When they emerged, team secretary Ed Eynon was first to greet them, bringing a big smile to Griffith's face. Mrs. Griffith was also there, and she rapturously embraced her husband. "The victory vindicates my faith in Bucky Harris," Griffith told a sportswriter. "I knew he could do it and he did. This team has been through the mill. A dozen times during the season they were in a position where they had to win—not win just a game, but a whole series—and they did it."[22]

Harris and Johnson, reported to be flattered by the turnout, had little to say before mysteriously vanishing from the scene. Sam Rice also said little and, like Harris and Johnson, he managed to avoid the crowd. When he arrived home on Allison Street, he was mobbed by neighbors, who surrounded him, shouting congratulations and questions. Children asked about tickets to the World Series; Rice pretended not to hear them. "I am glad I am on a winning team," he told his neighbors. "We all worked hard, especially Bucky. The trip was great and we fought like Trojans for every game."[23]

Roger Peckinpaugh managed in Harris's absence and started the reserves on a cold, misty day in Boston. With the Senators trailing in the season finale, 12–0, after six innings, Peckinpaugh appeased the small turnout, who kept yelling for Senators coach Nick Altrock to play. In the bottom of the seventh, Peckinpaugh sent the forty-eight-year-old Altrock to the mound and the former Major League pitcher allowed a run on four hits in two innings. In the top of the eighth, Altrock came to the plate and poked a hit over the Boston first baseman. When right fielder Shano Collins deliberately made a slow effort in retrieving the hit, Altrock rounded first and second and made it to third before deciding he was too winded to proceed.

With the Major League Baseball season and pennant races now in the books, the focus turned to the World Series. "Well, Washington should put a new thrill into the Series," Commissioner Landis said with a smile. "There was wonderful interest in the pennant races, and I am sure it will be a ripping Series."[24] The baseball commissioner was planning to arrive in Washington three days before the first game to inspect Griffith Stadium.

With the Senators on the road for the final few weeks of the season, a construction crew had been working on increasing the Griffith Stadium capacity. A few additional rows of bleachers were erected in front of the left field and center field bleachers, and the tall right field wall was disassembled to make room for more bleachers. The added seating increased the Griffith Stadium capacity to just short of thirty-six thousand and lessened the outfield dimensions. The new bleachers reduced the distance from home plate to the fence down the left field line from 424 to 375 feet, and center field was shortened from 421 to 400 feet.[25]

The emergence of the surprising Senators, the battle between New York and Brooklyn for the National League pennant, and the excitement of the coming World Series made for a wonderful 1924 baseball season. Major League Baseball had survived the Great War and Black Sox scandal and was now as strong as ever. Fans across the country were excited and looking forward to the World Series. But just when everything seemed to be going so well, another scandal emerged.

Before the Phillies–Giants game at the Polo Grounds on September 27, with the Giants one win away from clinching their fourth consecutive National League pennant, twenty-three-year-old Giants reserve outfielder Jimmy O'Connell approached Phillies starting shortstop, Heinie Sand.

"It will be worth five hundred dollars to you if you don't bear down too hard against us today," O'Connell told Sand.

"Get away from me. You must be crazy," replied Sand. "And don't ever say anything like that again to me—or to anyone else."[26] The Phillies shortstop immediately reported O'Connell's offer to his manager, Art Fletcher. Later that evening, after the Giants won, 5–1, to clinch the pennant, Fletcher phoned National League president John Heydler and requested a breakfast meeting the following morning to discuss an important matter he felt he couldn't discuss on the telephone. The next morning, Heydler, Fletcher, and Sand met for breakfast, and after the meeting, Heydler called Landis, who was preparing to travel from Chicago to Washington. The commissioner immediately changed his plans and headed to New York City. Shortly after arriving and checking into his room at the Waldorf Astoria, Landis conferred with Heydler before summoning Sand. Following his meeting with the Phillies shortstop, the commissioner phoned Giants owner Charles Stoneham and manager John McGraw, who said they were unaware of O'Connell's actions.

Jimmy O'Connell was at his rented room at New York's Embassy Hotel and looking forward to taking his wife to a show that evening when he received a phone call from someone who told him the commissioner wanted to meet with him at 4:00 that afternoon. The Giants outfielder was bewildered. Why would Commissioner Landis want to see him? He told his wife about the phone call and the scheduled meeting and said he would be back in about fifteen minutes. He took a cab ride to the Waldorf Astoria and went directly to the commissioner's room. O'Connell would later recall that it was an ordinary hotel room with a small davenport and a table in a sitting room. Landis sat on the davenport; O'Connell sat in a chair across from the commissioner. The young outfielder wasn't nervous. Landis asked some questions, and O'Connell didn't deny Sand's story and, in fact, admitted he had offered five hundred dollars in return for helping the Giants win.

"Do you understand, O'Connell, that as the result of what you are telling me, you will be expelled from baseball?" Landis said, wagging a finger at the young ballplayer.

By this time, O'Connell understood that what he had done was wrong and knew he was in trouble. "Yes, Judge; I know that," he replied.[27]

O'Connell explained that he was not alone. On the afternoon of September 27, he was in the clubhouse before the game when Giants' coach Cozy Dolan approached him and said, "If you can get Sand to let down in today's game, tell him there's five hundred in it for him." O'Connell asked where the money was going to come from; Dolan told him that New York City was going to pitch in and make up a purse. Shortly after his conversation with the coach, Giants center fielder Ross Youngs entered the clubhouse, walked over to O'Connell and asked if he had spoken with Dolan. O'Connell told him he had and said he planned to talk to Sand. "You go ahead because it's all right," said Youngs. A few minutes later, Giants second baseman Frank Frisch spoke with O'Connell and told him to tell Sand if he threw the game, he could have anything he wanted. Later, when on the field and standing by the batting cage during batting practice, Giants first baseman George Kelly encouraged O'Connell to speak to Sand. "If all these fellows are in on this, there's nothing strange about it, and it's all right for me, too," O'Connell thought.[28]

Following his discussion with O'Connell, Landis called for a stenographer and summoned the people O'Connell mentioned. Landis asked Cozy Dolan about his conversation with O'Connell, and the Giants coach said he couldn't recall it. "You can't recall it?" asked a surprised Landis. "Today is Tuesday. The conversation which I am asking you about between you and O'Connell, O'Connell says took place at the clubhouse at the Polo Grounds last Saturday. That is three days. And you can't recall such a conversation?" Landis kept asking and clarifying what O'Connell had said, and Dolan kept saying he couldn't recall. "That's the best answer you can give, just that you don't remember it?" asked a now angry Landis. "I don't remember," said Dolan.[29]

Ross Youngs, next to be interrogated, denied talking to O'Connell. "When is the first you heard of this?" Landis asked. "Just now, when you called me in," said Youngs. "The talk between him and Dolan that I am asking you about he said occurred last Saturday. This is Tuesday, only three days after," said Landis. "It is news to me," said Youngs.[30]

"Mr. O'Connell's statement was that he told you that Dolan had told him to see Sand and offer him five hundred dollars if he would 'not bear down on us' today," Landis explained to Frisch. "What did you say Frisch said to you after you told him what Dolan said to you?" Landis asked O'Connell, who was present for the questioning sessions. "Give him anything he wants," clarified O'Connell. "I never said that. That is news to me," said Frisch.[31] During the conference, Frisch said that there is "always a lot of kidding going on on every bench."[32]

Later that evening Landis called the investigation complete and made an announcement: "Player O'Connell and coach Dolan of the New York National League Baseball Club have been placed on the ineligible list."[33] Youngs, Frisch, and Kelly were exonerated and permitted to play in the World Series. "They were all in on it," said O'Connell. "I'm being made the goat." When asked why he went through with it, his answer was, "I didn't know what else to do."[34]

"For once in its history Washington will have a parade that will be its own," gloated a *Washington Post* journalist.[35] On the afternoon of October 1, 1924, around a hundred thousand turned out to celebrate the Washington Senators' American League championship. People lined the sidewalks on both sides of Pennsylvania Avenue and gathered at the Ellipse before the parade began. There were old men leaning on canes, white-haired women, called "Grandma" by the tots they escorted, women who were well dressed, women who were poorly dressed, and a band that entertained the turnout at the Ellipse before the parade progression arrived.[36] At 3:30, a committee met at the District building and headed to Griffith Stadium to meet the Washington ballplayers following their first practice in preparation for the World Series. The committee escorted the players to the Peace Monument.

At 4:30, eleven cars began to slowly advance westward on the north side of Pennsylvania Avenue. The first eight cars contained three ballplayers per car; Washington coaches Nick Altrock and Al Schacht occupied the ninth car; Clark Griffith, William Richardson, and Ed Eynon were in the tenth car, and team trainer Mike Martin and concessions manager Billy Smith were in the final car. As the parade moved along, the onlookers began to push, shove, and jostle for position. The crowd turned rowdy, and things became chaotic, with young women rushing forward, peaking into the automobiles, and shouting words of admiration. Boys also dashed to the automobiles and jumped onto the bumpers.

When the parade finally reached the Ellipse, the players joined the president on the stage amid shouts of "Bucky, Bucky, Bucky," "Oh you Goose," and "Yea-a-a Johnson."[37]

The president then addressed the crowd: "As the head of an enterprise which transacts some business and maintains a considerable staff in town, I have a double satisfaction in welcoming home the victorious Washington baseball team."[38]

The crowd responded to the president's words by erupting into hysteria. "Yee-eo-o-w!" yelled a stentorian-voiced gentleman. Then came a surge against the restraining ropes, calling for soldiers and police to hold the crowd in check.[39]

"The Washington team won because it deserved to win," continued Coolidge. "It had fought gamely year after year for a place at the front, never discouraged, always sure what better things were ahead. Manager Harris, I am directed by a group of your Washington fellow citizens to present you for the club with this loving cup. It is a symbol of deep and genuine sentiment. It is committed to you and your teammates in testimony of the feelings that all Washington has for you. With it goes the hardiest congratulations on victory already won and every wish for your success in the contest which is still ahead for you."[40]

Following the president's speech, Cuno H. Rudolph, the D.C. commissioner of the public utilities, presented Harris with a golden key to the city. As Commissioner Rudolph handed Harris the key, the president quietly left.

At 8:30 that evening, the Senators were honored at a banquet at Washington's Occidental Hotel. "This is the happiest moment of my baseball career," Griffith told the audience. When Harris went to the podium, he introduced every player, and proclaimed Ossie Bluege as "the best third baseman in the league." He introduced Walter Johnson as "the ace in the hole," and when the great pitcher rose, the crowd stood and gave a round of applause. When Harris announced Wade Lefler and complimented him for helping the team win, there were shouts of "I'll say he did."[41]

On Thursday, October 2, people from all over the country began to pour into the nation's capital, including the three who had preceded Harris as the Nationals manager. All three said they were pulling for Washington and believed the Senators would win. "I came here to see my last year's team hand the Giants a licking," said Donie Bush.[42] "I came here all the way from Clarksville [Texas] to watch the Nats trim those birds," said Clyde Milan.[43] "It's great to see a Washington team in the World Series and to see old Walter out there on the mound," said George McBride.[44] That evening, Bucky Harris and Walter Johnson went on the air over radio station WRC at the *Washington Times* radio studio. At 8:00, *Washington Times* sportswriter Louis Dougher introduced his guests, who thanked the listeners for their support and promised to work their hardest to win the World Series. "It's great to say 'hello' to everybody all at once like this," Harris said into the microphone. "It is something I always wanted to do ever since we returned to Washington and received the royal welcome that the fans have given us. I wanted to thank them in person."[45]

On October 3, the Senators held their final practice session before the start of the World Series and, afterward, Harris practiced swinging in front of a mirror for fifteen minutes. "There is a little hitch in my swing somewhere, and I find that doing this where I can see myself is a great little corrector," said Harris.[46] At 1:30 that afternoon, three young men from Charleston, South Carolina, arrived at the Griffith Stadium's Fifth Street general admission ticket window. The ticket office wouldn't open for business until 9:00 the following morning; however, the three young men were willing to trade a long wait through an uncomfortably cold evening for being first in line. Next in line were two young men who had traveled all the way from Portland, Oregon. Those who were willing to stand for the game lined up at the Griffith Stadium Georgia Avenue ticket window, with hopes of getting a standing-room ticket for $3.30. An eighteen-year-old George Washington University student was first in line at the Georgia Avenue counter. As more ticket seekers arrived and jumped into line with each passing hour, street vendors appeared and did well by selling hot dogs, coffee, pillows, and soap boxes. By 2:00 a.m. the lines had expanded to more than one thousand people wrapped in blankets and overcoats and who slept on flattened boxes made into mattresses.

On the eve of Game One, Walter Johnson, Roger Peckinpaugh, and Muddy Ruel went to dinner at the Wardman Park Hotel, the hotel where the New York Giants were quartering. Mrs. Johnson and Mrs. Peckinpaugh accompanied their husbands for supper, as did Ruel's father and sister. According to Mrs. Johnson, "the men registered good appetites." While having dinner in the hotel's dining room, the party encountered a few New York Giants ballplayers. "To me they appeared somewhat dejected," said Mrs. Johnson. "Certainly, there was no manifest glow of confidence on their faces."[47]

"The Giants aren't afraid of anything!" Frank Frisch snapped when asked if the Giants feared Walter Johnson. "That's not to boast; it's the truth. Look up the records; you'll find we always beat the best teams. So long as we know we're going into a real battle, we have the confidence that pulls out victories."[48]

Both managers were confident of victory. Harris, who expected the series to go at least six games, maybe seven, said there was no doubt in his mind that his team would win. McGraw said he wasn't big on predictions but warned that he had a fighting club and that it would take an awfully good team to beat his. When asked if the Jimmy O'Connell incident would have any effect on his team, McGraw said no. "The recent scandal has not affected the morale of my players."[49]

Based on having more experience and depth, the Giants were rated as World Series favorites, although some wondered if injuries would handicap the New Yorkers. Frisch missed the last week of the season due to a dislocated finger but was expected to be in the starting lineup. Giants third baseman Heinie Groh missed the last week of the season and would miss the World Series due to a knee injury. Taking over the hot corner for the Giants was rookie Fred Lindstrom. The eighteen-year-old batted just seventy-nine times this season, but according to his manager, he was a natural, possessed a great pair of hands, and was up to the task of performing in the World Series. "He is one of the greatest young players that ever came under my observation," said McGraw.[50]

The first two games in the best-of-seven 1924 World Series would be played in Washington; Games 3, 4, and 5 would be at New York. If necessary, the Series would move back to Washington for Game 6, and a coin toss would determine the home team for Game 7. Calvin Coolidge, planning to occupy Griffith Stadium's presidential box for Game 1, would make history by becoming the first president to attend a World Series opening game and the second to attend a World Series game.

Walter Johnson, looking forward to pitching in Game 1, said he was ready to go. He said he played some golf to help relax his nerves, worked out in his team's practices during the week, slept in every morning, and was well-rested. "I am in shape," Johnson assured them.[51]

When the sun rose on the morning of Game 1, the two ticket lines were said to be longer than eight blocks. There were no tickets for sale at Griffith Stadium's main gate, but more than one hundred waited there with reservation slips, including a man who had traveled more than eight hundred miles and claimed he had sent a check. Nine out of ten who had slips were turned down, told it was their own fault, and given little sympathy, including the man who journeyed eight hundred miles. When the ticket office finally opened for business, a mad scramble ensued, forcing Police Captain Robert Doyle and his force to use rough tactics to keep order.

CHAPTER 15

The 1924 World Series:
Games 1 and 2

> From the last ditch of his baseball career in his shinning
> buckler of the strongest affection ever given by any com-
> munity in sport, the great Walter Johnson fought and lost.[1]
>
> —Damon Runyon, sportswriter

Game 1

On Saturday, October 4, 1924, Griffith Stadium was packed beyond its fullest.
Every seat was taken and the spaces behind the back rows were filled with spectators who settled for standing room. The rooftops of the frail wooden buildings
that overlooked the field were crammed with hundreds who perched to view the
proceedings. When the attendance figures were added, the total was 35,760, the
largest gathering ever to witness a sporting event in Washington, D.C. Those
who were unable to be there but wanted to follow the game's play-by-play tried
to secure a good viewing spot before one of the city's electronic scoreboards.
An estimated seven thousand camped before the *Washington Post* scoreboard;
another five thousand watched the *Washington Star* scoreboard.

The fans inside the ballpark found the on-field pregame activities entertain-
ing. Shortly before the Senators took the field for fielding practice, Babe Ruth,
Ty Cobb, and George Sisler, attending the World Series as press syndicate reporters, posed for photographers in front of the Washington dugout. At 12:30,
Walter Johnson was applauded when he stepped out of the dugout and headed
to the batting cage. After the Senators took batting practice, they headed to their
clubhouse for a pregame meeting and pep talk from their manager. While the
American League pennant winners were listening to encouraging words from

Harris, photographers and reporters converged upon the two Mrs. Johnsons: Walter's wife and mother. Johnson's wife told a *Washington Star* reporter, "Please tell the Washington public whether Walter wins or losses, they can rest assured that he will put everything he has into the game to fulfill the supreme ambition of his life."[2]

At 1:30, the US Army Band, decked in gray and white uniforms, marched onto the field, circled once around the field while playing martial music and came to a halt beside home plate. Then two bright, shiny new automobiles—a Lincoln sedan and a Peerless touring car—were wheeled onto the field.

The Lincoln sedan, a gift for Walter Johnson from the local fans, had a horseshoe of chrysanthemums that adorned the radiator, gorgeous upholstery lining covered with flowers, and a District of Columbia license plate with a license plate number of "100,000." Johnson received a silver plate with the inscription: "To Walter Johnson, baseball's greatest pitcher, from his many friends of Washington, D.C., October 4, 1924."[3] Along with the new automobile came insurance for as long as the vehicle ran—courtesy of the Mutual Life Insurance Company.

Following Johnson's moment in the pregame spotlight, a prominent Cleveland businessman gifted Roger Peckinpaugh with the new Peerless, a present from the citizens of Peckinpaugh's hometown, Cleveland, Ohio. "It was certainly nice of them," said the flattered Washington shortstop.[4]

It was now close to 2:00, the scheduled starting time for Game 1, and everyone was ready for the first pitch. But there was a problem: the president had yet to arrive, and it didn't seem right to begin without him, even at the cost of delaying the start of the World Series.

President Coolidge had a lot on his to-do list. In addition to today being his nineteenth wedding anniversary, he had conferences scheduled for the morning hours, a monument dedication to attend, and Game 1 of the 1924 World Series. After sitting through the ceremony and making the dedicatory speech at the monument to honor the First Division of the US Army during World War I, it was already 1:00. Coolidge was hurried back to the White House where he changed and ate a quick lunch before being escorted by police to Griffith Stadium. At 1:55, the president and the First Lady arrived with their prestigious party, consisting of Speaker Frederick Gillet, Secretary Andrew Mellon, Secretary C. Bascom Slemp, and Major-General John Lejeune, and headed to the presidential box to the cheering of the capacity crowd and the playing of "Hail to the Chief" by the US Army Band. Shortly after the president entered his box, the two teams lined up, and the band broke into "The Star-Spangled Banner."[5] Coolidge made his ceremonial toss, and American League umpire Tommy Connolly made a leaping one-handed grab. Then Bucky Harris and Babe Ruth approached the box, and the Washington player-manager introduced the nation's idol to the president. A chubby-cheeked bat boy, wearing a white Senators uniform, next approached the president with a new baseball. "Please sign it; it may give us luck," the bat boy told Coolidge, who obliged by signing the baseball and handing it back.[6]

The Senators took the field to cheering that was greater than that for the president, but the greatest uproar came when Walter Johnson stepped onto the pitcher's mound. Ten minutes after the game was supposed to begin, Johnson twice swung his right hand over head, went into his windup, and made his first pitch of the game. The ball whistled toward the plate and hopped before smacking into Muddy Ruel's catcher's mitt.

Johnson retired the first two batters and threw two strikes past Ross Youngs, the dangerous left-handed-hitting center fielder who led the Giants with a .356 batting average this season. Johnson's next pitch was a slow-breaking curve over the inside corner of the plate, which Youngs took for strike three.

The starting pitcher for the Giants was Art Nehf, a crafty, five-foot-nine, thirty-two-year-old left-hander, who had been the Giants' best postseason pitcher during the previous three seasons. Although 1924 wasn't his best season, Nehf had experience and allowed only thirty-four hits and thirteen earned runs in fifty-eight and a third innings in seven World Series starts. In addition, he pitched a shutout against the Yankees in the 1921 and 1923 World Series and hurled a five-hit win against the Yanks in the 1922 Fall Classic.

After Nehf matched Johnson by sending the opponent down in order in their first at bat, Giants slugger George Kelly, who hit .324 with twenty-one homers and led the National League with 136 RBIs in 1924, led off the New York second. After incurring a full count, Kelly swung from his toes, connected on a Walter Johnson fastball, and sent a long fly ball to left-center field. Goslin drifted back to the base of the four-foot-high temporary bleachers barrier and accidentally back-flipped into the bleachers while the ball landed into the crowd for a home run.

The Giants 1–0 lead held through the first three innings, and the Senators, struggling against the Giants veteran left-handed hurler, didn't have a single hit. The Nats managed to put a man on base in the second inning and two on base in the bottom of the third, thanks to three walks, but were unable to deliver the big hit to score runs.

In the top of the fourth, Johnson retired Youngs on a called third strike for the second time, struck out Kelly on four pitches, and had two strikes on Giants rookie first baseman Bill Terry. Johnson's next pitch was a low fastball, and Terry golfed it into deep left field. The Senators' left fielder Goose Goslin backed up to the temporary bleachers (more conscious of them this time), leaped high, and missed a catch by less than a foot, Peckinpaugh said. Terry's drive dropped into the crowd to give the Giants another run.

The Senators finally made their first hit of the game in the bottom of the fourth, went three up three down in the bottom of the fifth, and still trailed, 2–0, when they came to bat in the bottom of the sixth. "This is going to be a game with nothing to write about but two home runs," a sportswriter said in the press box.[7]

Earl McNeely began the Washington sixth by poking a double down the left field line, advanced to third on a groundout, and came home on another groundout to put Washington on the board. The Senators put runners in scoring position in the bottom of the seventh and eighth, but Nehf managed to get the third out in both innings to maintain his team's one-run lead.

It didn't look good for Washington when Joe Judge led off the do-or-die Washington ninth by taking strike three. The next batter, Ossie Bluege, hitless in four trips to the plate, gave the home team a glimmer of hope with a single. Then Harris decided to take a chance on a hit-and-run, and his gamble paid off. As Bluege ran with the pitch, Peckinpaugh swung and drove a hit into left field. As the ball rolled toward the fence, Bluege scored all the way from first to ignite a wild outburst among the spectators. Some celebrated by throwing seat cushions and hats onto the field. Mrs. Coolidge cheered and waved her scorecard. The president stood, cheered, and smiled while looking at his distinguished guests, but refrained from tossing his pearl-blue hat.

The game was now tied, 2–2, there was only one out, and Peckinpaugh, representing the winning run, was on second base following his RBI double. Muddy Ruel and Walter Johnson, eight and nine in the batting order, were up next. It would have been a good time to call on Wade Lefler, who had been outstanding in his pinch-hitting role during the Washington pennant drive, but because the Senators purchased Lefler's contract after September 1, the pinch-hitting whiz was ineligible to participate in the World Series. Harris elected to stick with Ruel and Johnson, and they were retired to end the inning and send the game into extra innings.

Both teams put runners on base in the tenth inning, but failed to score, and the two teams went down in order in the eleventh. In the top of the twelfth, Giants catcher Hank Gowdy coaxed a walk and Art Nehf followed with a line drive to center field. Senators center fielder Earl McNeely charged forward and tried to make a diving catch rather than allow the hit, but though he had the ball in his hands, he dropped it before his body hit the ground. Gowdy, uncertain if the batted ball would result in a hit or an out, stayed close to the first-base bag, and when he saw the ball slip away from the center fielder's grasp, he sprinted toward second base. McNeely, who had a chance to recover and get the ball to second base ahead of Gowdy, reached for the ball but failed to get a grip on it. When he finally clutched it, he scrambled to his feet and made a hurried off-target throw, resulting in an error to allow Gowdy to advance to third and Nehf to take second. McGraw then sent up a pinch-hitter, who walked on four pitches to load the bases with nobody out. A now nervous crowd became very quiet as Frank Frisch, who hit .324 this season and had two hits in this game, came to the plate.

Frisch bounced one back to the mound. "When it left the bat, it looked like one of those made-to-order double plays that a pitcher often-times wishes for but seldom gets," a sportswriter assumed. "As the ball took its bounce it went far into the air over Johnson's head."[8] Harris fielded the grounder and made a snap throw to the plate in time for a force-out.

Johnson had a 1–1 count on the next batter, Ross Youngs, and threw a fastball on the outside corner of the plate, which Youngs reached for and blooped a Texas-League single into center field to score the go-ahead run. George Kelly followed with a fly ball that was deep enough to score another run for a 4–2 New York lead.

In the bottom of the twelfth, Mule Shirley, pinch-hitting for Johnson, made it to second base when Giants shortstop Travis Jackson muffed his pop fly. After McNeely flied out, Harris singled to score Shirley to cut the New York lead to 4–3. Then there was hope for a possible win when Rice followed with a single to center field to send Harris to third. Seeing center fielder Billy Southworth bobble the hit, Rice attempted to take an extra base, but Southworth recovered and threw to second base in time to retire the overeager Sam Rice. Instead of having runners on first and third with only one out, Harris was on third and the Senators were down to their last out.

The next batter, Goose Goslin, surprised the Giants by dragging a bunt to the right side of the infield. George Kelly, who started the game in center field before being switched to second base in the bottom of the twelfth, dashed in, made a barehanded pickup, and threw to first baseman Bill Terry, but Goslin beat the throw, or at least the Senators thought. First-base umpire Bill Klem signaled to indicate that Goslin was out. Washington first-base coach Nick Altrock immediately protested, and others joined in the argument. Harris said he did not have a good view of the play, "but everyone watching from the dugout believed Goose tied the throw to first," he said.[9] "He [Klem] was on top of the play," Peckinpaugh said when asked. "He was in better position to see whether Goslin had beaten the throw. He called him out, and that's that."[10]

"It was the most thrilling game and best game I ever watched," said Coolidge. "It was what baseball should be."[11] Following the game's last out, the president and his party walked through a private exit that shared the same walkway leading to the team clubhouses and the umpire's dressing room. When the presidential party was in the walkway, they witnessed an angry Joe Judge giving umpire Klem an earful.

In the Washington clubhouse, the Senators spoke about the loss, and each player mentioned a grievance about what they did or what they didn't do to contribute to the setback. Sitting on a chair in the corner, away from his team-mates, was Walter Johnson. "It sure was a disappointment for me," he said. "I'm disappointed not so much at being charged with the defeat in my first World Series game, but it hurts me to think I had to lose before my many friends who were at the game and watched the scoreboards throughout the country."[12] Harris told reporters that Johnson wasn't unhappy but wanted to win. "He deserved to win," added the Washington manager.[13] Even John McGraw expressed sympa-thy for the great hurler. "It was tough for Walter not to win, but I think Nehf out-pitched him," said McGraw.[14] Johnson pitched all twelve innings, threw a total of 165 pitches, and struck out a World Series record twelve batters. Win-ning pitcher Art Nehf also pitched twelve innings, and his dad, who attended the game, claimed to be the happiest man in town. "I'm sorry his mother wasn't here," Nehf's father said, "but I am sending a telegram to Terre Haute to tell her that Art beat the Mighty Johnson."[15]

"We went down fighting," said Harris. "I have no alibis to offer. The boys played well and I hope that we can turn the trick against the Giants with old Tom Zachary on the mound tomorrow."[16]

Smiling by the door leading to the Senators' clubhouse were Johnson's "pretty wife" and "attractive mother." Johnson's mom, who made the trip from Kansas so she could watch her son pitch in the World Series, was dressed in a sealskin coat and wore a blue velvet hat with the veil thrown back. She was described as tall, well-proportioned but not overweight, and was said to look younger than her years, convincing many to believe that she was Johnson's sis-ter. "Walter pitched a great game, didn't he?" Johnson's mother asked someone. "I'm terribly sorry he lost. I wanted so much for him to win that game. But he did wonderfully well, I think. I am so proud of my boy."[17]

"I did my best; I have no excuses," Johnson said when he emerged from the clubhouse in his street clothes. "It was a hard game to lose, but I did my best. The boys gave me wonderful support, and it's too bad we had to lose."[18] As he walked with his wife and mother to his new car, men, women, and children fol-lowed him, hoping to shake his hand or obtain his autograph. When Johnson got into the driver's seat, he mentioned his other automobile, the one he drove to the ballpark. A friend volunteered to drive it home for him. "Take it and keep it for the evening," said Johnson. "I'm going to stick with this one for a while."[19] Johnson started the engine of his new Lincoln and slowly paced his automobile through the crowd and smiled when the fans cheered and waved to him.

Game 2

The weather for Game 2 was better than the day before and perfect for a ball-game. There was lots of sunshine, a high in the upper seventies, and a gentle breeze coming from the Potomac River that straightened the flags atop the Griffith Stadium grandstand. For the second straight day, the standing-room sections were packed to capacity, the ramshackle rooftops that overlooked the field were jammed, and all but two seats in the stadium were occupied. The unoccupied seats were the two reserved for the president and First Lady, who passed up today's game for a day on a yacht called the *Mayflower* to celebrate their wedding anniversary. Although they would miss today's game, they would receive game updates via radio throughout the afternoon.

Before the start of the game, Bucky Harris and Giants captain Frank Frisch met at home plate, shook hands, and exchanged lineup cards. Today's home-plate umpire Bill Klem dusted off home plate with his whisk broom, E. Lawrence Phillips shouted the starting lineup through his megaphone, and Giants leadoff batter Fred Lindstrom emerged from the dugout with his bat in hand and headed to home plate. Senators starting pitcher Tom Zachary went into his windup and missed on his first pitch of the afternoon for ball one.

In 1924, Tom Zachary had his best year, winning fifteen games and finishing the season with a 2.75 ERA and fewer hits allowed than innings pitched for the first time in his career. In September, he won four and earned a save in a rare relief appearance. However, he was shaky in the previous week's start at Boston and began his first World Series start by yielding back-to-back singles. "Poor Zachary, he'll never know what hit him," said a sportswriter who thought the Senators left-hander had a long day in store.[20] Zachary, however, kept his composure, retired Ross Youngs on a pop out, and induced George Kelly to ground one to Harris. The Washington second baseman attempted to tag Frank Frisch, the baserunner heading from first to second, but Frisch evaded the tag to nullify any chance for a double play. Harris, hoping to at least get the force-out at second base, threw the ball to Peckinpaugh, who was covering second base, but the throw was high. Frisch was safe and Harris was charged with an error. With the bases loaded and only one out, Irish Meusel followed by grounding to Bluege, resulting in an inning-ending around-the-horn double play: Bluege to Harris to Judge.

The Senators came to the plate for their first at bat against Giants twenty-nine-year-old left-handed starter Jack Bentley, a former Senators pitcher who won sixteen for the 1924 Giants and possessed a unique pitching style of rotating his upper body toward center field during his windup then pitching the ball out of obscurity while rotating back toward home plate. Bentley handled McNeely and Harris to start the inning but was tagged for a single by Sam Rice and a long drive by Goose Goslin that sent Giants outfielder Ross Youngs racing to the short right field fence. As Youngs plowed into the barrier and began to fall into the temporary bleachers before regaining his balance, Goslin's drive fell into the crowd for a two-run homer to give Washington its first lead of the Series. In the top of the fifth, Harris got hold of a Bentley pitch and arched it into row three in section 109 of the temporary left field bleachers for the fourth home run of the series, a feat that failed to impress a New York sportswriter. "This ballpark is too small for World Series play," he mused.[21]

Washington now led, 3–0, and the way Zachary was hurling, a three-run lead appeared to be safe. Following an unsteady opening inning, the Senators veteran left-hander retired the Giants in order in the second, third, and fifth inning and faced just one over the minimum from the top of the second through the sixth.

In the top of the seventh, Kelly took ball four on a 3–2 pitch and advanced to third base when Meusel drilled a grounder that was too hot for Peckinpaugh to handle. With nobody out and runners on first and third following Meusel's hit, Giants center fielder Hack Wilson grounded into an around-the-horn double play, the third twin killing turned by the Washington infield in the game. Kelly scored from third on the play to register New York's first run of the day, a result accepted by the Senators, who gladly traded a run for two outs.

Zachary sent the Giants down in order in the top of the eighth, the fourth time the Washington left-hander pitched a three-up, three-down inning today. In the top of the ninth, Frisch drew a leadoff walk, Youngs popped out, and Kelly went to a full count when McGraw signaled for Frisch to run with the next pitch. As Zachary went into his stretch and delivered his next pitch, Frisch was off and running, and when Kelly drilled the pitch on a line into right-center field, the speedy Frisch rounded second and saw the Giants third-base coach signaling for him to keep running. Right fielder Sam Rice, running at full speed, fielded the hit and threw the ball to the cutoff man, Bucky Harris, who received the throw after Frisch had rounded third and was halfway down the third-base line. Harris winged the ball to Ruel, who caught the relay throw and jabbed the ball into Frisch's chest. Home-plate umpire Bill Klem called the runner safe, causing an uproar among the 35,922 fans, who hooted and hollered in protest.

The Washington lead was now 3–2; George Kelly, representing the tying run, was on first base and Irish Meusel, who drilled a single in his previous at bat, was at the plate. Meusel hit another hard grounder, this time to the right side of the infield. Harris quickly moved to his left, fielded the ball, and with only one play, threw to first base to retire the batter while Kelly safely advanced to second base. Giants rookie outfielder Hack Wilson, hitless on the day, came through by knocking a 2–2 pitch over the first base bag for a hit. The hit appeared to be heading for the right field corner, but Rice, once again, quickly got to the ball and threw to the plate. Kelly, determined to score on the play, rounded third, and just before Ruel received Rice's throw, he left his feet, fell over the Senators catcher, and "landed on his hands like on acrobat," a sportswriter described.[22] After Kelly tumbled, he managed to get both hands on the plate to tie the score, 3–3, and hushed the stunned Washington fans. Harris then motioned Zachary to the bench and signaled for a new pitcher. "It's all right. Here comes Marberry," a fan said.[23] As Marberry headed to the mound, Zachary, head down and looking dejected, walked to the Washington dugout.

The first batter Marberry faced was Giants shortstop Travis Jackson, and the Washington relief ace fired three consecutive strikes to end the inning. "You can't hit 'em when you can't see 'em, outfielder Ping Bodie used to remark. Jackson probably didn't see 'em," a sportswriter quipped.[24]

Joe Judge walked to lead off the Washington ninth in a tie game, and the crowd came out of its brief state of despair when Bluege followed with a successful sacrifice bunt to move Judge to second. As Roger Peckinpaugh headed to the plate for his turn at bat, Frank Frisch immediately looked to the New York dugout and shouted to McGraw for an intentional walk. The Giants manager answered by slowly shaking his head from side to side and ordered Bentley to pitch to the Washington shortstop. After fouling off a few and watching two balls go by, Peckinpaugh swung and sent a well-hit grounder between Lindstrom and Jackson. As left fielder Irish Meusel fielded the ball, Judge rounded third and beat the outfielder's swift throw to give the Senators a 4–3 win. The Series was now even and heading to New York City for the next three games. Walter Johnson said the home field advantage wouldn't favor the Giants, and the Senators would have a psychological advantage. "We beat the Yankees nine out of eleven games at Yankee Stadium, and the two we lost were by one run. So playing in the home of the Giants ought not to bother the boys much."[25]

Marberry was scheduled to be the Washington starting pitcher in Game 3 and Johnson was expected to start Game 4. "I look for Walter to win hands down the next time he faces those Giants," said Harris. "The excitement of the presentations on Saturday with the presence of President Coolidge and the high muckety-mucks was too much. The next time it will be just another ball game and that will make all the difference in the world."[26]

Following the game, the Senators taxied to Union Station and traveled by train to New York City. After checking into the Hotel Almanac that evening, Harris expressed confidence about winning on the road. "When we go home champions of the world, they'll have to bring out the soldiers from Fort Myer to get us through Union Station," Harris said.[27]

CHAPTER 16

The 1924 World Series:
Games 3, 4, and 5

Game 3

Would Roger Peckinpaugh play in Game 3? When running out his game-winning hit in Game 2, he strained a muscle in his left thigh, making him questionable for today's game. The absence of Peckinpaugh would be devastating. Not only was the smooth-fielding shortstop the heart and soul of the Washington infield, but the Senators lacked infield depth. To help increase Peckinpaugh's chances of playing, Mike Martin packed the shortstop's injured leg in ice for two hours. When Polo Grounds megaphone announcer George Levy blurted out the Game 3 starting lineups, he announced Peckinpaugh as Washington's shortstop.

Among the 47,608 who attended Game 3 was a large contingent of Senators fans. When the New York lineup was announced, the Washington fans inquired about the ineligible Giants outfielder and coach. "Where's O'Connell?" a Washington fan shouted. "What position is O'Connell playing?" another fan asked. Another fan yelled for the Giants to put Cozy Dolan in the coach's box.[1] Joining the Washington delegation in cheering on the Senators were several angry Giants fans, who not only wanted to see the underdog come through—they believed that O'Connell had followed orders, told the truth, and was abandoned by his teammates.

Back in Washington, drug stores, cigar stores, radio stores, and other stores attracted large crowds by attaching a loudspeaker to their radio sets. It was said that the radio was making ardent fans out of housewives, who formerly listened to or attended Senators homes games only to please their husbands. All government departments had small radio sets and quite a few were in use in the Senate office building. The radio at the White House was also tuned into the game, and Mrs. Coolidge was said to be an attentive listener.

Fred Marberry, the Senators' reliable reliever and sometimes starter, was Washington's Game 3 starting pitcher, and if the rookie was nervous, he certainly didn't show it when he retired three of the four New York batters he faced in the bottom of the first. Bill Terry began the Giants second inning with a line-drive single, but Marberry remained confident, struck out Hack Wilson, and got Travis Jackson to hit a ground ball to Senators third baseman Ossie Bluege, who made an off-target throw that pulled Harris off the second base bag. The Washington second baseman was charged with the error, "Which didn't seem right," according to a New York sportswriter.[2] "If I would have just gotten that ball a little higher, Stan would have caught it, we would've gotten a double play, and the Giants wouldn't have scored," Bluege confirmed after the game.[3] Hank Gowdy followed with a single to score Terry, and a wild pitch added another run. In the bottom of the third, Marberry was tagged for back-to-back singles to put baserunners on the corners, and as in Game 2, Hack Wilson drove in a run by grounding into a double play. When the inning ended with the Giants ahead, 3–0, Marberry's day was done. Harris sent Allen Russell to the mound in the bottom of the fourth, and he served up a homer to Giants relief pitcher Rosy Ryan for the fourth Giants run.

After the second inning, Peckinpaugh, who aggravated his injury when going for a grounder to his right in the first inning, withdrew from the game, forcing Harris to adjust the infield by shifting Bluege to shortstop and sending in Ralph Miller to play third base. Meanwhile, the Washington batters didn't have a hit through the first three innings against Giants starting right-handed pitcher Hugh McQuillan. In the top of the fourth, the Washington fans became boisterous, began to cheer for a rally, and their "Clap-clap-clap-clap-clap," echoed again and again across the field.[4] Following a walk to Sam Rice to begin the Washington fourth, Giants second baseman Frank Frisch quieted the Washington fans by running into right field and making a spectacular catch on Goose Goslin's fast-falling pop fly. The next batter, Joe Judge, got the Washington enthusiasts cheering again by advancing Rice all the way to third base with a double. Bluege followed with a walk to load the bases, and Ralph Miller, who had played in only nine games since joining the Senators in mid-season, came through with a sacrifice fly to score Rice and put Washington on the board. Two consecutive walks followed to score another run, making it 4–2. But after that, the Senators could produce only two infield singles and a walk in the next three innings.

In the bottom of the sixth, another Washington error, a sacrifice, and an RBI single by Lindstrom chalked one up for a 5–2 New York lead, which held until the Senators scored in the top of the eighth, on a single by Bluege, a walk by Miller, and a pinch-hit single by Mule Shirley. However, the Giants added another run in the bottom of the eighth to extend their lead back to three. In the top of the ninth, singles by Harris, Goslin, and Judge loaded the bases, and a walk to Bluege forced in a run. With the score now 6–4 and the bases loaded with only one out, McGraw signaled for a new pitcher. Sixteen-game winner Virgil Barnes and veteran Mule Watson were warming up in the bullpen. Barnes halted his warmup and headed toward the pitcher's mound, until he realized it was the other pitcher McGraw wanted. Watson slowly jogged onto the field, and when Frisch yelled impatiently, the relief pitcher broke into a trot.

Watson took the ball and gazed solemnly and impassively at Giants catcher Hank Gowdy. Ralph Miller, said to look uncomfortable at the plate in his first two plate appearances, swung at a high, inside pitch and lifted a popup, which third baseman Fred Lindstrom caught in foul territory. Muddy Ruel, still looking for his first hit in the Series, followed with a slow grounder to Lindstrom, resulting in the game's final out. "It wasn't a great game by any way of thinking—but certainly thrilling in the ninth inning," McGraw said after the game. "I'm pleased that my team won and that we have the upper hand again."[5]

The Senators were silent in their clubhouse following the game. It was assumed that everyone was thinking the outcome might have been different had Peckinpaugh been in there. "I don't know how long I will have to stay out," said Peckinpaugh. "I may be back tomorrow and I may not be back before the Series is over."[6]

"The injury to Peck is particularly tough," admitted Harris. "He's been going grand for us in the field and at bat. Pulling him out hurt immeasurably, breaking up our infield and weakening our batting. But what's the use in worrying about it now? We won the pennant by fighting, and we're going to keep right on scrapping to the end."[7]

Game 4

"Stand up there, you Goose Goslin—stand up there where the neighbors over in Salem, New Jersey can see you," wrote well-known newspaperman Damon Runyon after Goslin broke out of his World Series slump by going 4 for 4 with a homer and four RBIs in Washington's 7–4 Game 4 victory to even the World Series at two-games apiece.[8]

Before Game 3, Goslin surveyed the playing field at the Polo Grounds and smiled when he noted the short distance from home plate to the right field bleachers. "That right-field stand is just my dish," said Goslin.[9] But in Game 3, Goslin didn't homer, and through the first three games of the World Series the Washington cleanup hitter had just three hits in fifteen at bats.

Before Game 4, Babe Ruth, who was at the Polo Grounds to continue his job as a World Series syndicate reporter, stepped onto the field and approached Goslin. "Want to make some homers here?" Ruth asked.

"You're doggone right I do," answered Goslin.

"Well here's how to do it," said Ruth. "This park is made for you. Follow my instructions and you're bound to get a couple."[10]

Ruth had a good idea about hitting home runs at the Polo Grounds since the Yankees used to call the Manhattan ballpark home before moving into the brand-new Yankee Stadium in 1923. "Boy, how I used to sock 'em there," Ruth recalled. "I cried when they took me out of the Polo Grounds."[11] The Yankees slugger pointed to Goslin's faulty batting stance and illustrated how he should stand at the plate. He also demonstrated how he should time his swing. Following his lecture, he asked Goslin to try a few, and after going through the motions five times, Ruth gave his stamp of approval.

Would Walter Johnson be Washington's Game 4 starting pitcher? According to Runyon, Johnson was expected to start. "Everybody was quite flabbergasted when they saw warming up before the game the veteran left-hander George Mogridge, a thin, frail-looking chap of many years of experience in the big leagues," explained Runyon, and according to the admired newspaperman, the Washington manager's decision was an unpopular one. "There was a buzz of condemnation of Harris's judgment. Everybody said he ought to go with Johnson," wrote Runyon.[12]

In the opinion of most sportswriters, Mogridge wore out during the home stretch of Washington's pennant drive and wouldn't be a factor in the World Series. In mid-August, he allowed just six earned runs while pitching four complete-game victories and won eight of his final nine decisions of the season. But after pitching a five-hit complete game 2–1 victory on August 23, a fatigued Mogridge gave up an average of five earned runs per game during his final eight starts and failed to complete a game after September 6. "But Harris knew what he was doing," continued Runyon. "The thin Mogridge, with his old but lengthy left arm, held the Giants in check."[13]

The other question was whether Peckinpaugh would be in today's lineup. "Yes," Peckinpaugh said before leaving the Hotel Almanac and heading to the ballpark, but Harris and Mike Martin shook their heads negatively when asked.[14] "I would have been out there on the field assisting the boys in smacking the Giants for a few rows of buttercups, but they did very well without me," said Peckinpaugh.[15]

In the bottom of the first, Mogridge walked two, and a throwing error by shortstop Ossie Bluege led to a 1–0 New York lead. One inning later, Mogridge walked another batter and gave up a base hit but then shook off the World Series jitters. He retired Frank Frisch to end the Giants' threat, then retired nine of the next ten New York batters.

With the Nats still down by one in the top of the third, Goose Goslin came to the plate with two outs and two teammates on base. Giants starting pitcher Virgil Barnes made his first pitch to Goslin, a low curve ball, said to be a good pitch. As the pitch approached the plate, Goslin leaned to his left, cocked his bat behind his neck, then strode to his right while making a powerful arcing swing. "The crowd was up and in full cry at the crack," described Runyon. "They sensed something big was about to happen as soon as Goslin swung."[16] The drive traveled on a line, gradually rose, cleared the razor blade sign plastered to the right field fence, and landed in the bleachers for a three-run homer. Goslin went into his home run trot, and Babe Ruth looked at his agent, Christy Walsh, who was seated next to him in the press area, and grinned. Goslin's teammates cheered, waved their arms, and danced with joy. After Goslin crossed the plate and reached the Washington bench, his teammates pounded him on the back, praising the batting star for his second homer of the Series. In the top of the fifth, McNeely and Harris singled, and a wild pitch scored another Washington run. Then Goslin made his third hit of the game by drilling an RBI single for a 5–1 Washington lead. Later in the game the Washington slugger singled and scored when Judge and Bluege also singled. "Goslin was outstanding," McGraw said after the game. "He had a great time in banging our pitching staff around, didn't he?"[17]

Mogridge appeared to be confident as he stood on the mound, a huge wad of tobacco puffing one of his cheeks. His dazzling curveball and control surprised and continuously frustrated the Giants. "I'll admit that Mogridge had us fooled," confessed Frank Frisch. "The balls he chased up to us were easy to hit—but weren't easy to hit 'em safe."[18] The Giants managed to put another run across in the bottom of the sixth, but they went down in order in their half of the seventh and were trailing, 7–2, when they came to the plate in the bottom of the eighth.

Mogridge sandwiched an out in between two walks and threw two consecutive balls to the fourth batter of the inning. Harris decided to call on Marberry, even though he had been the starting pitcher in Game 3. The first batter he faced was Hack Wilson, and the Giants rookie outfielder sent a long drive that hit the right field barrier and bounced away from right fielder Sam Rice. Before Rice retrieved the ball, the lead New York baserunner easily scored from second base. Rice, thinking he might have a play on Wilson who was on his way to second base, threw the ball to Harris. Wilson easily beat the throw for a double; however, the other Giants baserunner, who was on first base before Wilson's hit, had rounded second and third and was attempting to score. Harris quickly fired the ball to Muddy Ruel, who received the manager's throw in time to tag the baserunner for a huge out. Marberry disposed of the next batter to end the inning. In the bottom of the ninth a hit, another Washington error, and another hit scored a run to reduce the Washington lead to 7–4. Then Marberry, not at his best today, walked a batter before getting the last two outs to finally end this ballgame.

"Johnson is ready for tomorrow and we ought to take the lead in the series," Harris said after the game.

"Give me a few runs tomorrow, that's all I need," Johnson said with a big smile.[19]

Game 5

The day began with overcast skies, but by ten o'clock, dark skies gave way to sunshine. The best-of-seven 1924 World Series was currently tied, 2–2, and was opened for either team to win it. But Bucky Harris, in great spirits the morning after his team won, 7–4, believed that his team had the upper hand. "Looks pretty good now, doesn't it?" he told reporters at the Hotel Almanac. "Here we are, even with the Giants and ready to cut loose with Johnson and Zachary. Walter ought to get them today, and Zachary has a great chance to take them in Washington tomorrow."[20]

"My arm feels fine," assured Johnson. "It never weakened because of those 12 innings on Saturday, and I honestly think that I'll be better at the Polo Grounds than I was in Washington. It's a darker field here you know, and that helps me."[21] According to Mrs. Johnson, her husband not only wanted to win to fulfill his lifelong dream, but he wanted to win for his team and appease his many fans who wanted him to be victorious. "I have to win," he kept repeating to his wife.[22] "The New York folk expected to see Walter win," a press editorialist noted. "They not only expected it, they virtually prayed for it."[23]

The Game 5 scheduled starting pitcher for the Giants was Art Nehf, the team's pitching ace who had matched Johnson for pitching twelve innings in Game 1. "I may not be able to pitch today," Nehf told the sportswriters. "I was hit on my pitching hand by a line drive in the first game at Washington and the injury has traveled to the joint of my thumb. I attempted to pitch a few curveballs before the game yesterday, but the injury became so painful, I had to quit."[24] Nehf also threw a few practice pitches before Game 5. "He was not fit to pitch today," McGraw declared. "He tells me that the injury is healing and he will be able to start tomorrow."[25]

Before 49,211 at the Polo Grounds, McGraw sent left-hander Jack Bentley, the losing pitcher in Game 2, to the mound, and he started off by sending the Senators down in order in the top of the first. Goose Goslin began the Washington second with a single, his fifth consecutive hit, but his teammates were unable to bring him home.

Fred Lindstrom, the New York eighteen-year-old third baseman who was filling in for the injured Heinie Groh, went 0 for 5 against Johnson in Game 1. He was 2 for 12 through the first three games, but McGraw didn't give up on him. In Game 4, Lindstrom went 3 for 4, and in Game 5 he singled in the bottom of the first. However, Johnson retired the next three batters to end the inning and retired the Giants in order in the bottom of the second. In the Washington third, Johnson received an ovation when he stepped in for his first at bat, described as "heart-warming" by a New York sportswriter.[26] He then belted a long fly that he thought would clear the fence. Thinking he had a home run, Johnson slowly trotted toward first base while admiring his long drive, but the ball fell short of the fence and landed in the outfield. Johnson turned on the speed, rounded first, but was out in his attempt to stretch his hit into a double. McNeely and Harris followed with infield singles, which likely would have scored Johnson had he safely reached base.

With the game still scoreless, Travis Jackson began the Giants' third with a grounder to the left side of the infield. Senators third baseman Ralph Miller should have made the play, but he got a slow jump and failed to reach the grounder before it rolled through the infield for a hit. After Johnson recorded his first strikeout of the day, Jack Bentley, noted as a good-hitting pitcher, singled to right to put runners on the corners with only one out. Fred Lindstrom followed with a slow roller, and once again, Miller got a sluggish start. The play resulted in another hit and allowed the runner on third to score the game's first run. The next batter grounded to shortstop Ossie Bluege, who fielded the ball and threw to Miller in what should have been a force-out at third base. But Miller was out of position and all New York runners were safe on the play. With the bases now loaded, Ross Youngs followed with a line drive directly at right fielder Sam Rice for the second out of the inning. The drive was deep enough to easily score Jack Bentley from third, but he was halfway to home when Rice made the catch and needed to retreat and tag up. Rice threw the ball to Johnson, who threw to Ruel in plenty of time to retire Bentley to complete the double play and end the inning. In the top of the fourth, a hit, a sacrifice, and an RBI single by Miller tied the game, 1–1. In the bottom of the fifth, Giants catcher Hank Gowdy singled and Bentley followed with a high pop fly down the right field line. In any other ballpark the fly ball would have been in play, but being only 257 feet down the right field line at the Polo Grounds, this routine pop fly ball landed in the upper deck for a two-run homer to give the Giants the lead. "Bentley caught one right over the plate and shot it high in the air toward the right field stand," Johnson explained after the game. "[Sam] Rice was up against the wall, waiting for the ball to come down, but he had no chance."[27]

After Miller's fourth-inning RBI hit tied the game, the Senators made only one hit and drew two walks through the next three innings. With one out in the top of the eighth, Goslin broke the drought by sending a drive into the upper tier in right field for his third World Series home run. Judge followed with a hit, but Bluege and Ruel grounded out to end the inning with the Nats trailing, 3–2.

There was still hope for Washington and for Walter Johnson to get the win. If Johnson could hold the Giants in the bottom of the eighth, perhaps the Senators could score a few in the top of the ninth and win this game. But when Johnson threw his first few pitches of the inning, it was clear that his fastball wasn't fast, and his curve wasn't sharp. According to Damon Runyon, Johnson's arm lifted wearily and fell wearily with each pitch. George Kelly began the inning with a line-drive single, and Bill Terry followed by coaxing a walk on four consecutive pitches. "This was evidence that Johnson was on the run and should've been taken out," opined a *New York Times* sportswriter. "But sentiment interfered. Harris had no intention of taking Johnson out."[28] The next batter, Hack Wilson, attempted a bunt to move up the baserunners, but bunted Johnson's pitch harder than he had intended. The ball quickly rolled toward the pitcher's mound and gave Johnson, the closest fielder, a chance to force-out the Giants' lead runner heading to third base. An exhausted Walter Johnson stepped forward, slowly lowered his glove to field the ball, but was unable to get a grip and was charged with an error. "Take him out!" a fan yelled.[29] American League umpire Billy Evans, a spectator at the game who had the utmost respect for Walter Johnson, heard the fan's remark and took exception. "It hurt me to hear someone shout that old line at a great pitcher like Walter Johnson," Evans said. "I can stand for anything they call me when I'm out there, but it's a shame to razz a man like Walter. He is a great player and is deserving of all the honors they shower upon him."[30]

With still nobody out and the bases loaded, a sacrifice fly and two singles scored three to seal Johnson's fate for another World Series loss. "There was a spirit of a dying gladiator in the air. The stands were silent; the spectators were stunned," described a World Series correspondent.[31]

Following a 6–2 Game 5 loss, reporters surrounded Johnson in the Washington dressing room. He showed the press a box containing several telegrams he had received from well-wishers. The great pitcher read a few of those telegrams to the sportswriters, including one from a couple in Alexandria, Virginia, who had named their newborn in his honor. "These telegrams make me feel worse," said Johnson. "I've received wires from all over the world telling me how everyone was pulling for me and I couldn't come through." Johnson confirmed his plans to retire and noted with sadness that he would finish his career with two World Series losses.[32]

Tom Zachary was slated to be Washington's starting pitcher in Game 6, and although Harris was uncertain whom he would start in Game 7, it was certain that Walter Johnson wouldn't be pitching the deciding game on just one day's rest. "I couldn't hold them," Johnson said apologetically. "I had two chances to beat them. I'm sorry but I couldn't hold them at any time."[33] Mrs. Johnson believed that the pressure for her husband to win was too great. "I feel sure his anxiety proved to be his undoing," explained Mrs. Johnson. "He was too eager to win."[34]

The Senators were now down, three games to two, in the Series, were playing without Roger Peckinpaugh, and would have to face Art Nehf in Game 6. "I've got a hunch if Art Nehf is in shape to start the sixth game there won't be any more season and there won't be any more World Series," predicted Babe Ruth.[35] But even with the odds against his team, Harris expressed confidence in Tom Zachary and winning the World Series. As Harris explained his reasoning to the sportswriters in the Washington clubhouse, he was summoned to the commissioner's box for the coin toss to decide which team would host Game 7 of the 1924 World Series, if necessary. "If Washington wins the coin toss, Washington will win the World Series," Griffith predicted after the Senators won Game 4 to even the series at 2–2.[36] Walter Kerr, the man who had hosted Harris, Johnson, and Peckinpaugh at his farm the day before Washington clinched the pennant, recently gave Griffith a vintage 1889 Canadian dollar to use for the coin toss. "This is my good-luck piece," Kerr told Griffith. "You can't lose the coin toss with that." As Harris and McGraw stood before the commissioner's box at the Polo Grounds, Griffith handed the commissioner the Canadian dollar. "What's this?" barked Commissioner Landis as he glared at the coin. "It's got a head and a tail, hasn't it?" replied Griffith.[37] Landis grabbed the coin and handed it to Harris. "Mr. McGraw, you call it," said Harris. The Washington player-manager then flipped the coin in the air. "Heads," called McGraw.[38] When the coin landed the tail end was facing up, meaning that Washington won the toss and would be at home if Game 7 happened.

Washington Herald sportswriter John Dugan thought about an exhibit at the 1915 San Francisco World's Fair and drew a comparison to Walter Johnson's disappointing Game 5 defeat. The exhibit was a statue of an old American Indian riding a worn-out horse. Both rider and horse, their heads hanging low, appeared to be disconsolate, dejected, and utterly routed by fate. Attached to the exhibit was a label with the words: *At the end of a long trail.*[39] Johnson, tears in his eyes, walked with his teammates along the train station's platform and headed to the team's Washington-bound train. During the trip, he sat next to a window and stared into the night. Griffith, hoping he could cheer him, sat in the seat next to him and offered words of encouragement, but it was no use. The great pitcher was inconsolable.

When the train arrived in Washington, Johnson was seen carrying his one-year-old daughter after disembarking and making his way along the roped-off path through the Union Station terminal. "Tough luck, Walter," was repeated by several among the five thousand fans who greeted the team upon arrival.[40] Johnson acknowledged the fans with a slight smile, but looked straight ahead as he kept walking. Then the great pitcher disappeared into the night.

CHAPTER 17

The 1924 World Series: Games 6 and 7

Game 6

It was a long night for the shivering fans who camped out in the line leading to the Griffith Stadium ticket window on the eve of Game 6. Bundled in woolen blankets, thick underclothing, heavy sweaters, and overcoats to combat the cold, they sacrificed a mattress, sweet dreams, and a hot breakfast for a place in line. First in line was a man from Falls Church, Virginia, and his fourteen-year-old son, a student at Ballston High School. "He was bound to see a World Series game, and his mother said that if I didn't take him, she would, so here I am," the man said.[1]

When morning arrived, a bright sun gradually dispelled the leftover chill from the previous night and warmed the park. Shortly after the Griffith Stadium box office window shutters were unlocked and the gates opened, the bleachers filled with fans who vented shouts and laughter. The grandstands also had some occupants, who read their newspapers or watched the red-capped ushers play catch in the outfield. At 11:00, Meyer Goldman and his band took the field and marched, playing "Take Me Out to the Ballgame." Less than five minutes before game time, some seats were still unoccupied, including the chairs in the presidential box. President Coolidge wasn't planning on attending today's game but changed his mind after some persuading by his wife, a die-hard Senators fan who had tuned in to all three broadcasts of the three games played at the Polo Grounds. Three minutes before game time, the president, First Lady, and their party arrived. As they walked down the aisle leading to their box, the crowd applauded, and players from both teams hurried from the dugouts to line up by the president's box. When the band broke into the national anthem, Coolidge abruptly halted in the aisle and removed his hat. Shortly after the presidential party got situated in their box, John McGraw, dressed in a sack suit and crush hat, looking more like a businessman than a baseball manager, approached the president's box with Commissioner Landis. The First Lady informed McGraw that she was pulling for the Senators, and the New York manager reacted with a smile. Harris also visited with the presidential party and chatted with Mrs. Coolidge. "I'm depending on you to win this game," she told Harris.[2]

The National League champions were so confident of victory in Game 6, most of the Giants packed a handbag instead of a suitcase for the trip. "It seems a cinch that the Series of 1924 comes to its end with the playing of the sixth game in Washington," assured Frank Frisch.[3] One game away from elimination and having to face Art Nehf in today's game, the pressure was on the Senators, but they received a boost: Peckinpaugh would be in the starting lineup. "With Peck playing today, we're going after those Giants," said Harris. "We'll have him coming to the plate every now and then and his steadiness and experience in the field will give us the edge we had over the Giants when this series started."[4] Peckinpaugh told the sportswriters that he would play in Game 6 "even if every step I take pains me. The leg feels fine, and no one is more anxious to play against the Giants than yours truly."[5] When E. Lawrence Phillips announced the starting lineups through his megaphone, he mentioned Peckinpaugh's name with increased volume. As the Washington shortstop limped to his position before the game, the home crowd cheered vociferously.

Art Nehf was ready and kept the Senators scoreless through the first four innings. In the bottom of the first, a single, a walk, and an error filled the bases for Washington, but Nehf struck out Joe Judge to end the inning. In the bottom of the second, Peckinpaugh came through with a one-out single, but Nehf retired the next two batters to end the threat then retired the Senators in order in the third and fourth. A double by Frisch and a single by Kelly scored one for the Giants in the top of the first, and the way Nehf was going, one run appeared to be all New York would need.

Peckinpaugh began the Washington fifth by lining one down the left field line. Giants left fielder Irish Meusel was hesitant and unsure if he should dash in or stay back. According to a New York sportswriter, "Meusel played the ball timidly and might have caught it with a little more forward dash and daring," and Peckinpaugh's drive dropped at the left fielder's feet for a single.[6] Ruel, 0 for 15 in the series, sacrificed the Washington shortstop to second and Tom Zachary moved Peckinpaugh to third with a groundout. Then Nehf walked the next batter, Earl McNeely, on four consecutive balls that weren't even close to the plate. "The fourth ball was so wide, it looked intentionally wide," wrote Damon Runyon.[7]

With runners on first and third with two outs, Harris stepped to the plate, and the Senators saw an opportunity to score two runs on one hit and take the lead. Peckinpaugh was in scoring position on third, and McNeely, if he could advance to second base, was fast enough to advance two bases on a single. On the first pitch to Harris, McNeely was off and running. Giants catcher Hank Gowdy was a bit slow to react but made a fast throw. Second baseman Frank Frisch ran to cover the base, caught Gowdy's throw with both hands, but missed the tag "by a hair," described a *New York Times* sportswriter.[8] Washington was now a hit away from taking the lead.

Nehf's first two pitches to Harris were strikes, but then the New York star hurler missed on his next three. With a full count, Harris asked for time. He stepped out of the batter's box, rubbed some brown dirt on his hands, and pulled down his cap. When he reentered the batter's box, he purposely leaned over the plate to reduce the strike zone. Nehf aimed his next pitch for the outside corner, and as the pitch approached the plate, it looked as if it would be outside for ball four, but Harris leaned in, swung, hit the ball off the end of his bat and between the Giants first and second basemen. As the ball rolled into right field, Peckinpaugh easily scored, and McNeely rounded third and beat the outfielder's throw to the plate. Griffith Stadium erupted in a delirium of joy. Hats, canes, and programs filled the air. People pounded one another in an enthusiasm that was called madness. "The ensuing racket must have rocked the Washington Monument," wrote Runyon.[9] All occupants in the presidential box were on their feet, and smoke poured from Coolidge's cigar more profusely than at any other time during the game.

With Washington now ahead by a run and five innings in the books, everyone wondered if Zachary could hold the Giants for four more innings. The Washington starting pitcher had allowed just one run on five hits through the first four innings, sent the Giants down in order in the fifth, and seemed to be getting stronger as the game progressed. His changeup, said to be his best pitch of the day, kept the New York batters off balance, and his curve ball was sharp.

The Giants went three up and three down in their half of the sixth, and Zachary retired the first batter in the top of the seventh before Hack Wilson singled to snap the Washington starting pitcher's string at eight. After Wilson's base hit, Giants shortstop Travis Jackson fouled out and Hank Gowdy popped out to finish the inning. In the top of the eighth, Zachary once again sent the Giants down in order. "His control was absolutely perfect, and he was never in a hole," complimented Ty Cobb, seated next to Babe Ruth in the Griffith Stadium press area.[10]

Zachary looked as if he might have an easy inning in the top of the ninth, until George Kelly executed a one-out single to keep the Giants' hopes alive. Irish Meusel followed with a grounder that appeared to be heading through the middle of the infield for another New York hit, but Peckinpaugh headed it off by darting to his left, reaching down, and making a glove-hand stop behind the second-base bag. As the shortstop's momentum began to carry him past second base, he jerked a backhanded toss to Harris in time to force out the baserunner. After making the play, Peckinpaugh stumbled, tumbled to the ground, and rolled over, wincing in pain. As his swarthy complexion distorted in agony, he rolled over a second time. He got up under his own power and limped toward the Washington dugout, but when he reached the halfway point, he couldn't go a step further. Two teammates hurried to the injured player and helped him walk the rest of the way.

Following his arrival in Washington through a trade with the Red Sox in 1922, Peckinpaugh started slowly and was deemed a disappointment, but now the Washington baseball fans greatly appreciated his good work during the 1924 season, the pennant drive, and in the World Series. As Peckinpaugh hobbled off the field, the Griffith Stadium fans stood and applauded.

Hack Wilson took a strike and swung and missed on two more pitches for the game's final out. When the game concluded, several fans stepped onto the field and headed for the center field exit. A fan dressed in a raincoat made a remark as he brushed past Wilson, and Wilson responded by swinging a fist. Hank Gowdy intervened and shoved Wilson in the direction of the dressing rooms. After a few more shoves and encouraging words, a calmer Wilson walked with Gowdy and disappeared into the tunnel.

"We have fought for this chance. Now watch us go and get 'em" Harris said.[11] But who would pitch in Game 7? The fans were hoping for Walter Johnson, but that was unlikely since he would be working on one day's rest. The obvious choice was Fred Marberry, who didn't appear in Games 5 and 6 and was assumed to be well rested, or George Mogridge, the winning pitcher in Game 4. Babe Ruth felt the best choice was Mogridge. "This much is certain: Mogridge and Zachary proved the Giants heavy artillery can't do much damage against southpaw pitching," he said.[12] But Harris surprised everyone by announcing Curly Ogden. "I have great faith in Curly," said Harris. "He is always cool and collected out there in the box. That counts for a lot in an important game. I am banking on Curly to fool the Giants and clinch this championship for us."[13] Ogden had a sore arm, pitched in only two games in September, and was recently warned by a medical expert to lay off pitching for three to four weeks. The last time he pitched was at Chicago on September 24, when Harris started him as a decoy to trick the White Sox into starting their heavy-hitting left-handed batters.

Following his postgame discussions with the sportswriters, Harris was last to leave the clubhouse and was greeted by more than a hundred autograph-seeking female fans. "Oh, you Bucky," they yelled as they surrounded the Washington player-manager. Then as hands pushed out programs, pencils, baseballs, fountain pens, there were shouts of "sign this! Here! Here! Here!"

"Ladies, you will have to excuse me," said Harris. "I will be glad to sign all day long after tomorrow." He then hurried to his automobile and slowly drove his car through the crowd. When he reached Vermont Avenue, he stepped on the accelerator. "Gee, that was a trying experience," he said.[14]

Game 7

"We've been listening to every game of the Series," said Mrs. W. C. McNeely, the mother of Washington's rookie center fielder Earl McNeely. The McNeelys lived almost three thousand miles from Griffith Stadium and the Polo Grounds, yet due to the rapid progress of technology during the 1920s, Earl's parents heard every play of the 1924 World Series through their homemade radio in the living room of their vine-covered cottage in Alameda, California. Accompanying the McNeelys were Earl's eighty-three-year-old grandfather and seventy-four-year-old grandmother. "Of course, we take turns [using the radio set headphones to hear the play-by-play announcements], but whoever is listening in tells the rest of us what is happening," clarified Mrs. McNeely.[15]

Could the Senators win without Roger Peckinpaugh? The morning after his heroics and injury in Game 6, the star shortstop visited a physician, who ordered him to bedrest for a week. Peckinpaugh balked at the doctor's instructions. He understood about sitting out today's game and postponing his hunting trip booked for next week, but there was no way he wouldn't attend today's game. His teammates needed his encouragement, and the best way he could support them was to sit on the dugout bench in his street clothes and cheer his team on to victory. The doctor was reluctant but understood and gave his OK for attending Game 7.

During Peckinpaugh's absence in Games 3, 4, and 5, Harris moved Ossie Bluege to shortstop and inserted Ralph Miller into the lineup; however, Miller's shakiness at the hot corner and anxiety at the plate convinced the Washington manager to start Tommy Taylor at third base, even though the backup infielder had a bandage on his right hand due to an injury sustained when tripping over the dugout steps during Washington's practice session two days before Game 1. "You know, I broke in as a pitcher. I intend to make all my throws with two fingers like a pitcher," explained Taylor, who said he was thrilled about being granted the Game 7 starting assignment. "I appreciate that Harris thinks I can help him win."[16]

Not wanting to miss a moment of today's game, the president and his party arrived ten minutes before game time. Mrs. Coolidge, yearning for a Senators victory from the bottom of her heart, was wearing her lucky necklace, the same one she had worn during the elections of her husband's political career. Shortly after the president's arrival, both teams formed a *V* before the president's box for a photograph. Coolidge smiled broadly as a panorama picture was taken.

During Washington's pregame warmup, Harris ordered Mogridge and Marberry to throw in the bullpen and instructed Ogden to warm up in front of the Washington dugout. Was Harris really going to start a sore-armed pitcher? Some hometown fans thought he was joking. Others mentioned Ogden's last start at Chicago and suspected Harris was up to something.

Following Washington's Game 6 victory, sportswriter Frank Morse, who had warned Harris last spring about the Senators generally playing out their schedule come midsummer, asked the Washington manager who was going to pitch in Game 7.

"You will tell no one?" asked Harris.

"No sir," promised Morse.

"I'll give 'em the works. I'll take a chance. I'm going to get Terry out of the lineup," Harris told Morse.

McGraw platooned the left-handed-batting Bill Terry at first base, used him almost exclusively against right-handed pitching, and the result was Terry was 6 for 11 against Washington's right-handed pitchers. If Harris started the right-handed-throwing Ogden and quickly switched to the left-handed Mogridge, McGraw might pull Terry from the game, or if the Giants' manager elected to keep Terry in the game, he would have to bat against Mogridge.

"And when George can go no further, I'll put in Marberry," Harris continued, "and if they get to Marberry, I'll put in Walter. And Walter will win for us."[17]

Later that evening, Harris went to Griffith's home and told his boss about his game plan. "I like the idea," replied Griffith.[18]

Ogden began the game by striking out Fred Lindstrom, then began to walk toward the Washington dugout. Harris, who had planned to let Ogden pitch to only one batter, decided to let his starting pitcher face another, but after Ogden walked the next batter, Harris called on Mogridge, who struck out Ross Youngs and finished the inning by retiring George Kelly on a groundout. Mogridge started the top of the second by inducing the feared Bill Terry into grounding to Harris for an easy out. Two innings later, when Terry stepped in for his second plate appearance, Mogridge struck him out.

Game 7 began as a pitcher's duel. Mogridge allowed only two infield hits, struck out three, and blanked the Giants through the first four innings. Giants starting pitcher Virgil Barnes retired the Senators in order in the first three innings and started the bottom of the fourth by striking out McNeely. The next batter, Bucky Harris, worked the count to 3–2, then brought the crowd to its feet when he connected on a fastball, lifting a long fly ball to deep left field. At the crack of the bat, Giants left fielder Hack Wilson turned, headed toward the

fence, and backed up to the waist-high, green wooden barrier before the temporary bleachers. Glove-hand extended skyward, he leaped and started to tip into
the crowd, while a score of hands reached out to save him from falling. Despite
Wilson's gallant effort, the ball managed to elude his reach and find a place in
the bleachers for a 1–0 Washington lead.

As Harris made his circuit around the bases, the home crowd went wild. All
occupants in the presidential box jumped to their feet, and Coolidge applauded
with plenty of vigor. In left field, Wilson's body disappeared among the fans
in the bleachers, except for his legs draped over the fence. Fearing that the left
fielder might be injured, six New York pitchers sprinted out of the bullpen and
Giants center fielder George Kelly ran from his position to aid Wilson. After his
teammates helped him out of the bleachers and to his feet, Wilson rubbed his
head and paced a bit. He then signaled toward the dugout to let his manager
know he was OK.

Mogridge blanked the Giants in the top of the fifth to maintain Washington's 1–0 lead, but this wasn't enough to convince Harris that his experienced
hurler could go the distance. Before the game entered the sixth inning, Harris
ordered Marberry to start throwing in the bullpen. During his warmup, Walter
Johnson walked from the dugout to the bullpen, which convinced some that he
was going to warm up. However, Johnson just said something to Marberry and
returned to the dugout.

Ross Youngs began the New York sixth with a walk and advanced to third
when George Kelly singled. Bill Terry, the next scheduled batter, began to make
his way to the plate for another turn at bat, then did an about-face and headed
back to the Giants' bench. Irish Meusel, a right-handed batter, emerged from
the New York dugout and was announced as a pinch-hitter. Harris had accom-
plished his goal: Bill Terry was now out of the game.

As Meusel stepped up to the plate, the youthful Washington manager called
on Marberry to pitch; however, it was Meusel who won the righty-versus-righty
matchup by hitting a fly ball deep enough to score Youngs from third to tie the
game, 1–1. Hack Wilson followed with a single to once again put Giants baserunners on the corners. Then Travis Jackson tapped a dribbler toward first base.
Washington's reliable first baseman Joe Judge charged in and, hoping to head
off Kelly who was trying to score from third, attempted to scoop Jackson's slow
roller off the ground. "Had he fielded the ball, he probably would have got Kelly
with plenty to spare, but he fumbled the ball," insisted a New York reporter. "He
recovered the ball quickly but not in time to get Kelly at the plate. He still had
time to get Jackson at first, but Joe seemed bewildered by his fumble, and stood
still while Jackson safely reached first."[19] Hank Gowdy followed with a grounder
in the direction of shortstop Ossie Bluege, "who had been playing sensational

ball up to this time," Runyon reported.[20] But Bluege botched the play for another Washington error, and another New York baserunner crossed the plate.

The 3–1 Giants lead hushed the Griffith Stadium crowd. Mrs. Coolidge, said to be the most interested in the game among the occupants of the presidential box, appeared very worried. "The joy which had been on Mrs. Coolidge's face seemed to disappear, and she clasped her two hands tightly," observed a *New York Times* sportswriter.[21]

Muddy Ruel, who had played in every game since July 20, was still hitless in the World Series when he stepped in to lead off the Washington sixth, and when Barnes retired him on a ground out, the exhausted Washington catcher was now 0 for 18 in the Series. Barnes also handled the next two Washington batters to end the inning.

Harris gave the hometown fans hope when he began the bottom of the seventh with a single for Washington's first hit since the fourth inning, but Barnes retired the next three to conclude the inning. Ossie Bluege began the Washington eighth with a foul out, "and the crowd moaned in deep misery," claimed a New York sportswriter.[22] Harris then sent Nemo Leibold to pinch-hit for Tommy Taylor, and the veteran outfielder came through by slicing a hard grounder that grazed the third-base bag and rolled down the left field line, resulting in a double. Ruel advanced Leibold to third by finally reaching base on a hard grounder between first and second, which Giants second baseman Frank Frisch knocked down but recovered too late to make a play. Washington baserunners were now on first and third with only one out, and suddenly the Washington fans were reenergized. They cheered louder when Bennie Tate, pinch-hitting for Marberry, drew a walk to load the bases. Then the crowd let out a deafening cheer when McNeely took ball one. On the next pitch, the rookie center fielder lined one directly to left fielder Irish Meusel, who had remained in the game after pinch-hitting for Terry, for the second out of the inning, and "the Giants breathed easier," wrote a New York sportswriter.[23] The crowd responded by quieting again, and Mrs. Coolidge, visibly suffering under the strain of her team's trailing, clenched a fist and smacked it against the palm of her other hand.

The bases were still loaded with two outs, leaving it up to the next batter, Bucky Harris, to come through to keep Washington's hopes intact. Before the Washington player-manager settled into the batter's box, Giants catcher Hank Gowdy called time out, walked over to the Giants' dugout, and had a word with McGraw before returning to his position. As Giants pitcher Virgil Barnes lifted his arm, Harris took two steps toward the pitcher's mound, swung, and grounded one toward Giants third baseman Fred Lindstrom for what looked like a sure out. "It looked like an easy chance for young Lindstrom, who set himself to take the ball on the bounce," described Runyon. "In nine cases out of ten, the bounce would have been directly into Lindstrom's hands. This was the tenth case, and the ball bounced over his head and into left field for a hit."[24] Leibold easily scored from third, and Ruel rounded third and crossed the plate to tie the game, 3–3. The crowd erupted into mass hysteria. Bells and whistles sounded from all corners of the ballpark. The president dropped his cigar, came to his feet, and pounded his hands together.

Washington was now a hit away from claiming the lead, and Sam Rice, Washington's hottest batter in September, was due to bat. Deciding that he now had to go with his best, McGraw called Art Nehf out of the bullpen, and his reliable hurler took care of Rice. Game 7, deadlocked at 3–3, now headed into the ninth inning with a question that was heavy on everyone's mind: who would pitch for Washington? The fans were aware that Harris had lifted Marberry for a pinch-hitter during the eighth-inning rally and a new pitcher would be on the mound in the top of the ninth. Walter Johnson's mother, seated a row behind the presidential box, had a pretty good idea as to who would be on the mound. "They'll put him in now, I think," she said.[25]

CHAPTER 18

Conclusion of the 1924 World Series

> When future generations are told about this game they will not hear about Barnes, or Frisch, or Kelly, or even about Harris or McNeely. But the boy with his first glove and ball crowding up to his father's knee, will beg: "Tell me about Walter Johnson."[1]
>
> —Bill Corum, sportswriter

"Loose-jointed and lumbering, he ambled to the center of the diamond," described Bucky Harris.[2] "Walter! Walter! Walter!" the crowd cried out.[3] President Coolidge and other high-ranking government officials joined in the ovation that was so loud, megaphone announcer E. Lawrence Phillips could hardly be heard: "Johnson, now pitch-ing for Wash-ing-ton."[4] Here was one last chance for Walter Johnson to pitch a World Series victory. One last chance to come through for all those fans who had messaged their support and best wishes and told the great pitcher they were cheering for him.

"You're the best we got, Walter. We've got to win or lose with you," Harris told Johnson, handing him the baseball.

"I didn't have much confidence in myself," Johnson would later recall. "I was thirty-six years old, and that's pretty far gone to be walking into the last game of the World Series—especially when you've lost two starts already. I remember thinking 'I'll need the breaks,' and if I didn't actually pray, I sort of was thinking along those lines."[5]

Leading off the New York ninth was Fred Lindstrom, who'd had a great game against Johnson two days ago. "Lindstrom seemed to like my pitching," Johnson said after Game 5. "He cracked me for four hits and three of them were good, hard cracks."[6] This time the eighteen-year-old rookie got under a fastball and popped up to the left side of the infield. Ralph Miller, who had just entered

185

the game as a substitution for Tommy Taylor at third base, looked nervous as he trotted forward, camped under the ball, and caught it for the first out. Next to the plate was Frank Frisch, and he belted a waist-high fastball into the gap in right-center field for his tenth hit of this series. "The ball never seemed to stop rolling and I was crazy for fear Frisch would come clear home," Muddy Ruel would later say.[7] After McNeely retrieved the extra-base hit and returned the ball to the infield, Frisch was standing on third with only one out and the number three and four hitters in the Giants lineup due up.

It was happening to Walter Johnson again. A tough-luck loser in Games 1 and 5, he was now in danger of losing again. During his career, he had won the love and respect of baseball fans for his greatness, modesty, and sportsmanship. The fans were sympathetic when it appeared the great pitcher would finish his career without ever pitching in a World Series. They cheered for Washington throughout this season so Johnson could finally pitch for a pennant winner and were thrilled when he was named the 1924 American League MVP. They hoped he would win a World Series game. But now it sadly seemed as if it wasn't meant to be.

Harris instructed Johnson to intentionally walk the next batter, Ross Youngs, to put runners on first and third for George Kelly, the 1924 National League RBI leader. Standing six feet, three inches, and weighing 190 made him a menacing sight at the plate. Johnson, knowing it was do or die, blew a pair of fastballs by the Giants slugger for two strikes. He then reached back and followed through with everything he had for another blazing fastball. Kelly swung and missed for strike three, and as the crowd roared its approval, Walter's mother began to cry. With two outs and runners on the corners, Irish Meusel came to the plate.

The Senators paid no attention to the baserunner on first, and Youngs took advantage by stealing second without a play—but it wouldn't matter. Meusel grounded to Miller, causing the Griffith Stadium fans to gasp. Ralph Miller was the last person they wanted to see handling the ball, but the Washington substitute third baseman successfully fielded the grounder and threw the ball to first. The throw was off target, and first baseman Joe Judge was forced to make a long stretch while keeping a foot in contact with the base but made the grab to end the crisis.

With the game still tied in the Washington ninth, Judge reached base with a one-out single and advanced to third when a Giants attempt to turn Bluege's grounder into a fielder's choice resulted in an error. Ralph Miller came to the plate with a chance to become a hero. However, before the right-handed-hitting Miller stepped in against left-hander Art Nehf, McGraw signaled to his bullpen, and Giants right-hander Hugh McQuillan came on to pitch. The move paid off for New York, as McQuillan induced Miller into rapping a tailor-made double-play ground ball to shortstop Travis Jackson. The Giants turned in an inning-ending twin killing—Jackson to Frisch to Kelly. For the second time in World Series history, extra innings would be needed to decide the final game.

After Hack Wilson began the New York tenth by drawing a walk, Johnson got a big out by striking out Travis Jackson. When home plate umpire Bill Dineen called strike three, Jackson dropped his bat and expressed his disapproval by putting his hands on his hips and staring at the arbitrator. Hank Gowdy, who had seven hits in the series, followed by grounding one back to the pitcher's mound, where Johnson gloved the ball, turned, and threw to Ossie Bluege, who was covering second base. Bluege received the throw, then threw to Judge to complete an inning-ending double play.

Once again, the Senators had a chance to win with one run in the bottom half of the inning but went down in order. Ruel, who had finally gotten his first hit of the Series during Washington's two-run rally in the eighth, grounded out, and Johnson followed by putting his shoulders behind a heavy swing and sending a long fly ball to deep left-center field. Thinking the drive might clear the fence, Walter's mom let out an "o-o-o-h" before Hack Wilson corralled the drive. "I thought he made a home run," confessed Mrs. Johnson.[8] McQuillan then struck out McNeely to end the inning.

In the top of the eleventh, McGraw sent thirty-five-year-old Heinie Groh to pinch-hit for his pitcher. Groh, a thirteen-year veteran who was known for his famous bottle-shaped bat, was the Giants starting third baseman in the 1922 and 1923 World Series. He was New York's starting third baseman during the 1924 season as well, until a knee injury sidelined him in mid-September, but he came through in his only 1924 World Series at bat with a leadoff single. Lindstrom followed with a sacrifice to put the potential winning run on second for the dangerous Frank Frisch, "but Johnson, calling on all he had, struck out Frisch," reported America's leading sportswriter Grantland Rice. "It had been three years since any pitcher had struck out the keen-eyed Frisch [in a World Series]. But today Frisch was facing the Johnson that used to be the Johnson that nailed them all, with a fastball that few could see and fewer could hit."[9]

After Frisch became Johnson's fourth strikeout victim of the game, Harris, once again, instructed Johnson to purposely walk Ross Youngs and take his chances with George Kelly, a decision that drew boos from a few spectators. Kelly swung at and missed Johnson's first offering. Johnson then threw another fastball, and Kelly swung again, this time getting a piece of the ball and tapping it foul for strike two. Then Johnson wasted a pitch, which Kelly took for a ball. Now with a count of one ball and two strikes, Johnson surprised Kelly with a curve ball, and Kelly flailed and whiffed to end the inning.

"Gee, Walter is pitching beautifully," said Mrs. Johnson.[10]

"I don't recall that I ever witnessed a battle between pitcher and hitter on the diamond that thrilled me as did the contest between Johnson and Kelly," said an impressed Ty Cobb. "Kelly was a brimful of determination both times. No batter likes to have the player preceding him purposely passed in a pinch. George Kelly, no doubt, would have given anything he's possessed to make a hit, but the old master of the pitching art foiled him."[11]

The game now headed into the bottom of the eleventh with the Senators still needing only one run to win. Since he had lifted his pitcher for a pinch-hitter, McGraw needed a new pitcher, and knowing that the heart of the Senators batting order—left-handed batters Rice, Goslin, and Judge—were coming to the plate, the Giants manager sent left-hander Jack Bentley to the mound. Goslin became the potential winning run when he hit a two-out double but would be left on base. McGraw ordered Bentley to intentionally walk Judge and let the left-handed Bentley focus on the lighter-hitting, right-handed batting Bluege, and the strategy paid off, as Bluege grounded out.

As the game moved into the twelfth inning, the Griffith Stadium fans were on the brink of exhaustion. How many more innings could Walter Johnson pitch? Would he get the one run he needed to win this ballgame? Probably not— or at least not in this inning. Due up in the Washington half of the twelfth were Ralph Miller, who had failed in the clutch in the bottom of the ninth; Muddy Ruel, with just one hit in the Series; and Johnson. Therefore, if Washington was going to win this game, Johnson would have to hurl two more shutout innings, and the Senators would have to wait to bat in the bottom of the thirteenth, when the top of the order and the clutch-hitting Harris would be coming to the plate.

For the third straight inning, the Giants leadoff batter reached base. Irish Meusel gave New York hope by hitting Johnson's first pitch into right field for a single, and Babe Ruth, seated in the press area, immediately expressed his concern about Johnson's weakening. But once again Johnson dashed the Giants' hopes by retiring the next three batters.

Ralph Miller began the Washington twelfth by tapping a grounder to Frisch for an easy out, and when Muddy Ruel followed by popping one over home plate, the crowd let out a groan, thinking this would be another out. New York's veteran catcher Hank Gowdy camped under the ball and showed his anxiety by vigorously shuffling his feet. He then made a catcher's cardinal sin by dropping his mask directly before his feet rather than tossing it to one side where it would be out of his way. The result was that Gowdy stepped on his mask, then shook it off his foot, stepped on the mask again, stumbled while extending his glove hand for an attempt to make the catch and flat out missed the ball for an error. After the ball "fell to mother earth with a joyous plop," reported *Washington Star* sportswriter Harold Phillips, the crowd let out a sigh of relief.[12] Ruel had received a reprieve, and given another chance he "slammed a vicious drive inside the third base line," described a New York sportswriter.[13] Fred Lindstrom moved to his right and lunged for Ruel's hard grounder, but couldn't reach the ball before it hopped past third base and down the left field line. Ruel put his tired legs into motion, rounded first, and scurried to second base for a double. "The stands in Griffith Stadium rocked and shook with the raving of the multitude of 35,000," wrote Irving Vaughan in the *Chicago Tribune*. "To them that 'break' was the beginning of the end."[14]

With one out and the potential winning run on second, Mrs. Johnson closed her eyes and began to move her lips as if in prayer while her son made his way to the plate for his turn at bat. Johnson smacked a hard grounder to shortstop Travis Jackson, "and I made as if to run past Travis then turned around and scuttled back to second," recounted Ruel.[15] Perhaps he was distracted by Ruel, but Jackson fumbled the ball for an error.

Washington runners were now on first and second, and there was still only one out with Earl McNeely at the plate. Back in Alameda, California, hovering over his homemade radio, Mr. W. C. McNeely, who was keeping score, looked down at his notepad. He knew the circumstances of his son's at bat. After a pause, the McNeely who wore the radio headphones heard the announcer report the first pitch to Washington's center fielder: "Foul ball, strike one."[16] The McNeelys impatiently waited out the broadcast's pause between pitches.

Giants pitcher Jack Bentley went into his windup, rotated his body toward center field, and then turned toward the plate as he followed through with the pitch. McNeely swung, connected, and hit a routine grounder toward third baseman Fred Lindstrom for what looked like would result in an inning-ending double play. "I saw Freddy hold his hands ready at his chest for the ball," recalled Ruel, "then I saw him jump up."[17] As on Harris's two-run single in the bottom of the eighth, the grounder took a high hop over Lindstrom and rolled into left field. As Ruel ran for third base, he saw Senators third-base coach Al Schacht waving his arm "like a runaway windmill," Schacht later said, the signal for Ruel to round third and head for the plate.[18] Ossie Bluege, watching from the Washington dugout, saw Meusel field the hit and anticipated a play at the plate. "[Ruel] wasn't too fast as most catchers are," Bluege said years later.[19] Standing and cheering next to Bluege was Nemo Leibold, who yelled, "C'mon, Muddy! C'mom, Muddy!" and pumped his arm, as if he were trying to push Ruel across home plate.[20] The play at the plate never happened. "He—stuck it in his pocket—" a surprised Bluege said about Meusel. "He walked off the field with the ball in his pocket, and that was that."[21] Walter Johnson advanced on McNeely's hit, and when he reached second base, "I turned and saw Ruel crossing the plate," he remembered years later. "Tears were in my eyes. We'd won. I'd won. I felt so happy that it didn't seem real."[22]

Epilogue

As soon as Ruel crossed the plate with the winning run, there was an uproar "that must have echoed against the Virginia Hills across the Potomac," chronicled an out-of-town sportswriter.[1] Then a mass of humanity spilled out of the stands, and thousands of wild-eyed fans screamed with glee as they rushed across the field. Spectators who poured out of the bleachers skipped, danced, and turned handsprings of joy. Hats, programs, and seat cushions were hurled into the air. Paper torn to pieces snowed down from the upper deck. And Walter's mom wept tears of joy. "I was never so happy before in all my life," she said. "I knew Walter wouldn't fail Washington."[2] Coolidge cheered as he watched the mad celebration from his box. The Secret Service officers were ready to escort him and his party to his private exit and his motorcade but had to wait. The president wanted to stay and watch the jubilation. After a few minutes, Coolidge left his box and headed for the exit unnoticed.

"Flash: Washington wins," the radio announcer said. Mr. McNeely dropped his notepad. Then came the report about Earl McNeely's single to score Ruel. "We could hardly believe it," said Mrs. McNeely. "Father had to telephone the local newspaper to make certain."[3]

The policemen on duty at Griffith Stadium had their work cut out for them in trying to protect the Washington players and usher them to the safety of the tunnel leading to the clubhouse. The crowd mobbed the players and blocked the tunnel entrance, forcing the officers to use force to clear the way. Earl McNeely, the buttons ripped off his jersey by souvenir hunters and the top half of his jersey torn to shreds, was surrounded. According to a reporter, female fans were screaming and "fighting like wildcats to get near him."[4] Two policemen rushed to the scene, pushed their way through the mob, grabbed McNeely, and guided him to safety. A few men in blue rushed toward second base to rescue Walter Johnson and shield him while he fled to the clubhouse. After Johnson made

191

it to the tunnel and headed through the walkway leading to the Washington clubhouse, he encountered Coolidge, who had just walked through his exit and was on his way to his motorcade. The president passed a pleasant word to the winning pitcher.

Inside the security of the Washington clubhouse, the players cheered, sang, danced, and congratulated Johnson with handshakes and pats on the back. "I'm the happiest man in the world," said Johnson.[5]

"I can't realize that it's over and that we are world champions," Harris announced.[6]

"A great end to a great season, boys," shouted Joe Judge.[7]

"Champions! Hot dog! I can hardly believe it," said Sam Rice.[8]

"I wouldn't trade places with President Coolidge today," said Earl McNeely.[9]

Clark Griffith, unable to refrain from crying, embraced his manager. "I'm certainly proud of you, Bucky boy," he said, and hugged Harris again like a proud father.[10] "I don't know what to say," Griffith told the sportswriters. "The credit goes to Harris and the team. Harris has been wonderful all through the season and his players have been almost as wonderful. That's all I wanted to do for Washington. Win a pennant and World Championship. I am satisfied now."[11] Then Griffith, tears still streaming down his checks, made his way through the clubhouse, shook hands, slapped a few backs, and voiced his congratulations.

As he approached Al Schacht, the Washington third-base coach grinned. "Just a minute, Griff. How about the three hundred?" asked Schacht.

"Good God!" cried Griffith. "You can have it!"[12]

"I can't praise the boys enough," said Harris. "They never quit. When Roger Peckinpaugh had to leave the lineup, a lot of fans probably thought we were done, but we weren't. It was too bad to lose Roger, but Bluege played a fine game in his place."[13]

"Gosh, wouldn't I have liked to be in that game today," said Peckinpaugh. "It was literal agony to sit there, unable to help, when the Giants got into the lead, but I had the wonderful satisfaction of knowing better than the fans could know that the team was never going to give up no matter what the odds. Wasn't Walter great?"[14]

The fans continued to celebrate on the field and search for souvenirs. A man picked up third base, stuck it under his coat, and snuck away. First base and second base were also swiped, and somebody ripped the American flag off the barrier in front of the president's box. Several bats and balls were looted from the Washington dugout, and a few urchins dug their fingernails under home plate and tried to yank it out of the ground but were unsuccessful.

Mrs. Johnson remained in her seat for thirty minutes after Ruel crossed the plate and watched the fans celebrate on the field. "Isn't it wonderful?" she asked and then started to cry again. She got up from her seat and made her way up the aisle and toward the exit. She said she would be heading back home to Coffeyville, Kansas, in the morning. "I am happy I came here," she mentioned.[15]

"We did it! We did it!" Harris shouted when he appeared fresh from his shower. "And Muddy was the boy to make the hit and run that counted. I'm glad for Muddy's sake, for he had not been hitting during the Series. He was saving his hits for when they counted."[16] A few sportswriters trailed Harris as he headed toward his locker. "Did Walter insist on going this afternoon?" a writer asked. "Why do you ask me that?" Harris harshly replied. "The public is anxious to know if Walter felt he could come back after those two defeats," the writer answered. "Walter was my best bet," Harris said while searching for his underwear. "That's why I put him in. Anyone who thought Walter was through was a fool. I knew he was all right."[17] By this time, a large crowd had gathered outside the Washington clubhouse, and they were so loud, their cheers and screams could be heard inside the clubhouse. "We want Walter! We want Walter!" they chanted. "We won't go home until Walter comes out," a fan yelled.[18]

Harris continued to talk to sportswriters. "Most of all I'm happy Walter got into a winning game in this Series," Harris said. "Now he knows how it feels to win a decisive game. He may not come back to us next year. He says he wants to quit and stay out on the coast, probably buying a ball club. Well, be that as it may, he now knows the thrill of being with a World Championship ball club and I feel sure he will remember that next spring and will change his mind about leaving until he has had at least one season with the topmost team in baseball."[19] Johnson would be back and would win twenty games in 1925 with the Senators when they repeated as American League champions.

As the Senators continued to enjoy the moment, there was a loud knock on the clubhouse door, and when Johnson answered, he found Frank Frisch standing in the doorway. "You did wonderful, Walter boy," Frisch said while shaking Johnson's hand. "I'd rather have you beat us than anyone else."[20]

Hank Gowdy also stopped by to congratulate the winning team. "Put it there, scout," he said before shaking Harris's hand. "You sure gave us a fight, and that's what we wanted. It was a great series, wasn't it? Here's hoping that we'll be hooked up again next year."[21] Gowdy also congratulated a few others, including the game's winning pitcher. "Walter, now that we lost, I am truly happy it was you that pitched us out. I shall never regret losing to you."[22]

Irish Meusel, Ross Youngs, and John McGraw also paid a visit to the Washington clubhouse.

"I want to congratulate you, Bucky," McGraw said.

"Thank you, Mr. McGraw," replied Harris, as the two managers clasped hands and pressed hard.[23]

Washington, D.C., reveled in what many said was a greater celebration than the one following the Armistice six years earlier. As downtown crowds climbed into the thousands while darkness descended, small cannons firing, pistol shots, firecrackers, sirens, horns, drums, shouts, and happy fans beating tin pans while marching through the streets were audible throughout the city. Newspapers torn into flakes were released from the upper windows of tall office buildings and fluttered to the streets. Automobiles jammed the blocks from Pennsylvania Avenue to F Street and Ninth to Fourteenth Streets. Where did so many horns and so much confetti come from, someone wanted to know. "How could anyone be angry about anything?" somebody asked. "Everyone was wearing a smile that couldn't come off," wrote a reporter.[24] At the dinner hour, people buzzing with excitement packed every restaurant and café, but they were in no mood to eat. People crowded into theaters and hotel lobbies. They all discussed the great Washington victory in detail—from the time Ogden toed the rubber to begin the game to McNeely's game-winning hit. By this time, people who were at the game began to arrive, and they were asked repeatedly about what they had witnessed. A few white ribbons bearing the words *I told you so* appeared and soon they were everywhere, as if by magic.[25] Street vendors appeared out of nowhere and reaped a harvest. Newspaper boys sold every paper they could get their hands on.

Back at Griffith Stadium, Walter Johnson spoke to the sportswriters. "Tell everyone I'm tickled to death and everything along those lines you can think of," he said. "I'll stand behind everything you say as I can't express my feelings in words at all right now." Johnson then walked over to talk to Harris. "Bucky, I've got to shake your hand again," Johnson said as his eyes began to fill. "Your playing and leadership turned the trick, and I want to thank you for letting me go today."[26] When Johnson finally exited the clubhouse, he was greeted by a huge audience and followed by a seemingly endless stream of humanity to his automobile. "Mrs. Johnson and I slipped away to a quiet little restaurant where I used to eat on Vermont Avenue, and you know that before we were through with our dinner, two hundred telegrams had been delivered there," Johnson said.[27]

Bucky Harris and Mike Martin were the only two remaining in the Washington clubhouse. Harris, still undressed as he stood before a mirror, combed his black hair into a careful part. Martin, worried that the player-manager might drive himself to a nervous breakdown, urged Harris to calm down. "Get away from me, Mike," Harris laughed. "There's nothing the matter with me, but I've just got to blow off steam. You can't blame me for that, can you?"[28]

Later that evening, Harris headed downtown and joined the rest of Washington's citizenry in enjoying the victory. He was riding with a few friends in a taxi when a traffic cop ordered the driver to stop the vehicle. "Only the president can get by here!" bellowed the officer. "I got Bucky Harris in this bus," the driver said. "Why didn't you say so. On your way!"[29] said the policeman, and he let the taxi through. That's when Bucky Harris knew he had reached the top of the baseball world.

Notes

Introduction

1. "Senators Win Championship, Johnson Pitching Team to Victory over Giants, 4–3, in 12 Innings," *New York Times*, 11 October 1924, 1.

2. Frank Young, "Nine Years Ago When Boy Manager Led "'Team of Destiny' to Victory," *Washington Post*, 10 February 1933, 16.

3. Henry W. Thomas, *Walter Johnson: Baseball's Big Train* (Washington, DC: Phenom Press, 1995), 33.

4. Shirley Povich, "Bucky Harris—Chapter Nine," *Washington Post*, 16 January 1939, 14.

Chapter 1

1. "Capital Hails 1924 with Noisy Acclaim," *Washington Post*, 1 January 1924, 1.

2. "Business Reported Good in Most Lines during This Year," *Washington Post*, December 30, 1923, 13.

3. "Sports Due in Time to Supersede Wars," *Washington Evening Star*, 30 December 1923, part 4, page 1.

4. Stanley Harris, *Playing the Game: From Mine Boy to Manager* (New York: Grosset & Dunlap Publishers, 1925), 175.

5. "City Hails New Year; Hotels Filled with Revelers," *Washington Post*, 1 January 1924, 14.

6. Shirley Povich, "Bucky Harris—Chapter Eight," *Washington Post*, 15 January 1939, sec. 4, 1.

7. Harris, *Playing the Game*, 176.

8. Harris, 176.

9. Henry W. Thomas, *Walter Johnson: Baseball's Big Train* (Washington DC: Phenom Press, 1995), 33.

10. Norman Baxter, "In the Press Box," *Washington Post*, 12 February 1924, S-3.

11. Denman Thompson, "'Billy' Richardson Is a Fan as Well as Man of Business," *Washington Star*, 14 December 1919, 26.

12. "Griff Admits He May Be Next Pilot of Nats," *Washington Herald*, 13 December 1923, 1-S.

13. John Dugan, "Peck Is Now Likely to Head Griffs," *Washington Herald*, 18 January 1924, 1-S.

14. Denman Thompson, "Nationals Are Woefully Lacking Infielders," *Washington Evening Star*, 12 March 1924, 28.

15. "Catcher Hargrave and Pitcher Wingfield Sign Contract," *Washington Herald*, 12 January 1924, 18.

16. Henry B. Plant Museum tour audio, Tampa, Florida.

17. Henry Castor, *Teddy Roosevelt and the Rough Riders* (New York: Random House, 1954), 76.

18. Steve Rajtar, *A Guide to Historical Tampa* (Columbia, SC: History Press, 2007).

19. "Pair of Homers Win and Lose It," *Tampa Tribune*, 2 April 1919, 4.

20. "Ruth's Drives Marks Giants to Defeat and Makes Them Drink Too, B'gads," *Tampa Tribune*, 5 April 1919, 10.

21. "Tampa's New Grandstand Described for Benefit of Washington Baseball Fans," *Tampa Tribune*, 15 March 1923, 8-A.

22. "Tampa's New Grandstand."

23. Jack Smiles, *Bucky Harris: A Biography of Baseball's Boy Wonder* (Jefferson, NC: McFarland, 2011), 74.

24. Harris, *Playing the Game*, 174.

25. Povich, "Bucky Harris," sec. 4, 1.

26. "Eddie Collins Admits He Has Been Placed on Market," *Washington Herald*, 11 December 1923, 2-S.

27. "Griffith Unable to Land Collins from White Sox," *Washington Herald*, 12 December 1923, 2-S.

28. "Griffith Unable to Land Collins."

29. "Collins Will Not Be Pilot of Nats," *Washington Herald*, 13 December 1924, 1-S.

30. John Dugan, "Nats Looks Same as Last Year," *Washington Herald*, 29 January 1924, 2-S.

31. John Dugan, "Jack Barry May Be Named to Pilot Washington Club," *Washington Herald*, 31 January 1924, 1-S.

32. Dugan, 1-S.

33. "Barrow Turns Down Job as Washington Manager," *Tampa Tribune*, 7 February 1924, 10A.

34. Harris, *Playing the Game*, 178.

35. Smiles, *Bucky Harris*, 71.

36. Harris, *Playing the Game*, 179.

37. Shirley Povich, *The Washington Senators: An Informal History* (New York: G.P. Putnam's Sons, 1954), 107.

Chapter 2

1. Ray Parmley, "Griff's Manager to Take New Job with Confident Attitude," *Tampa Daily Times*, 10 February 1924, 6; "Stanley Harris Will Manage Washington Senators," *Tampa Tribune*, 10 February 1924, 10-E.

2. Denman Thompson, "Stanley R. Harris Is Named New Manager of Nationals," *Washington Evening Star*, 10 February 1924, pt. 4, 1.

3. Denman Thompson, "On the Sidelines," *Washington Evening Star*, 10 February 1924, pt. 4, 1.

4. Louis Dougher, "Harris Has Yet to Sign Contract as Pilot," *Washington Times*, 10 February 1924, 20.

5. Shirley Povich, "Clark Griffith: Fifty Years in Baseball—Chapter Twenty-Six," *Washington Post*, 10 February 1924, 19.

6. Frank Smith, "Cubs Picked Third and White Sox Fifth, but Expert Has His 'Alibi' Ready," *Chicago Tribune*, 13 April 1924, pt. 2, 1.

7. Louis Dougher, "Harris to Superintend Hot Springs Training," *Washington Times*, 14 February 1924, 24.

8. Thompson, "Stanley R. Harris Is Named."

9. Denman Thompson, "Grind Began by Nationals Rookies," *Washington Evening Star*, 18 February 1924.

10. Denman Thompson, "Harris Is Confident of Success," *Washington Evening Star*, 19 February 1924, 24.

11. Denman Thompson, "Manager Harris Is Confident Nationals Will Be Stronger Than Last Season," *Washington Evening Star*, 10 March 1924, 24.

12. Jack Smiles, *Bucky Harris: A Biography of Baseball's Boy Wonder* (Jefferson, NC: McFarland, 2011), 73.

13. Frank Young, "Nats Get Down to Work at Hot Springs Today," *Washington Post*, 22 February 1924, sec. 2, 3.

14. "Peck Confident Harris Will Succeed as Pilot," *Washington Evening Star*, 26 February 1924, 22.

15. "Walter Johnson Is in Great Trim," *Washington Evening Star*, 23 February 1924, 20.

16. "Walter Johnson Is in Great Trim."

17. "Harris Facing Problem of Filling Right Field," *Washington Evening Star*, 24 February 1924, pt. 4, 1.

18. "Griffs at Hot Springs Not Wasting Any Time," *Washington Evening Star*, 25 February 1924, 26.

19. "Heilmann Not Making Any Rash Predictions," *Washington Evening Star*, 28 February 1924, 30.

20. John Kieran, "Sport of the Times," *New York Times*, 16 February 1927, 21.

21. "Ruth Threatened with Pneumonia," *Washington Herald*, 1 March 1924, 1-S.

22. Denman Thompson, "Nationals Are Woefully Lacking in Infielders," *Washington Evening Star*, 12 March 1924, 28.

23. Thompson.

24. "Plans of Johnson News to Griffith," *Washington Evening Star*, 29 February 1924, 30.

25. Thompson, "Manager Harris Is Confident," 24.

26. Al Schacht, *Clowning through Baseball* (New York: A.S. Barnes and Company, 1941), 103–4.

27. Denman Thompson, "'Tabasco' Shirley Peps Up Tampa Practice," *Washington Star*, 4 March 1924, 24.

28. "Griffs Now Ready for the Real Work," *Washington Herald*, 10 March 1924, 1-S.

29. Schacht, *Clowning through Baseball*, 105–10.

30. John Dugan, "Bush Breaks Nats' Winning Streak," *Washington Herald*, 26 March 1924, 1-S.

31. John Keller, "Harris Seeks More Pep on Coaching Lines," *Washington Star* 29 March 1924, 12.

32. Keller, 12.

33. Keller, 12.

34. John Dugan, "Chesbro Will Act as Scout for Griffmen This Summer," *Washington Herald*, 2 April 1924, 2-S.

35. John Keller, "Goslin Suspended by Manager Harris," *Washington Star*, 8 April 1924, 28.

36. Bryan Morse, "New Infield for Griffmen for Next Year," *Washington Herald*, 17 December 1923, 2-S.

37. Bryan Morse, "Johnson Slated to Pitch His Fifteenth First Game," *Washington Herald*, 15 April 1924, 1-S.

38. Stanley Harris, *Playing the Game: From Mine Boy to Manager* (New York: Grosset & Dunlap Publishers, 1925), 187–88.

39. "Team Will Fight Always—Harris," *Washington Herald*, 15 April 1924, 1-S.

Chapter 3

1. Babe Ruth, "Ruth Sees Better Clubs in Eastern Half," *Washington Times*, 30 April 1924, 15.

2. Bryan Morse, "30,000 See Nationals Defeat Athletics, 4 to 0," *Washington Herald*, 16 April 1924, 1.

3. "25,581 See Johnson Hurl Nats to 4–0 Win in Opener," *Washington Post*, 16 April 1924, 1.

4. John Dugan, "Griffmen Produce First Class," *Washington Herald*, 28 April 1924, 2-S.

5. "Fans Roasting Not Helping Athletics Climb Ladder," *Washington Times*, 31 May 1924, 23.

6. J. G. Taylor Spink, *Judge Landis and Twenty-Five Years of Baseball* (New York: Thomas Y. Crowell Company, 1947), 111.

7. David Fleitz, "Shoeless Joe Jackson," Society for American Baseball Research Bioproject, https://sabr.org/bioproj/person/shoeless-joe-jackson/.

8. "Johnson Hurls Nats to Victory in Opener," *Washington Post*, 16 April 1924, 4.

9. "Johnson Hurls Nats to Victory," 4.

10. "President Watches Walter Blank Macks," *Philadelphia Inquirer*, 16 April 1924, 20.

11. "Altrock Attracted by Coolidge's Curve," *Washington Times*, 16 April 1924, 22.

12. John Dugan, "Elaborate Ceremonies Mark Inaugural in Washington," *Washington Herald*, 15 April 1924, 1-S.

13. "Caught by the Fly," *Washington Evening Star*, 16 April 1924, 28.

14. "President Watches Walter Blank Macks," 20.

15. "Johnson Hurls Nats to Victory," 4.

16. John Dugan, "Freak Delivery Not Solved by Harris and His Players," *Washington Herald*, 16 April 1924, 2-S.

17. Frank Young, "Zahniser's Bone in Eighth Inning Aid to Mackmen," *Washington Post*, 18 April 1924, sect. 2, 1.

18. Miller Huggins, "Manager of Yanks Thinks His Team Is Sure to Repeat," *New York World*, 13 April 1924, 17.

19. "Monitor Sees Another World Series for New York," *New York World*, 13 April 1924, 18.

20. "Harris with Rocky Road Ahead," *New York Times*, 13 April 1924, sec. 10, 4.

21. Will Wedge, "Yankees in Washington Today," *New York Sun*, 19 April 1924, 20.

22. John Dugan, "Nationals Face Campaign with Rosy Prospects," *Washington Herald*, 13 April 1924, 32.

23. Denman Thompson, "Only Yanks and Indians Have Big Edge on Griffs," *Washington Evening Star*, 13 April 1924, pt. 4, 1.

24. Baseball Almanac, www.baseball-alamanac.com; "Sam Rice, Goslin, Marberry Are Merriwells to Auths," *Washington Post*, 11 October 1925, 23.

25. Tim Hagerty, "Joe Martina," Society for American Baseball Research Bioproject, https://sabr.org/bioproj/person/joe-martina/.

26. Louis Dougher, "Mackmen Made Debut at Home in Series with Harris' Hustlers," *Washington Times*, 23 April 1924, 20.

27. Will Wedge, "Ruth's Homer Not Enough," *New York Sun*, 21 April 1924, 28.

28. Babe Ruth, "Babe Ruth First Home Run Is a Big Load off Chest," *Washington Times*, 23 April 1924, 21.

29. Frank Young, "Johnson Leads Nats to Another Victory," *Washington Post*, 21 April 1924, sec. 2, 1.

30. W. B. Hanna, "Ruth's First Circuit Blow Is Wasted," *New York Tribune-Herald*, 21 April 1924, 16.

31. Louis Dougher, "Mackmen Made Debut," 20.

32. Dougher, "Mackmen Made Debut, 20."

33. Dougher, "Mackmen Made Debut. 20."

34. W. B. Hanna, "Concentrated Attack Enables Hugmen to Triumph," *New York Tribune-Herald*, 22 April 1924, 15.

35. Louis Dougher, "Mackmen Made Debut," 20.

36. "Briefs," *New York Tribune-Herald*, 22 April 1924, 15.

37. Denman Thompson, "Marberry to Make Debut in Box Today," *Washington Evening Star*, 23 April 1924, 28.

Chapter 4

1. Louis Dougher, "Looking 'Em Over," *Washington Times*, 23 April 1924, 21.
2. John Foster, "Team's Punch Bolstered by Strand and Simmons," *Washington Evening Star*, 13 March 1924, 30.
3. Thomas Cummiskey, "Mr. Al Simmons of Macks Looks Like a Star," *Washington Herald*, 13 April 1924, 32.
4. Denman Thompson, "Harris's Troubles Begin This Afternoon," *Washington Evening Star*, 16 April 1924, 28.
5. Bob Addie, "Bob Addie's Column," *Washington Post*, 11 August 1923, A-15.
6. "A Tough Ball to Handle, Says Mack," *Philadelphia Inquirer*, 25 April 1924, 22.
7. John Dugan, "Griffs Beat Mackmen by 4 to 3 Count," *Washington Herald*, 25 April 1924, 1-S.
8. Louis Dougher, "Griffs Beating Self, Opines Expert," *Washington Times*, 26 April 1924, 22.
9. John Dugan, "Griffmen Produce First Class," *Washington Herald*, 28 April 1924, 2-S.
10. John Dugan, "Howling Wolves Are Baffled as Nats Pounce on Hurlers," *Washington Herald*, 28 April 1924, 1-S.
11. Louis Dougher, "Mackmen Make Debut at Home in Series with Harris' Hustlers," *Washington Times*, 23 April 1924, 20.
12. John Dugan, "Harris Has Improved Club for Race," *Washington Herald*, 13 April 1924, 1-S.
13. John Dugan, "Nats Open Series with Yankees Today," *Washington Herald*, 1 May 1924, 1-S.
14. Dugan, 1-S.

Chapter 5

1. "Yankees Streak Ended by Senators," *New York Times*, 2 May 1924, 23.
2. John Dugan, "Marberry Rescues Johnson, Holding Huggins' Men Safe," *Washington Herald*, 2 May 1924, 1-S.
3. Babe Ruth, "Ruth Sees Better Clubs in East," *Washington Times*, 30 April 1924, 15.
4. "Caught at the Plate," *New York Times*, 2 May 1924, 23.
5. Will Wedge, "Walter Johnson Talks Ball," *New York Sun*, 5 May 1924, 28.
6. "Rice Hits Home Run Which Beats Yankees," *New York Times*, 3 May 1924, 10.
7. "Yanks Rally in 8th; Beat Senators, 5–4," *New York Times*, 4 May 1924, sec. 10, 1.

8. "Yanks Rally in 8th," sec. 10, 1.

9. Bryan Morse, "Mack's Left-Hander, Meeker, Is Generous to Nationals," *Washington Herald*, 5 May 1924, 2-S.

10. Louis Dougher, "Griffmen Play Minor League Baseball," *Washington Times*, 6 May 1924, 22.

11. Dougher.

12. John Dugan, "Nationals Again Lose to Red Sox," *Washington Herald*, 9 May 1924, 1-S.

Chapter 6

1. Frank Young, "Rally in Eighth Gives Nats Win over Tigers," *Washington Post*, 11 May 1924, S-1.

2. Stanley Harris, *Playing the Game: From Mine Boy to Manager* (New York: Grosset & Dunlap Publishers, 1925), 165.

3. Harry Salsinger, "Ty Cobb Day? Reading Day? Poet Day?" *Detroit News*, 11 May 1924, pt. 4, 1.

4. Harry Salsinger, "34-Year Old Recruit and Youngster Beat Tigers, 3–2," *Detroit News*, 11 May 1924, pt. 4, 1.

5. "Statesmen Laud Cobb at Baseball Banquet," *Washington Evening Star*, 11 May 1924, pt. 4, 1.

6. Harry Salsinger, "Tigers Repeat 1923 Start in East by Losing to Senators," *Detroit News*, 14 May 1924, 38.

7. John Dugan, "Tribe Finds Holes in Griffs Infield," *Washington Herald*, 16 May 1924, 1-S.

8. "Griffith Says White Sox Should Win Series Title," *Washington Evening Star*, 30 August 1919, 8.

9. "'What a Team,' Says Nemo Leibold, Recalling Black Sox Crew of 1919," *Sporting News*, 27 December 1961.

10. "Joe Judge Discloses Tipoff about Black Sox," *Washington Evening Star*, 10 August 1959, A18.

11. Bruce Allandice, "'Playing Rotten, It Ain't That Hard to Do': How the Black Sox Threw the 1920 Pennant." Society for American Baseball Research, https://sabr.org/journal/article/playing-rotten-it-aint-that-hard-to-do-how-the-black-sox-threw-the-1920-pennant/.

12. "Kid Gleason Is Not Discouraged," *Tampa Tribune*, 22 March 1921, 9.

13. James Crusinberry, "Walter Johnson of Old Days Stops Sox with One Hit," *Chicago Tribune*, 24 May 1924, 9.

14. Frank Young, "Doubleheader Will Put Pitchers to Test," *Washington Post*, 1 June 1923, 18.

15. "Meteoric Browns Here to Play Griffs," *Washington Evening Star*, 18 May 1924, pt. 4, 1.

16. Babe Ruth, "Ruth Expects Trouble This Season," *Washington Times*, 21 May 1924, 17.

17. W. B. Hanna, "Champions Win Opener but Take Slam in Second," *New York Herald-Tribune*, 29 May 1924, 14.

18. John Dugan, "Zachary's Win over Yankees Gives Nats Clean Break," *Washington Herald*, 29 May 1924, 1-S.

19. Dugan, "Zachary's Win over Yankees," 1-S.

20. Harris, *Playing the Game*, 194.

Chapter 7

1. Al Schacht, *My Own Particular Screwball* (Garden City, NY: Doubleday, 1955), 158.

2. Schacht, 157.

3. Schacht, 158.

4. Schacht, 158–59.

5. Schacht, 160.

6. Al Schacht, *Clowning through Baseball* (New York: A. S. Barnes and Company, 1941), 81.

7. Schacht, *My Own Particular Screwball*, 161–62.

8. John Dugan, "Griffs Lose More Than Boston Game," *Washington Herald*, May 7, 1924, 1-S.

9. "Griff Pitchers Who Are Aching for a Chance in Big Series," *Washington Evening Star*, 2 October 1924, 28.

10. "Joins Mound Staff of Nationals," *Washington Evening Star*, 24 May 1924, 23.

11. John Dugan, "Ogden, Macks Castoff, Beats Sox, 8–2," *Washington Herald*, May 27, 1924, 2-S.

12. "Mack Expects More Hitting by A's," *Washington Times*, June 2, 1924, 27.

13. "Fans Roasting Not Helping Athletics Climb Ladder," *Washington Times*, 31 May 1924, 14.

14. Harry Salsinger, "Tigers Over-Press Luck and Draw Penalty," *Detroit News*, 4 June 1924, 37.

15. "Tom Zachary Holds Tigers as Nationals Win, 11–1," *Washington Herald*, 4 June 1924, 1-S.

16. Salsinger, "Tigers Over-Press Luck," 37.

17. John Dugan, "Nationals Beaten by Tigers in Tenth," *Washington Herald*, 5 June 1924, 2-S.

18. Louis Dougher, "Looking 'Em Over," *Washington Times*, 6 June 1924, 16.

19. Dougher, 16.

20. "Johnson Faces Jungleers in final," *Washington Times*, 6 June 1924, 22.

21. Ford Frick, "Teach Boys to Play Is Advice of Yankee," *Washington Times*, 7 June 1924, 18.

22. John Keller, "Nationals Slide a Notch in Flag Race," *Washington Evening Star*, 16 June 1924, 27.

23. Irving Vaughn, "Sox Cop 9–8 Win," *Chicago Tribune*, 17 June 1924, 25.

24. Thomas, *Walter Johnson: Baseball's Big Train* (Washington DC: Phenom Press, 1995), 197.

25. Larry Woltz, "Senators and Umpire Beat White Sox," *Chicago Herald and Examiner*, 19 June 1924, 13.

26. John Keller, "Griffs Prove Consistent '50-50' Team," *Washington Evening Star*, 20 June 1924, 30.

27. John Keller, "Marberry Proving Star as Rescuer," *Washington Evening Star*, 21 June 1924, 8.

28. Louis Dougher, "Griffmen Making Fight to Stay up around League Top," *Washington Times*, 22 June 1924, 18.

29. "Johnson Too Much for Mackmen, Who Lose 6th Straight," *Philadelphia Inquirer*, 22 June 1924, 17.

Chapter 8

1. Ford Frick, "Walter Johnson Will Face Yankees in Third Game," *Washington Times*, 24 June 1924, 20.

2. "Caught at the Plate," *New York Times*, 4 May 1924, sec. 10, 2.

3. Al Schacht, *My Own Particular Screwball* (Garden City, NY: Doubleday, 1955), 115.

4. "Griffs Consistent with Yankees for Lead," *Washington Evening Star*, 23 June 1924, 22.

5. Louis Dougher, "Griffmen Making Fight to Stay up around League Top," *Washington Times*, 23 June 1924, 18.

6. Dougher, 18.

7. "Griffs Consistent with Yankees for Lead," 22.

8. "Griffs Consistent with Yankees for Lead," 22.

9. "Griffs Consistent with Yankees for Lead," 22.

10. Babe Ruth, "Ruth Realizes Yankees Are in Precarious Circumstances," *Washington Times*, 25 June 1924, 19.

11. Frick, "Walter Johnson Will Face Yankees," 20.

12. W. B. Hanna, "Yankees Lose Twice and Fall to Second Place," *New York Herald-Tribune*, 24 June 1924, 20.

13. "All of D.C. Enthused as Nationals Rise," *Washington Evening Star*, 25 June 1924, 1.

14. "Johnson to Be Ready to face A's Tomorrow," *Washington Evening Star*, 25 June 1924, 30.

15. John Keller, "To Seek Final from Yanks Today to Stay in Front," *Washington Evening Star*, 25 June 1924, 30.

16. Joseph Rogers, "Eighth Straight Victory Recorded by Harris Club," *Washington Herald*, 25 June 1924, 1-S.

17. Rogers, 1-S.

18. "Yanks Lose in 10th; Senators in Lead," *New York Times*, 25 June 1924, 18.

19. Will Wedge, "Griffith Elated over Team," *New York Sun*, 25 June 1924, 37.

20. Schacht, *My Own Particular Screwball*, 168.

21. "Ruth's Homer Fails to Check Senators," *New York Times*, 26 June 1924, 27.

22. John Keller, "Griffs Face Real Test at Long Stay at Home," *Washington Evening Star*, 26 June 1924, 30.

23. "Ruth's Homer Fails to Check Senators," 27.

24. "Caught at the Plate," *New York Times*, 26 June 1924, 27.

25. Louis Dougher, "Looking 'Em Over," *Washington Times*, 26 June 1924, 24.

26. "Fans Accord Nationals a Noisy Welcome at Home," *Washington Evening Star*, 26 June 1924, 30.

27. Arthur Knapp, "Washington Team Given Tumultuous Welcome by 8,000," *Washington Post*, 26 June 1924, S-1.

28. John Dugan, "Harris All Smiles on Return Home in First Place," *Washington Herald*, 26 June 1924, 2-S.

29. Knapp, "Washington Team Given Tumultuous Welcome," S-1.

30. Shirley Povich, "Happy and Tough to Beat Is Harris's Picture of Nats Sentiments," *Washington Post*, 26 June 1924, S-1.

31. Francis Daily, "30,000 Rabid Nats Fans Jam Stadium for Baseball Holiday," *Washington Herald*, 27 June 1924, 1-S.

32. Daily, 1-S.

33. Daily, 1-S.

34. Harry Stringer, "Fans Enjoy Thrill of Leading League," *Washington Post*, 27 June 1924, S-4.

35. Denman Thompson, "Nationals Boost Margin of Lead in Race," *Washington Evening Star*, 29 June 1924, pt. 4, 1.

36. Louis Dougher, "DeWolf Hopper Tonight Honor Griffmen with 'Casey at the Bat,'" *Washington Evening Star*, 30 June 1924, 25.

37. Calvin Coolidge, *The Autobiography of Calvin Coolidge* (Chatsworth, CA: The National Notary Association, 1955), 173–77.

38. John Dugan, "Zahniser Blanks Boston, 5 to 0," *Washington Herald*, 3 July 1924, 1-S.

Chapter 9

1. Babe Ruth, "Griffmen Are Second Choice of Ruth to Win Pennant," *Washington Times*, 4 July 1924, 15.

2. Harry Cross, "Yankees Get New Thrill at Midseason," *Washington Times*, 7 July 1924, 16.

3. Babe Ruth, "Must Create Breaks of Game, Says Ruth," *Washington Times*, 5 July 1924, 14.

4. Al Schacht, *My Own Particular Screwball* (Garden City, NY: Doubleday, 1955), 166–67.

5. Babe Ruth, "Babe Ruth Is Puzzled by Pennant Fight," *Washington Times*, 9 July 1924, 16.

6. "Yankees Break Even and Fail to Advance," *New York Times*, 6 July 1924, 23.

7. "Caught at the Plate," *New York Times*, 10 July 1924, 16.

8. "Yankees Split with Senators, Winning 2–0 and Losing 7–2," *New York Tribune-Herald*, 6 July 1924, C1.

9. "Yankees Break Even," 23.

10. "Yankees Break Even," 23.

11. "Yanks' Four in 9th Beat Senators, 7–4," *New York Times*, 7 July 1924, 13.

12. "Yanks' Four in 9th," 13.

13. Babe Ruth, "Yankees Sigh Relief as They Near Top Rung," *Washington Times*, 7 July 1924, 16.

14. Louis Dougher, "Yankees Win Heartbreaker in Final," *Washington Times*, 7 July 1924, 1-S.

15. "Error Paves Way to Hugmen's Winning Rally," *New York Tribune-Herald*, 7 July 1924, 12.

16. "Western Telegram," dated July 7, 1924, sent to Mrs. Hills. On file at the Calvin Coolidge Presidential Library and Museum, Northampton, MA.

17. John Keller, "Tigers Hope to Hammer Way to Championship," *Washington Evening Star*, 10 March 1924, 24.

18. John Foster, "Cobb Annoyed by Deafness of Rival Pilots," *Washington Evening Star*, 27 December 1924, 24.

19. "Bush Sorry Friendship Has Crept into Baseball," *St. Paul Pioneer Press*, 3 May 1935, 12.

20. Shirley Povich, *The Washington Senators: An Informal History* (New York, NY: G.P. Putnam's Sons, 1954), 114.

21. Louis Dougher, "Taylor Will Remember His First Chance in Major Leagues," *Washington Times*, 10 July 1924, 20.

22. Louis Dougher, "Looking 'Em Over," *Washington Times*, 8 August 1924, 12.

23. Dougher, "Taylor Will Remember," 20.

24. Harry Salsinger, "Earl Whitehill's Wildness Costs Detroit Double Victory," *Detroit News*, 11 July 1924, 34.

25. John Dugan, "Tigers Defeat and Tie Nationals," *Washington Herald*, 11 July 1924, 1-S.

26. John Keller, "Griff Have Five Games with Tribe in Four Days," *Washington Evening Star*, 11 July 1924, 20.

27. Salsinger, "Earl Whitehill's Wildness," 34.

28. Salsinger, 34.

29. Louis Dougher, "Looking 'Em Over," *Washington Times*, 14 July 1924, 21.

30. Harry Salsinger, "Tigers Blunder on Bases Is Turned into Victory," *Detroit News*, 12 July 1924, 12.

31. John Dugan, "Nationals Lose Final to Tigers," *Washington Herald*, 12 July 1924, 1-S.

32. Stuart Bell, *Cleveland Plain Dealer*, 13 July 1924, 1-D.

33. Louis Dougher, "Manager Harris May Be Suspended Today," *Washington Times*, 14 July 1924, 21.

34. "Here's Lowdown on Harris Run-in with Umps during Fray," *Washington Herald*, 14 July 1924, 1-S.

35. "Harris Made Goat of Umpire's Decision," *Washington Herald*, 15 July 1924, 2-S.

36. John Keller, "Ogden's Shift Brings Form Reversal," *Washington Evening Star*, 15 July 1924, 30.

Chapter 10

1. John Foster, "His Work at First Base Unhurt by Faulty Vision," *Washington Evening Star*, 15 March 1924, 23.

2. "Sisler Sure of Playing with Team," *Washington Herald*, 4 March 1924, 2-S.

3. "Impairment of Sight Was a Blow to Sisler," *Washington Post*, 14 April 1924, S-1.

4. "Matthews to Return to Griff Lineup," *Washington Evening Star*, 14 July 1924, 24.

5. Norman Baxter, "In the Press Box," *Washington Post*, 17 July 1924, S-3.

6. Louis Dougher, "Looking 'Em Over," *Washington Times*, 14 July 1924, 21.

7. Dougher, 21.

8. John Foster, "Scott Expected to Help Bucks at Bat," *Washington Evening Star*, 21 July 1924, 22.

9. Frank Young, "Browns Rally in Ninth to Ring Up 7 to 6 Victory," *Washington Post*, 19 July 1924, S-1.

10. John Dugan, "Umps Misinterpret Ground Rule When Harris Hits Homer," *Washington Herald*, 20 July 1924, 1-S.

11. Frank Young, "Griffith Will Protest Browns 16-Inning Victory," *Washington Post*, 20 July 1924, S-1.

12. Frank Young, "Washington Win Final of Series from St. Louis," *Washington Post*, 21 July 1924, S-1.

13. Young, 21.

14. Babe Ruth, "Anybody's Pennant, Bambino Says," *Washington Times*, 13 July 1924, 16.

15. "Caught at the Plate," *New York Times*, 9 July 1924, 16.

16. Joe Villa, "Setting the Pace," *New York Sun*, 13 September 1924, 16.

17. "Yanks Regain Lead as Ruth Hits No. 29," *New York Times*, 24 July 1924, 8.

18. Fred Lieb, "Mr. Cobb May Be Biting Hand That Feeds Him," *Washington Times*, 25 July 1924, 11.

19. "Yanks Regain Lead," 8.

20. "Yanks Beaten, 6–5; Lose Lead," *New York Times*, 25 July 1924, 9.

21. Wilton Farnsworth, "Farnsworth," *Washington Herald*, 28 July 1924, 2-S.

22. Bert Walker, "Favored by Schedule, Tigers Should Win, Declares Cobb," *Washington Times*, 25 July 1924, 16.

23. Stuart Bell, "Sherry Smith Turns In Best Hurling of Year," *Cleveland Plain-Dealer*, 27 July 1924, 1-D.

24. Frank Young, "Harrismen again Tied with Yanks for Second Place," *Washington Post*, 28 July 1924, S-1.

25. Frank Young, 'Washington Loses Final Game of Indians Series," *Washington Post*, 30 July 1924, S-1.

26. John Keller, "Nationals Open Series with Tigers Tomorrow," *Washington Evening Star*, 29 July 1924, 19.

27. "Caught on the Fly," *Washington Evening Star*, 30 July 1924, 28.

28. "Caught on the Fly," *Washington Evening Star*, 31 July 1924, 30.

29. Frank Young, "Washington within Half Game of Lead," *Washington Post*, 1 August 1924, S-1.

Chapter 11

1. Norman Baxter, "In the Press Box," *Washington Post*, 5 August 1924, S-3.

2. "Griffs Expect Much of Earl McNeely, Outfielder," *Washington Herald*, 5 August 1924, 1-S.

3. Shirley Povich, *The Washington Senators* (New York: Putnam, 1954), 115.

4. Louis Dougher, "Brownies Win Griff Leader's Respect," *Washington Times*, 5 August 1924, 14.

5. "Griffith Confident Johnson to Grant Protest of Contest," *Washington Post*, 6 August 1924, S-1.

6. "Pickups and Putouts," *New York Times*, 9 July 1925, 15.

7. Frank Young, "St. Louis Takes First of Series with Harrismen," *Washington Post*, 4 August 1924, S-1.

8. Babe Ruth, "Ruth Says Yankees Are on Way to Another Flag," *Washington Times*, 6 August 1924, 19.

9. Harry Salsinger, "Whitehill Stops Ruth and Tigers Win First Game," *Detroit News*, 22 July 1924, 26.

10. John Dugan, "Griff and Harris Confident Team Will Resume Winning," *Washington Herald*, 7 August 1924, 1-S.

11. Louis Dougher, "Looking 'Em Over," *Washington Times*, 5 August 1924, 15.

12. Heinie Miller, "Sports on Sports," *Washington Herald*, 8 August 1924, 1.

13. Dugan, "Griff and Harris Confident," 1-S.

14. Frank Young, "Johnson's Hurling Wins Opening Game from Eversmen," *Washington Post*, 8 August 1924, S-1.

15. Shirley Povich, "Clark Griffith 50 Years in Baseball: Chapter Twenty-Six," *Washington Post*, 10 February 1938, 19.

16. Povich, *The Washington Senators*, 115.

17. Frank Young, "Griffith Offers $5,000 to Retain Wid Matthews," *Washington Post*, 10 August 1924, S-1.

18. Louis Dougher, "Sparky Totters Twixt Majors and Minors," *Washington Times*, 9 August 1924, 12.

19. John Dugan, "Spark Plug Wid Matthews Goes to Coast After All," *Washington Herald*, 11 August 1924, 1-S.

20. John Dugan, "Nats Take First Game from Indians," *Washington Herald*, 13 August 1924, 1-S.

21. Denman Thompson, "Harris Sure McNeely Will Make Good Here," *Washington Evening Star*, 13 August 1924, 26.

22. Frank Young, "Nats Beat Indians," *Washington Post*, 15 August 1924, S-1.

23. Frank Young, "Cobbmen Take Series Opener from Nats, 5 to 2," *Washington Post*, 17 August 1924, S-1.

24. Frank Young, "Johnson Hurls Nats to 6 to 1 Win over Tigers," *Washington Post* 18 August 1924, S-1.

25. "Johnson's 8–1 Win Keeps Bucks on Heels of Tigers," *Washington Evening Star*, 18 August 1924, 19.

26. Frank Young, "Nats Win Twin Ball and Go Back to Second Place," *Washington Post*, 20 August 1924, S-3.

27. "Here's Evidence Griff Has Some Flag Hopes," *Washington Evening Star*, 25 July 1924, 18.

28. "Yanks Lose in 12th to Tigers, 8–6," *New York Times*, 23 August 1924, 6.

29. Frank Young, "Zach's Spell over Sox Still Not Working," *Washington Post*, 25 August 1924, S-1.

30. Louis Dougher, "Matthews Shines on Coast for Sacramento," *Washington Times*, 23 August 1924, 13.

31. "Notes of the Nats," *Washington Post*, 27 August 1924, S-3.

32. Frank Young, "Nats Forced Back in Race on Eve of Yankees Series," *Washington Post*, 28 August 1924, S-1.

33. John Dugan, "Nationals Lose to Browns in Eleventh," *Washington Herald*, 28 August 1924, 1-S.

Chapter 12

1. Louis Dougher, "Looking 'Em Over," *Washington Times*, 28 August 1924, 16.

2. Ford Frick, "Fighting Spirit Regains Lead for Senators," *New York Evening Journal*, 29 August 1924, 15.

3. John Dugan, "Nats Confident of Victory in Pennant Race," *Washington Herald*, 31 August 1924, 3-S.

4. "Yankees Lose Lead; Ruth Hits 2 Homers," *New York Times*, 29 August 1924, 7.

5. Frick, "Fighting Spirit Regains Lead," 15.

6. "Yankees Lose Lead," 7.

7. "Yankees Lose Lead," 7.

8. Frank Young, "Nats Beat Yankees by 8-Run Rally and Go into Lead," *Washington Post*, 29 August 1924, S-1.

9. Sam Crane, "Diamond Dust," *New York Evening Journal*, 30 August 1924, 15.

10. Crane, 15.

11. "Yankees Again Lose to Senators, 5–1," *New York Times*, 30 August 1924, 5.

12. John Keller, "Bucks Seek Third in a Row over Hugmen," *Washington Evening Star*, 30 August 1924, 19.

13. Louis Dougher, "Looking 'Em Over," *Washington Times*, 4 September 1924, 20.

14. Louis Dougher, "Looking 'Em Over," *Washington Times*, 30 August 1924, 13.

15. Frank Young, "Yankees Nose Out Griffmen in Ninth," *Washington Post*, 31 August 1924, 1.

16. Frank Young, "45,000 Fans See Nationals Capture Final Game from Yankees," *Washington Post*, 1 September 1924, 1.

17. "Caught at the Plate," *New York Times*, 1 September 1924, 10.

18. Louis Dougher, "Looking 'Em Over," *Washington Times*, 1 September 1924, 16.

19. Young, "45,000 Fans," 1.

20. John Kieran, "Senators Down Yankees in 10-Inning Battle, 4–2," *New York Tribune-Herald*, 1 September 1924, 9.

21. Dougher, "Looking 'Em Over," 16.

22. "Griffs Receive Warm Welcome," *Washington Herald*, 1 September 1924, 2-S.

23. "10,000 Fans Greet Victorious Nationals," *Washington Herald*, 1 September 1924, 1.

24. "Harris and His Men Get Big Reception upon Arrival Home," *Washington Post*, 1 September 1924, S-1.

25. "Harris and His Men."

26. "10,000 Fans," 1.

27. John Dugan, "Fighting Nats Take Two from Macks before Record Throngs," *Washington Herald*, 2 September 1924, 2-S.

28. J. H. Keen, "Miss Washington Throws Out First Ball at Matinee Game," *Washington Herald*, 2 September 1924, 1-S.

29. Frank Young, "Nats and Red Sox to Battle Today," *Washington Post*, 4 September 1924, S-1.

30. John Dugan, "Johnson Hurls His Farewell Game," *Washington Herald*, 5 September 1924, 1-S.

31. Frank Young, "Nats Beat Fohlmen," *Washington Post*, 5 September 1924, S-1.

32. "Notes of the Nats," *Washington Post*, 5 September 1924, S-3.

33. Dougher, "Looking 'Em Over," 20.

34. John Dugan, "Mogridge Will Face Ehmke Today," *Washington Herald*, 6 September 1924, 1-S.

35. Babe Ruth, "Ruth Never Saw Yankees Fall Down So Badly," *Washington Times*, 1 September 1924, 16.

36. Frank Young, "Mogridge Pitches for Nats against Fohl Nine Today," *Washington Post*, 6 September 1924, S-1.

37. "Yanks Fear Western Clubs May Assist Griff Triumph," *Washington Times*, 7 September 1924, 13.

38. Louis Dougher, "Griffs to Battle Macks in Four Contests," *Washington Times*, 8 September 1924, 12.

39. John Dugan, "Griffmen Lose, League Standing Unchanged," *Washington Herald*, 8 September 1924, 1.

Chapter 13

1. Louis Dougher, "Griff Gives Bucky Full Credit for Triumph," *Washington Times*, 25 September 1924, 20.

2. Lawrence S. Ritter, *The Glory of Their Times* (New York: Macmillan, 1966), 151.

3. Lee Poe Hart, "Johnson Visualizes Self on Mound in Series," *Washington Herald*, 8 September 1924, 1-S.

4. John Dugan, "Nationals Resume Chase after Flag with Red Sox," *Washington Herald*, 6 September 1924, 1-S.

5. Louis Dougher, "Looking 'Em Over," *Washington Times*, 9 September 1924, 12.

6. "Ruth Knocks 44th Homer while Bush Puzzles Red Sox," *Washington Post*, 9 September 1924, S-1.

7. Gordon McKay, "'Old Fox' Says Senators Will Gallop Away with Flag," *Philadelphia Inquirer*, 10 September 1924, 20.

8. S. O. Grauley, "Senators Share with Mackmen," *Philadelphia Inquirer*, 11 September 1924, 18.

9. Louis Dougher, "Hometown Gang Gives Bucky Big Reception," *Washington Times*, 12 September 1924, 20.

10. "Johnson Deeply Feels the Honor Paid to Him," *Washington Evening Star*, 14 September 1924, pt. 4, 1.

11. Frank Young, "Johnson Hangs Up His Twenty-First Victory of Season," *Washington Post*, 14 September 1924, S-1.

12. John Dugan, "Nationals Defeat Detroit, 6–4," *Washington Herald*, 14 September 1924, 1.

13. Louis Dougher, "Harris Shows Ability in Wrangle over Zach," *Washington Times*, 15 September 1924, 18.

14. Dougher, 18.

15. "Shaute's Injury Lucky Break for Griffs," *Washington Times*, 16 September 1924, 16.

16. Louis Dougher, "Indians Appear Easier for Griffmen Than Browns for Yankees," *Washington Times*, 16 September 1924, 16.

17. "Shaute's Injury Lucky Break," 16.

18. Stuart Bell, "Senators Defeat Indians, 6 to 2, and Take First Place," *Cleveland Plain-Dealer*, 17 September 1924, 18.

19. Dent McSkimming, "Huggins Thinks St. Louis-Washington Series Key to Pennant," *St. Louis Post-Dispatch*, 19 September 1924, 44.

20. "Yankees Lose in 9th; Fall Back in Race," *New York Times*, 20 September 1924, 10.

21. Dent McSkimming, "Nationals Play Poorly but Regain Lead," *St. Louis Post-Dispatch*, 20 September 1924, 6.

22. Al Schacht, *My Own Particular Screwball* (Garden City, NY: Doubleday, 1955), 168.

23. Frank Young, "Marberry Tosses Away Griff's Game in Last of Tenth," *Washington Post*, 21 September 1924, 1.

24. Louis Dougher, "Dolan Sent by Giants to Spot Griffs," *Washington Times*, 22 September 1924, 18.

25. Larry Woltz, "Griffs Trim Sox," *Chicago Herald and Examiner*, 23 September 1924, 15.

26. Louis Dougher, "Harris Sees His Team in Pennant by Saturday Night," *Washington Times*, 25 September 1924, 20.

27. James O'Leary, "Senators Hopeful of Victory," *Boston Globe*, 26 September 1924, 16.

28. John Keller, "Three Wins and the Flag," *Washington Evening Star*, 27 September 1924, 21.

29. James O'Leary, "Red Sox Defeat Senators, 2–1," *Boston Globe*, 27 September 1924, 8.

30. Frank Young, "Griffmen Beat by Red Sox, 2–1," *Washington Post*, 27 September 1924, 1.

31. Burton Whitman, "American League Race Gets Closer as Red Sox Beat Washington, 2 to 1," *Boston Herald*, 27 September 1924, 1.

32. Whitman, 1.

33. Burton Whitman, "Senators Stumble into 7 to 5 Victory," *Boston Herald*, 28 September 1924, B-5.

34. "Boston Fans Cheer Nats on to Victory," *Washington Post*, 28 September 1924, S-1.

35. Louis Dougher, "Cows and Chickens Aid Griff Vets to Relax," *Washington Times*, 29 September 1924, 18.

36. Frank Young, "Harris Sees Little Trouble in Taking One from Red Sox," *Washington Post*, 29 September 1924, S-1.

37. John Dugan, "'Zach' Promises to Clinch Flag Today," *Washington Herald*, 29 September 1924, 1-S.

38. "The Old Sports Musings," *Philadelphia Inquirer*, 29 September 1924, 18.

39. John Dugan, "Griffith Gives Full Credit to 'Little Scrap Iron,'" *Washington Herald*, 29 September 1924, 2-S.

Chapter 14

1. Irving Vaughan, "Senators Step over Red Sox to First Title, 4–2," *Chicago Tribune*, 30 September 1924, 19.

2. Louis Dougher, "Cows and Chickens Aid Griff Vets to Relax," *Washington Times*, 29 September 1924, 18.

3. Frank Young, "15,000 Boston Fans Cheer Nats as Game Ends in Big Victory," *Washington Post*, 30 September 1924, 2.

4. Young, 2.

5. Louis Dougher, "Marberry Wipes Out St. Louis Blunder Is Happiest Griff," *Washington Times*, 30 September 1924, 20.

6. Paul Shannon, "Walter Johnson to Hurl Today," *Boston Post*, 26 September 1924, 16.

7. "Thousands in Rain Shout with Joy as Team Romps Home," *Washington Post*, 30 September 1924, S-1.

8. "Rejoicing Capital Banishes Gloom as Griffmen Win," *Washington Evening Star*, 30 September 1924, 2.

9. Burton Whitman, "Washington Clinches A.L. Pennant by 4 to 2 Victory," *Boston Herald*, 30 September 1924, 16.

10. Whitman, 16.

11. John Dugan, "Players Weep for Joy When Victory Gives Them Banner," *Washington Herald*, 30 September 1924, 1.

12. John Dugan, "Tears in Eyes of Happy Vets," *Washington Herald*, 30 September 1924, 1-S.

13. "Debonaire Capital Delirious over Victory of Senators," *Boston Herald*, 30 September 1924, 16.

14. "Capital Still Excited," *New York Times*, 1 October 1924, 1.

15. "Mack and Huggins Wish Harris Luck," *Philadelphia Inquirer*, 30 September 1924, 18.

16. Al Schacht, *Clowning through Baseball* (New York: A. S. Barnes and Company, 1941), 83.

17. "Harris and Griffith Due in Washington Today," *Washington Post*, 30 September 1924, S-3.

18. Stanley Woodward, "Harris, Griffith and Johnson Look Ahead to World Series," *Boston Herald*, 30 September 1924, 16.

19. Louis Dougher, "Marberry Wipes Out St. Louis Blunder," 20.

20. Frank Young, "Griffmen Defeat Red Sox, 4–2, as Rain Routes Yanks," *Washington Post*, 30 September 1924, 1.

21. Woodward, "Harris, Griffith and Johnson," 16.

22. "Bucks Will Win, Declares Griffith," *Washington Evening Star*, 1 October 1924, 2.

23. Arthur Knapp, "Quartet of Nats Greeted by Fans upon Arrival," *Washington Post*, 1 October 1924, S-4.

24. "Judge Landis Arrives in Washington Today," *Washington Post*, 1 October 1924, 1.

25. "Sam Rice, Goslin, Marberry Are Merriwells to Auths," *Washington Post*, 12 October 1925, pt. 4, 1.

26. J. G. Taylor Spink, *Judge Landis and Twenty-Five Years of Baseball* (New York: Thomas Y. Crowell, 1947), 130.

27. Spink, 132.

28. "O'Connell, Confessing, Says He Is 'Goat' in Bribery Plot," *Washington Evening Star*, 2 October 1924, 2.

29. *New York Herald-Tribune*, 1 January 1925. Article from the Cozy Dolan file, Giamatti Research Center, Cooperstown, New York,

30. *New York Herald-Tribune*.

31. *New York Herald-Tribune*.

32. Spink, *Judge Landis*, 133.

33. Universal Service, "O'Connell Confesses Offering $500 to Throw Game," *Washington Herald*, 2 October 1924, 1.

34. "O'Connell Says He Thought All Were in on Scheme," *Washington Evening Star*, 2 October 1924, 1.

35. "District to Pay Homage to Victorious Team in Big Parade," *Washington Post*, 1 October 1924, 1.

36. "Washington Is Exceedingly Happy over What President Says in Welcoming Team," *Washington Post*, 2 October 1924, 1.

37. "Washington Is Exceedingly Happy," 1.

38. "Coolidge's Address," *Washington Herald*, 2 October 1924, 2.

39. "Washington Is Exceedingly Happy," 1.

40. "Coolidge's Address," 2.

41. "Big Banquet Ends Day's Celebration," *Washington Post*, 3 October 1924, 2.

42. "Harris and McGraw Issue Statements on Eve of Big Classic," *Washington Post*, 3 October 1924, S-1.

43. "Harris and McGraw Issue Statements," S-1.

44. "Former Griffs Pilots Here for Series," *Washington Times*, 3 October 1924, 24.

45. "Nats Stars Are Heard via Radio," *Washington Times*, 3 October 1924, 3.

46. "Bucky Harris Does Bat Swinging in Front of Mirror," *Washington Post*, 4 October 1924, S-4.

47. Mrs. Walter Johnson, "Public's Inspiring Support Will Help Nats' Victory," *Washington Post*, 4 October 1924, S-3.

48. "Frisch Says Walter Hasn't Got Goats of Giants," *Washington Times*, 2 October 1924, 22.

49. "Harris Expects Series to Go 6 Games," *Washington Times*, 4 October 1924, 2.

50. "Frisch Will Be Seen at Second Base for Giants," *Washington Post*, 1 October 1924, S-3.

51. Walter Johnson, "Walter Keen for Opening Battle," *Washington Times*, 4 October 1924, 1.

Chapter 15

1. Damon Runyon, "Giants Win Opener, 4-3," *Washington Herald*, 5 October 1924, 1.

2. "'Did My Best, No Excuses,' Johnson Says after Game," *Washington Evening Star*, 5 October 1924, pt. 1, 5.

3. "Washington Fans Give Johnson a Car," *New York Times*, 5 October 1924, 29.

4. "Admirers Give Autos to Johnson and Peck," *Washington Post*, 5 October 1924, S-3.

5. "President Takes Place among Fans," *Washington Evening Star*, 5 October 1924, pt. 1, 3.

6. "Coolidge's Cheers for 'Home Team,'" *New York Times*, 5 October 1924, 1.

7. Norman Baxter, "Circuit Drives by Kelly and Terry Give New York Hard-Fought First Contest," *Washington Post*, 5 October 1924, 1.

8. John Dugan, "Nationals Show Plenty of Fight," *Washington Herald*, 5 October 1924, 3-S.

9. "Harris Has No Alibi; Expects Victory Today," *Washington Herald*, 5 October 1924, pt. 1, 2.

10. Roger Peckinpaugh, "Peckinpaugh Says Breaks Gave Giants Victory," *Washington Herald*, 5 October 1924, 2-S.

11. "40,000 Fans, Including Coolidge, See Giants Defeat Senators," *New York Times*, 5 October 1924, 28.

12. "Sorry Friends Disappointed, Says Johnson," *Washington Herald*, 5 October 1924, 2.

13. "Harris Believes His Team Destined for World Title," *Washington Evening Star*, 5 October 1924, pt. 1, 1.

14. "'Tough Break' for Johnson, Says McGraw," *Washington Herald*, 5 October 1924, 2.

15. "Harris Believes His Team Destined," pt. 1, 1.

16. "Harris Has No Alibi; Expects Victory Today," *Washington Herald*, 5 October 1924, pt. 1, 2.

17. "'Did My Best, No Excuses,'" pt. 1, 5.

18. "'Did My Best, No Excuses,'" pt. 1, 5.

19. "'Did My Best, No Excuses,'" pt. 1, 5.

20. "Washington Defeats in Second Game and Evens Series," *New York Times*, 6 October 1924, 14.

21. "Washington Defeats."

22. "Washington Defeats."

23. "Washington Defeats."

24. Damon Runyon, "As Runyon Saw Griffs' Second Game Win over Giants," *Washington Herald*, 6 October 1924, 26.

25. Walter Johnson, "Johnson Sure of 7 Games in Series," *Washington Times*, 6 October 1924, 1.

26. Johnson, 1.

27. Louis Dougher, "Marberry and Ogden Ready to Hop on McGraw's Giants," *Washington Times*, 6 October 1924, 16.

Chapter 16

1. "Giants Win, 6–4; Crowd Sets Record for Polo Grounds," *New York Times*, 7 October 1924, 1.
2. "Giants Win, 6–4," 1.
3. "Interviews with Nationals Give Their Views of Game," *Washington Post*, 7 October 1924, 2.
4. "Giants Win Cheers from Hostile Fans," *New York Times*, 7 October 1924, 17.
5. "Peck's Leg Baked; He May Play Today," *Washington Herald*, 7 October 1924, 1.
6. "Injury May Keep Peck Idle," *New York Times*, 7 October 1924, 17.
7. "Peck's Leg Baked," 1.
8. Damon Runyon, "Foes Halted by Marberry, as Mogridge Slips in 8th," *Washington Herald*, 8 October 1924, 1.
9. "45,000 Howling Fans See New York Game," *Washington Evening Star*, 6 October 1924, 1.
10. Louis Dougher, "Looking 'Em Over," *Washington Times*, 9 October 1924, 20.
11. Frank Graham, "Babe Grumbles at His Record," *New York Sun*, 14 May 1927, 17.
12. Damon Runyon, "Left-Hander Holds Giants," *Washington Herald*, 8 October 1924, 4.
13. Runyon, "Left-Hander Holds Giants," 4.
14. Denman Thompson, "Johnson Chosen to Capture Fifth," *Washington Evening Star*, 8 October 1924, 1.
15. Roger Peckinpaugh, "'Giant Pitcher Won Great Game,'" *Washington Herald*, 8 October 1924, 2-S.
16. Runyon, "Left-Hander Holds Giants," 4.
17. "Nehf May Not Hurl Again in the Series," *New York Times*, 8 October 1924, 13.
18. Frank Frisch, "'Mogridge Had Us Fooled,' Says Frisch," *Washington Herald*, 8 October 1924, 1-S.
19. "Senators Morale at a High Pitch," *New York Times*, 8 October 1924, 13.
20. John Keller, "'Looks Pretty Good Now,' Harris Declares," *Washington Evening Star*, 8 October 1924, 27.
21. Louis Dougher, "Harris to Rely on Speed King," *Washington Times*, 8 October 1924, 1.
22. "Johnson Too Eager to Win to Justify Friends, Says Wife," *Washington Post*, 8 October 1924, 2.
23. Robert Small, "New Yorkers Expected Johnson to Be Victorious," *Washington Evening Star*, 9 October 1924, 26.
24. Denman Thompson, "'Johnson Chosen to Capture Fifth,' Harris Declares," *Washington Evening Star*, 8 October 1924, 1.
25. "Giants Confident of Victory Today," *New York Times*, 9 October 1924, 19.
26. "Giants Again Hit Johnson with Ease," *New York Times*, 9 October 1924, 1.
27. Walter Johnson, "Johnson Has No Alibi in Defeat," *Washington Times*, 9 October 1924, 2.

28. "Giants Again Hit Johnson," 18.

29. "Slur on Johnson Starts Near Fight," *New York Times*, 9 October 1924, 19.

30. Herbert Corey, "Billy Evans Rushes Jeerer of Johnson," *Washington Times*, 9 October 1924, 26.

31. Robert T. Small, "New Yorkers Expected Johnson to Be Victorious," *Washington Evening Star*, 9 October 1924, 26.

32. "Senators Whistle in Face of Disaster," *New York Times*, 9 October 1924, 19.

33. "Johnson Defeated Second Time, May Retire as Player," *Washington Post*, 9 October 1924, 2.

34. "Johnson Too Eager," 2.

35. Babe Ruth, "Babe Ruth Hunch It'll All Be Through after Battle Here Today," *Washington Times*, 9 October 1924, 21.

36. Louis Dougher, "Peckinpaugh Is Hopeful of Putting Griffs Back Even," *Washington Times*, 9.

37. Dougher, 9.

38. "Harris Wins Toss for Seventh Game," *Washington Herald*, 9 October 1924, 1.

39. John Dugan, "Walter Johnson's Failure to Win Is Game's Tragedy," *Washington Herald*, 9 October 1924, 1-S.

40. "5,000 Fans Welcome Team in Washington," *New York Times*, 10 October 1924, 18.

Chapter 17

1. "Hundreds Defy Cold to Get in Bleachers," *Washington Evening Star*, 9 October 1924, 2.

2. "Thousands in Line All Night to Obtain Precious Tickets," *Washington Herald*, 10 October 1924, 5.

3. Frank Frisch, "Outlook Mighty Rosy, Says Frisch," *Washington Herald*, 9 October 1924, 1-S.

4. Louis Dougher, "Peckinpaugh Is Hopeful of Putting Griffs Back Even," *Washington Times*, 9 October 1924, 20.

5. John Keller, "Johnson's Failure Laid to Undue Mental Strain," *Washington Evening Star*, 9 October 1924, 27.

6. "Senators Win from Giants, 2 to 1," *New York Times*, 10 October 1924, 14.

7. Damon Runyon, "Yesterday's Griffs Victory as Seen by Damon Runyon," *Washington Herald*, 10 October 1924, 4-S.

8. "Senators Win from Giants," 14.

9. Runyon, "Yesterday's Griffs Victory," 4-S

10. Ty Cobb, "Ty Cobb Has Praise for Zachary's Mastery," *Washington Times*, 10 October 1924, 20.

11. Louis Dougher, "Twirling Problem Facing McGraw," *Washington Times*, 10 October 1924, 1.

12. Babe Ruth, "Ruth Glad to Call Peck His Old Yankee Teammate," *Washington Times*, 10 October 1924, 21.

13. Dougher, "Twirling Problem," 1.

14. "Harris Is Besieged by Female Fans," *Washington Herald*, 10 October 1924, 5.

15. "McNeely's Folks Listen When Earl Wins Game," *San Francisco Chronicle*, 10 October 1924, 2H.

16. John Dugan, "Curley Ogden to Pitch; Tom Taylor on Third Base," *Washington Herald*, 10 October 1924, 1-S.

17. Bryan Morse, "Inspiration Gives Victory to Harris," *Washington Herald*, 11 October 1924, 5.

18. John Carmichael, *My Greatest Day in Baseball* (New York: A.S. Barnes & Company, 1945), 56.

19. Damon Runyon, "Baseball's Dramatic Final as Seen by Damon Runyon," *Washington Herald*, 11 October 1924, 4-S.

20. Runyon, 4-S.

21. "Mrs. Coolidge Glad That Senators Won" *New York Times*, 11 October 1924, 9.

22. "Senators Win Its First World's Series, Beating Giants, 4–3," *New York Times*, 11 October 1924, 9.

23. "Senators Win."

24. Runyon, "Baseball's Dramatic Final," 4-S.

25. John Kennedy, "Johnson's Mother Cried over Victory," *Washington Herald*, 11 October 1924, 5.

Chapter 18

1. Bill Corum, "Johnson of Old Too Much for Giants," *New York Times*, 11 October 1924, 9.

2. Stanley "Bucky" Harris, *Playing the Game* (New York: Grosset & Dunlap, 1925), 1.

3. Heywood Broun, "Johnson Comes Back from Baseball 'Grave' to Pitch Senators to Title," *Evening News* (Harrisburg, PA), 11 October 1924, 11.

4. Harris, *Playing the Game*, 1.

5. Doris Townsend, *This Great Game* (Englewood Cliffs, NJ: Prentice-Hall, 1971), 141.

6. Walter Johnson, "Johnson Has No Alibi in Defeat," *Washington Times*, 9 October 1924, 2.

7. John P. Carmichael, *My Greatest Day in Baseball* (New York: A.S. Barnes, 1945), 61.

8. John Kennedy, "Johnson's Mom Cries over Victory," *Washington Herald*, 11 October 1924, 5.

9. Grantland Rice, "Johnson of Old Brings Back His Fastball to Defeat Giants, 4 to 3," *San Francisco Chronicle*, 11 October 1924, 1H.

10. Kennedy, "Johnson's Mom Cries," 5.

11. Ty Cobb, "Walter's Four Innings Tough Ones, says Cobb," *Washington Times*, 11 October 1924, 18.

12. Harold Phillips, "Capital Celebrates Bucks' Great Victory in Joyous Delirium," *Washington Evening Star*, 11 October 1924, 1.

13. "Washington Wins Its World's Series, Beating Giants, 4–3," *New York Times*, 11 October 1924, 9.

14. Irving Vaughan, "Senators Take World Title," *Chicago Tribune*, 11 October 1924, 17.

15. Carmichael, *My Greatest Day*, 62.

16. "McNeely's Folks Listen When Earl Wins Game," *San Francisco Chronicle*, 11 October 1924, 2H.

17. Carmichael, *My Greatest Day*, 62.

18. Al Schacht, *My Own Particular Screwball* (Garden City, NY: Doubleday, 1955), 170.

19. John Devaney and Burt Goldblatt, *The World Series: A Complete Pictorial History* (Chicago: Rand McNally, 1981), 106.

20. Jane Leavy, "On Opening Day, Ossie Bluege Remembers Life with the Senators," *Washington Post*, 8 April 1985, B1.

21. Devaney and Goldblatt, *The World Series*, 106.

22. Townsend, *This Great Game*, 141.

Epilogue

1. Irving Vaughan, "Senators Triumph," *Los Angeles Times*, 11 October 1924, 1.

2. John Kennedy, "Johnson's Mother Cries over Victory," *Washington Herald*, 11 October 1924, 5.

3. "McNeely's Folks Listen When Earl Wins Game," *San Francisco Chronicle*, 11 October 1924, 2H.

4. Francis Daily, "Crazed by Thrills, Mad Mob Engulfs Heroes after Game," *Washington Post*, 11 October 1924, 2.

5. "Griffs Tear Loose after Game and Celebrate Like Schoolboys," *Washington Evening Star*, 11 October 1924, 4.

6. "Team's Spirit Won, Says Bucky Harris," *New York Times*, 11 October 1924, 10.

7. "Team's Spirit Won," 10.

8. "What Nats Say," *Washington Post*, 11 October 1924, 4.

9. "What Nats Say," 4.

10. "Griffs Tear Loose," 4.

11. Louis Dougher, "Fighting Hearts of Griffs Stand Tests in Triumph," *Washington Times*, 11 October 1924, 17.

12. Al Schacht, *My Own Particular Screwball* (Garden City, NY: Doubleday, 1955), 170.

13. Louis Dougher, "Fighting Hearts of Griffs," 17.

14. "Griffs Tear Loose," 4.

15. Kennedy, "Johnson's Mother Cries," 5.

16. Dougher, "Fighting Hearts of Griffs," 17.

17. "Griffs Tear Loose," 4.

18. Kennedy, "Johnson's Mother Cries," 5.

19. Dougher, "Fighting Hearts of Griffs," 17.

20. "Gowdy First Giant to Extend Greeting," *Washington Evening Star*, 11 October 1924, 2.

21. Dougher, "Fighting Hearts of Griffs," 17.

22. John Keller, "Clout Worth That Sum to Washington Players," *Washington Evening Star*, 11 October 1924, 13.

23. "John McGraw Shakes Hands with Young Pilot of Nats," *Washington Herald*, 11 October 1924, 1-S.

24. "Carnival Spirit Grips Fans Celebrating Nats Triumph," *Washington Post*, 11 October 1924, 2.

25. "Carnival Spirit Grips Fans," 2.

26. "Griffs Tear Loose," 4.

27. John P. Carmichael, *My Greatest Day in Baseball* (New York: A.S. Barnes, 1945), 141.

28. "Griffs Tear Loose," 4.

29. Jack Smiles, *Bucky Harris* (Jefferson, NC: McFarland & Company, 2011), 18.

Bibliography

Books

Carmichael, John P. *My Greatest Day in Baseball.* New York: A.S. Barnes, 1945.

Castor, Henry. *Teddy Roosevelt and the Rough Riders.* New York: Random House Books, 1954.

Coolidge, Calvin. *The Autobiography of Calvin Coolidge.* Chatsworth, CA: The National Notary Association, 1955.

Devaney, John, and Burt Goldblatt. *The World Series.* Chicago, Rand McNally, 1981.

Harris, Stanley "Bucky." *Playing the Game.* New York: Grosset & Dunlap, 1925.

Leavengood, Ted. *Clark Griffith.* Jefferson, NC: McFarland & Company, 2011.

Povich, Shirley. *The Washington Senators.* New York, Putnam, 1954.

Ritter, Lawrence S. *The Glory of Their Times.* New York: Macmillan, 1966.

Schacht, Al. *Clowning through Baseball.* New York: A. S. Barnes, 1941.

———. *My Own Particular Screwball.* Garden City, NY: Doubleday, 1955.

Smiles, Jack. *Bucky Harris.* Jefferson, NC: McFarland & Company, 2011.

———. *"Ee-Yah": The Life and Times of Hughie Jennings, Baseball Hall of Famer.* Jefferson, NC: McFarland & Company, 2005.

Spink, J. G. Taylor. *Judge Landis and Twenty-Five Years of Baseball.* New York: Thomas Y. Crowell, 1947.

Thomas, Henry W. *Walter Johnson: Baseball's Big Train.* Washington, DC: Phenom Press, 1995.

Townsend, Doris, *This Great Game.* Englewood Cliffs, NJ: Prentice-Hall/Benjamin Co., 1971.

Internet

Baseball Almanac. https://www.baseball-almanac.com.
Baseball Reference. www.baseballreference.com.

Newspapers

Boston Globe
Boston Herald
Boston Post
Chicago Herald Examiner
Chicago Tribune
Cleveland Plain Dealer
Detroit News
Evening News (Harrisburg, PA)
Los Angeles Times
New York Evening Journal
New York Sun
New York Times
Philadelphia Inquirer
St. Louis Post-Dispatch
St. Paul Press
San Francisco Examiner
Tampa Daily Times
Tampa Tribune
Washington Herald
Washington Post
Washington Star
Washington Times

Index

About the Author

Gary Sarnoff has been an active member of Society of American Baseball Research since 1994. He is the former beat writer of the Silver Spring-Takoma Thunderbolts and the former chairman of the Ron Gabriel Award Committee. In addition, he has authored two other baseball books: *The Wrecking Crew of '33* and *The First Yankees Dynasty*. He currently resides in Alexandria, Virginia.

www.ingramcontent.com/pod-product-compliance
Lightning Source LLC
Chambersburg PA
CBHW030302100426
42812CB00002B/541